A GUIDE TO CIVIL RESISTANCE

A GUIDE TO CIVIL RESISTANCE:
A Bibliography of Social Movements and Nonviolent Action

VOLUME TWO

EDITED BY
APRIL CARTER, HOWARD CLARK
AND MICHAEL RANDLE

Published by Green Print, an imprint of the Merlin Press,
in association with the Centre for Trust, Peace
and Social Relations, Coventry University

Published in 2015 by Green Print
an imprint of
The Merlin Press Ltd
99B Wallis Road
London
E9 5LN

www.merlinpress.co.uk

in association with the Centre for Trust, Peace and Social Relations,
Coventry University

ISBN. 978-1-85425-113-8

A substantially revised and expanded edition of *People Power and Protest
Since 1945: A Bibliography of Nonviolent Action* published in 2006 by
Housmans Bookshop Ltd

Catalogue in publication data is available from the British Library

Printed in the UK by Imprint Digital, Exeter

Contents

Preface and Acknowledgements

The purpose of this volume is to provide an introduction to the history of major social movements – including Occupy and the Global Justice Movement, significant green campaigns, peace and anti-war resistance and feminist and LGBT struggles – over the last 70 years, and to signpost contemporary developments in these movements. It provides brief background summaries and a range of references from movement periodicals and websites, scholarly journals and books by activists as well as academic studies. It is part of a wider survey of movements employing the methods of nonviolent action – for example marches, strikes, boycotts, sit-ins, blockades and civil disobedience – to achieve political, economic or social justice. (Volume 1 focused primarily on people power movements against repressive or authoritarian regimes.) This is, however, designed as a 'stand alone' volume. We hope it will be a valuable resource for movement activists, students and teachers engaged in studying social movements and for those exploring the potential of nonviolent action.

There is a particular focus on nonviolent (or predominantly nonviolent) resistance, including more symbolic protests such as fasts or 'kiss-ins' and constructive forms of action and organization, such as land occupations and squatting in empty buildings. But social movements comprise a range of tactics, so lobbying for policy and constitutional reform, intervention in the electoral process and forms of legal action are covered as well in the commentaries and references.

Contemporary movements are usually global in scope, and we have included a global dimension. But given the enormous range of campaigns around the world we have only been able to indicate and reference some of them. In some sections we have chosen to represent a global issue such as corruption by focusing on campaigns in one country: in this case India. This volume covers movements since the Second World War (with some explanatory background on earlier history where relevant), but gives weight to movements since 2010 – for example the resistance to government authoritarianism and neoliberal policies in Chile, Bulgaria, Turkey and Brazil.

Bibliographies need constant updating. So whilst this printed guide brings together a wide range of information and sources, this volume will be made available in fully searchable form on the website: http://civilresistance.info and duly updated. Volume 1 has been searchable on this website since early 2015, and is already being updated there. In due course we plan to add new campaigns to the web Guide. Andreas Speck, formerly of War Resisters' International, has been devoting his skills to developing this website and we are extremely grateful for his constructive role in expanding the availability and usefulness of this Guide.

We are indebted to many who have helped us to compile Volume 2. Above all we owe a great debt to our colleague Howard Clark, a former coordinator and chair of War Resisters' International and scholar of civil resistance, who played a major role in compiling and editing Volume 1 and whose researches have contributed significantly to this volume. We have thought it appropriate to keep his name on the list of compilers, but his sudden and most untimely death in November 2013 has meant that we have lost his enormous range of knowledge about social movements in completing Volume 2.

We have, however, had generous advice on different sections of this volume from a number of individuals with expertise on particular topics who have commented on drafts and provided references for us. We are therefore most grateful to: Fionnuala O Connor, Fay Gadsen, Javier Garate, Veronica Kelly, Brian Martin, John Osmond, Robin Percival and Eugene Walsh. Particular thanks are due to Robyn Fitzharris for her work on the LGBT section and to Andreas Speck for his additions to several sections.

As promised at the end of Volume 1, we have included lists of important references in three major European languages: French, German and Spanish in an Addendum to this volume. In due course (if resources are available) we will add many more foreign language titles to the website http://civilresistance.info and make it multilingually searchable. Meanwhile, we are extremely grateful to Veronique Dudouet, Christine Schweitzer, Jesus Castanar and Javier Garate for finding time, despite their many other commitments, to work on these initial lists of titles.

Finally, we would like to thank two organizations that have made an important financial contribution to the publication of this Guide. The Joseph Rowntree Charitable Trust in York has made it possible for us to cover the printing costs of both volumes; and the International Center for Nonviolent Conflict in Washington has enabled us to make Volume 1 available in fully searchable form on the web.

April Carter and Michael Randle

The Compilers

April Carter has lectured at the universities of Lancaster, Oxford and Queensland, Australia. Her publications include *The Politics of Women's Rights* (Longmans, 1988), *Peace Movements* (Longmans, 1992) and *The Political Theory of Global Citizenship* (Routledge, 2001). She was a senior editor of the *Oxford International Encyclopedia of Peace* (Oxford University Press, New York, 2010). Her interest in nonviolent action dates from the late 1950s, when she became active in the direct action wing of the nuclear disarmament movement, and she has written on direct action and nonviolent resistance since the 1960s. Her latest books are: *Direct Action and Democracy Today* (Polity, 2005) and *People Power and Political Change: Key Issues and Concepts* (Routledge, 2012).

Howard Clark, who died unexpectedly in December 2013, was a nonviolent activist from 1968 engaging in campaigns at a local, national and international level. He was coordinator for War Resisters' International from 1985-97 and its chair from 2006-2013. He was a research fellow at the Albert Einstein Institute (1997-99) and at the Coventry University Centre for Peace and Reconciliation Studies from 2000 to his death. His publications include: *Making Nonviolent Revolution* (Peace News, 1978, 1981 and, 2012), *Civil Resistance in Kosovo* (Pluto 2000), *Handbook for Nonviolent Campaigns* (co-editor, War Resisters' International 2009) and *People Power: Unarmed Resistance and Global Solidarity* (editor, Pluto 2009). He also played a major role in compiling Volume 1 of the *Guide to Civil Resistance*.

Michael Randle has been involved in the anti-war movement in Britain since the 1950s and in 1958 was one of the organizers of the first Aldermaston March against Britain's nuclear weapons. A former chairperson of War Resisters' International, and subsequently co-ordinator of the Alternative Defence Commission, he has been a visiting research fellow at the Department of Peace Studies, University of Bradford. Until 2009 he co-edited the quarterly review of the Committee for Conflict Transformation Support. His publications include: *People Power: the Building of a New European Home* (Hawthorn, 1991), *Civil Resistance* (Fontana, 1994), *Challenge to Nonviolence* (editor, Department of Peace Studies, Bradford University, 2002), and *Jubilee 2000: The Challenge of Coalition Campaign* (Centre for Peace and Reconciliation Studies, Coventry University).

Note to Readers

1. Availability of titles referenced

This Guide covers movements stretching back to the 1950s and 1960s, which means that some of the books, articles and pamphlets produced at the time may be difficult to find. We have indicated later editions or web versions of some sources. We have also done some checking on the availability of titles second hand, and quite a number can still be acquired. We have also indicated where we know there are paperback versions (pb) as these should be cheaper.

We have attempted to combine movement-based sources and academic studies. The latter are likely to be available in some academic and national libraries. For more specialized movement accounts and materials, a good resource for researchers in the UK is: The Commonweal Collection, J.B. Priestley Library, University of Bradford, Richmond Road, Bradford, West Yorkshire, BD7 1DP.

Its online address is: http://www.bradford.ac.uk/library/libraries-and-collections/commonweal-collection

Commonweal has especially good collections on Gandhi, nonviolence in theory and practice and peace movements, but also covers environmental, social justice and other campaigns. In addition it has an outstanding collection of movement periodicals.

Important materials and records are also available at: the London School of Economics, Houghton Street, London, WC2A 2AE. LSE now houses the Women's Library, a major collection of British feminist history, and also has Greenham Women and Women in Black archives, as well as *Feminist Review* from the 1970s. See: http://www.lse.ac.uk/library/collections/featuredcollections/women'slibrary.aspx

In addition LSE has a good LGBT collection, including archives of lesbian and gay activism. The LSE Collections are open to anyone who wishes to do some research.

For those seeking to buy movement books and pamphlets – including those published some time ago – a key source in the UK (and from abroad) is: Housmans Bookshop, 5 Caledonian Road, London, N1 9DX: http://www.housmans.com Books can be ordered online, and Housmans can also supply lists of titles on various topics.

NB. A few important out of print books and pamphlets are available free from our website: http://civilresistance.info

2. Web References

This is primarily a print bibliography, but ebooks and web sources are becoming increasingly important. We have drawn attention to a range of relevant organizational websites in relation to particular movements and also noted the availability of some journal articles online. We have also relied upon online sources for information on a number of recent campaigns, such as the anti-fracking movement, and made quite frequent references to the online journal *openDemocracy*. In many cases we have referred to websites (which tend to have a longer lifespan) and not given detailed (more changeable) online addresses; but where these were checked at the end of 2014, or the web reference is the only source, we have sometimes included the full address.

There are now a number of very useful general websites covering nonviolent action, which we listed in Vol. 1. section A.7. (now online in fully searchable form at: http://civilresistance.info).

Introduction

Social movements have historically played an important role in bringing about political change and have voiced the hopes of those suffering from inequality and discrimination. The trade unions and socialist parties of the 19th and 20th centuries, for example, organized workers to demand the right to vote, shorter hours, and better wages and conditions at work, and a more equal society, and peace campaigns and feminist activism both began in the 1800s and gained momentum in the 1900s.

In recent decades, however, campaigns on a wide range of economic, social and cultural issues have become increasingly frequent round the world, and the ideas and demands generated – for example an end to racial discrimination, full equality for women, and the rights of gays and lesbians – have become part of political discourse, even if they are very far from being wholly achieved. The Green movement has helped to put issues of pollution, saving the rainforests and the dangers of climate change on the international agenda. Indigenous peoples round the world have increasingly asserted their political and cultural rights and are stubbornly resisting destruction of their local environments by mining, oil and logging companies. Peace activists have campaigned against specific wars – notably Vietnam. They have also resisted conscription and protested against nuclear and other weapons and bases. Citizens in many parts of the world are challenging corruption and the failure to meet democratic standards, or resisting policies that dispossess the poor or fail to make major corporations accountable. This volume focuses primarily on movements since the Second World War, but does make brief reference to earlier history in some cases.

Although significant movements with different priorities have emerged, their members have also tended to come together to campaign for common ends. For example, the Global Justice Movement, that first captured international attention with the demonstrations against the World Trade Organization at Seattle in December 1999, brought together trade unionists resisting the neoliberal policies promoted by international economic bodies, with small farmers, green activists and many others. The organizational links created by this movement also helped promote transnational protest against the Iraq War of 2003.

Students have often played an important part in resistance to governments and in social movements on a wide range of issues. They were prominent for example in the US Civil Rights Movement and in many of the rebellions against dictatorial regimes covered in Volume 1 of this Guide. Students often protest about their own specific problems, but may also ignite a wider movement, as in Chile in 2011-12 (see Section H.1.a.). A major student movement erupted in many countries in 1968, often closely linked to the ideas of the New Left, But, although there were student demonstrations in 2011 in Britain, students were mainly active in national and international movements in 2011, from Occupy to the Arab Spring – as indicated in some of the references under 1.a. below. Therefore, we have not covered student movements as a separate category. (The1968 student movement will be included in due course on the Guide's website: http://civilresistance.info.)

In the past, movements by workers and small farmers have quite often used tactics of non-cooperation, such as strikes, boycotts and tax refusal; or undertaken direct unarmed intervention such as land occupations and takeover of factories. But they have also resorted to violent rioting, or have systematically taken up arms. In recent decades the proliferation of popular campaigns has been linked to a greater tendency to use methods of nonviolent action. News stories have made marches, sit-ins, road blocks, strikes, boycotts, civil disobedience and many other forms of nonviolent dramatic protest familiar. Many more nonviolent protests that do not feature in the mainstream press and television are covered in movement journals and websites and publicized via today's social media,. Some demonstrations or occupations of key sites or buildings do turn into rioting and use of stones and Molotov cocktails, and sometimes essentially nonviolent tactics are linked to willingness to engage with security forces. Nevertheless, social movements now often rely primarily on forms of nonviolent action to publicize their cause and to try to achieve their goals. The widespread use of nonviolent action can be linked to long term social trends, including the vulnerability of complex modern societies to social disruption and the role of media of communication in publicizing protest and encouraging others to do the same.

An important role has also been played by specific movements in promoting the idea of nonviolence whilst devising challenging and dramatic forms of nonviolent protest. The US Civil Rights Movement, with its specific commitment to nonviolence for many years and its use of bus boycotts, sit-ins at segregated facilities, marches in defiance of local bans and many other forms of nonviolent challenge to segregation and inequality was publicized around the world. Peace movements, in keeping with their general commitment to promote nonviolence, also used a range of nonviolent tactics to oppose military policies and protest at military bases (for example at Greenham Common) and their protests were also widely reported, photographed and filmed. The Green movement has been particularly innovative in using ships at sea, and devising technologies to enhance physical obstruction, for example of tree felling.

The primary focus of this volume is on the use of nonviolent forms of protest by social movements in the last 70 years, but it also encompasses constructive initiatives to deal with specific problems (for example women's refuges from domestic violence), and covers more conventional forms of political campaigning. Changing the law is often central to the aims of a movement. Use of the law (both nationally and internationally) can also be an important element in campaigns of nonviolent action, both to establish the legitimacy of the protests and (sometimes) to secure victory on specific issues.

The first volume of this Guide (now available in fully searchable form at: http://civilresistance.info) had an introductory section on nonviolent action (including Gandhi and the US Civil Rights Movement), but was focused on consciously nonviolent or effectively unarmed popular struggles against colonial rule, military occupation, dictatorship or 'semi-authoritarian' regimes with the aim of achieving an independent and democratic form of government. This volume covers social movements seeking economic and social justice or an end to discrimination against sections of the population. It also covers movements opposing war (or specific weapons or wars), environmental threats and corruption.

This distinction is not absolute. Resistance to authoritarianism may initially be expressed obliquely, for example through environmental protest. Some more limited protests in authoritarian regimes are therefore referenced in Volume 1 (for example under China and Russia). Moreover resistance to global economic policies may be manifested through sectional and community protests, but can escalate into a full scale rebellion against national governments implementing these policies (as has happened in Argentina, Bolivia and Ecuador, all covered in Volume 1).

Most of the social movements included here are nationally based but have a transnational dimension. As this Guide is compiled and published in the UK we have included important struggles and campaigns here, for example the 1984-85 Miners Strike and the Poll Tax rebellion in 1989-90, and given weight to the peace, green, feminist and LGBT campaigns in this country. We have focused in particular depth on Northern Ireland, where the role of nonviolent action has been important but complex in the context of the wider politics and role of armed struggle, and which has international significance in terms of the peace process there. We have also provided many references giving an indication of the global extent of protest and resistance – especially in peace movements, but a comprehensive global coverage is beyond our scope. This volume should be seen as an introduction to important campaigns and modes of nonviolent action in movements round the world.

1. General Introductory Books on Social Movements

The rise of so many social movements employing a wide range of tactics has prompted a growing theoretical literature since the 1970s Whilst this literature has largely developed independently of the study of nonviolent action, some more recent studies do take note of civil resistance or cover movements employing nonviolent methods. The emphasis of this Guide is on sources which give prominence to nonviolent tactics, major campaigns or examples of protest, but some of the references are books or articles written within a theoretical framework drawn from the social movement literature. Others draw on theories of nonviolent action, or on wider political and social perspectives.

A preliminary selection of titles covering both nonviolent action and social movements was published in Volume 1 (A.6.) and can be found at: http://civilresistance.info. The references on transnational or national movements listed below under 1.a. and 1.b. are additional titles directly relevant to Volume 2, with an emphasis on recent publications.

There are, however, a number of books listed in Volume 1 which are particularly relevant to various movements and campaigns covered in this volume, and which are cited under these movements. For ease of reference for those using this printed version of Volume 2 we have listed these titles in full under 1.c. below.

1.a. Transnational and Continent-wide Movements and Networks

1. Castells, Manuel, *Networks of Outrage and Hope: Social Movements in the Internet Age*, Cambridge, Polity, 2012, pp. 200.

Well known theorist of global networks examines the mass uprisings across the world in 2011, giving account of events in 'Arab Spring' and the reaction to the bank collapse and austerity policies in the west in Iceland, Spain, Greece and the USA, and stressing the causal role of the internet.

2. Della Porta, Donatella, *Social Movements in Times of Austerity: Bringing Capitalism Back into Protest Analysis*, Cambridge, Polity and Wiley, 2015, pp. 216.

Analyzes movements since 2008 (Iceland) challenging corruption and inequality and situating them within the crisis of neoliberalism. Covers Spain, Greece and Portugal anti-austerity movements, but also Peru, Brazil, Russia, Bulgaria, Turkey and Ukraine.

3. Edwards, Michael and John Gaventa, eds., *Global Citizen Action*, London, Earthscan Publications, 2001, pp. 327.

Discusses transnational civil society, its impact on financial institutions, and a range of specific campaigns, e.g. to ban landmines, Jubilee 2000, campaigns against corporations.

4. Feigenbaum, Anna, Fabian Frenzel and Patrick McCurdy, *Protest Camps*, London, Zed Press, 2013, pp. 272.

Examines protest camps as key tactic of movements from Tahrir Square to Occupy Wall Street; includes Red Shirts in Thailand and teachers in Oaxaca.

5. Jacobsson, Kerstin and Steven Saxonberg, eds., *Social Movements in Post-Communist Europe and Russia*, London, Routledge, 2015, pp. 128.

Examines social movement strategies and how they differ to fit national circumstances and considers activism related to the environment and sustainability, animal rights, human rights, women's rights and gay rights. Reconceptualizes the relationship between state and civil society under post-communism. Based on special issue of *East European Politics*.

6. *Mobilization: an International Quarterly*, vol. 9 no. 3 (Oct. 2004) Special issue on Latin America: Democratization, Globalization and Protest Culture

7. Reydams, Luc, ed., *Global Activism Reader*, London, Macmillan, 2011, pp. 420, pb.

Main focus on contemporary transnational activism, including case studies of labour, environmental, human rights, women's rights, social justice and peace campaigns. Readings include theoretical perspectives and critical views. A companion website provides information on further reading, films and documentaries and activist websites.

8. Snow, David A., Donatella Della Porta, Bert Klandermans and Doug McAdam, eds., *The Wiley Blackwell Encyclopedia of Social and Political Movements*, Oxford, Wiley-Blackwell, 2013, 3 vols. (organized A-Z), pp.1544.

Covers period since the French Revolution, but also contains summary accounts of numerous contemporary movements and organizations, including many included in this volume.

9. Solomon, Clare and Tania Palmieri, eds., *Springtime: The New Student Rebellions*, London, Verso, 2011, pp. 256, pb.

Focuses on the widespread student protests in Britain in 2010, but also extends to Italy, France, Greece and the USA, as well as the beginning of the Arab uprisings in Tunisia. Includes texts from the past and reminders of 1968, as well as coverage of contemporary events, and political and theoretical commentaries from established and new voices.

10. Weiss, Meredith Leigh and Edward Aspinall, *Student Activism in Asia: Between Protest and Powerlessness*, Minneapolis MN, University of Minnesota Press, 2012, pp. 318.

Comparative examination of student-led protest challenging governments in Asia since the Second World War, with a focus on Burma, China, Hong Kong, Japan, Taiwan, South Korea, Indonesia, Malaysia, Thailand and the Philippines

I.b. National Studies

11. Burgmann, Verity, *Power, Profit and Protest: Australian Social Movements and Globalization*, Crows Nest NSW, Allen and Unwin, 2003, pp. 393.

12. Gosse, Van, *The Movements of the New Left 1950-1975: A Brief History with Documents*, New York, Bedford/St. Martins, 2004, pp. 224.

Uses a very broad definition of the New Left, and examines common features in Civil Rights, peace, anti-war, student, feminist and gay/lesbian movements in the USA.

13. Koopmans, Ruud, *Democracy from Below: New Social Movements and the Political System in West Germany*, Boulder CO, Westview Press, 1995, pp. 300.

Analyzes range of social movements and over 3,000 'protest events' between 1965-1989 in the context of West German institutional arrangements, drawing comparisons with the Netherlands and Switzerland.

14. Tyler, Imogen, *Revolting Subjects: Social Abjection and Resistance in Neoliberal Britain*, London, Zed Books, 2013, pp. 224.

Begins with forced eviction (despite their resistance) of about 500 travellers from their homes in 2011, and explores exclusion and labelling of a range of 'abjected' groups (treated as scapegoats) and denigration of their resistance. Main focus on Britain, but makes comparisons with other oppressed groups, such as those in the Niger Delta.

15, Valocchi, Stephen, *Social Movements and Activism in the USA*, New York and London, Routledge, 2009, pp.200.

Examines what can be learned from social movement activists, focusing on community, labour, feminist, gay and lesbian, peace and anti-racist groups in Hartford Connecticut.

16. Wittner, Lawrence, *Working for Peace and Justice: Memoirs of an Activist Intellectual*, University of Tennessee Press, 2012, pp. 288.

Lively account of peace, racial justice and labour activism in USA from the 1960s to 2000s by author of major study of transnational movement against nuclear weapons from 1945 (442-445 D.3.b).

Ic. Titles included in Volume 1, but also cited in Sections of Volume 2

For the convenience of those using this volume, we are including these titles (which are already listed in Vol.1) in alphabetical order of author but unnumbered (and marked +). Where applicable in later references, readers will be referred back to this section for full publication details.

+Clark, Howard, ed., *People Power: Unarmed Resistance and Global Solidarity*, London, Pluto Press, 2009, pp. 237.

+Cohen, Robin and Shirin M. Rai, *Global Social Movements*, London, Athlone Press, 2000, pp. 231.

+Deming, Barbara, *Revolution and Equilibrium*, New York, Grossman, 1971, pp. 269.

+Epstein, Barbara, *Political Protest and Cultural Revolution: Nonviolent Direct Action in the 1970s and 1980s*, Berkeley C A, University of California Press, 1991, pp. 327.

+Escobar, Arturo and Sonia Alvarez, eds., *The Making of Social Movements in Latin America*, Boulder CO, Westview Press, 1992, pp. 383.

+Hare, Paul A. and Herbert H. Blumberg, eds., *Liberation Without Violence: A Third Party Approach*, London, Rex Collings, 1977, pp. 368.

+Hewison, Kevin, ed., *Political Change in Thailand: Democracy and Participation*, London, Routledge, 1997, pp. 301.

+Keck, Margaret and Kathryn Sikkink, *Activists Across Borders: Advocacy Networks in International Politics*, Ithaca NY, Cornell University Press, 1998, pp. 240.

+Klein, Naomi, *Fences and Windows: Dispatches from the Front Lines of the Globalization Debate*,London, Harper Collins/Flamingo, 2002, pp. 267, pb.

+Kolb, Felix, *Protest and Opportunities: The Political Outcomes of Social Movements*, Frankfurt Mainz, Campus Verlag, 2007, pp. 360.

+Martin, Brian, *Justice Ignited: The Dynamics of Backfire*, Lanham MD, Rowman Littlefield, 2007, pp. 236.

+McManus, Philip and Gerald Schlabach, eds., *Relentless Persistence: Nonviolent Action in Latin America*, Philadelphia PAS, New Society Publishers, pp. 312.

+Moser-Puangsuwan, Yeshua and Thomas Weber, eds., *Nonviolent Intervention Across Borders: A Current Vision*, Honolulu, Spark M. Matsunaga Institute for Peace, 2000, pp. 369.

+Perry, Elizabeth J. and Mark Selden, eds., *Chinese Society: Change and Resistance*, London, Routledge, [2003] 2010 (3rd edition.).

+Randle, Michael, ed., *Challenge to Nonviolence*, Bradford Department of Peace Studies, University of Bradford, 2002, p. 304. Online at: http://civilresistance.info

+Routledge, Paul, *Terrains of Resistance: Nonviolent Social Movements and the Contestation of Place in India*, Westport CT, Praeger, 1993, pp. 170.

+Sharp, Gene et al. *Waging Nonviolent Struggle: Twentieth Century Practice and 21st Century Potential*, Boston MA, Porter Sargent, 2005, pp. 598.

+Solnit, Rebecca, *Hope in the Dark: The Untold History of People Power*, London, Canongate Books, 2005, pp. 181.

+Talbot, John, *The War Without a Name: France in Algeria 1954-1962*, New York, Alfred Knopf, 1980, pp. 305.

+Tracy, James, *Radical Pacifism from the Union Eight to the Chicago Seven*, Chicago IL, Chicago University Press, 1996, pp. 196.

+Zunes, Stephen, Lester B. Kurtz and Sarah Beth Asher, eds., *Nonviolent Social Movements: A Geographical Perspective*, Oxford, Blackwell, 1999, pp. 330, pb.

A. Campaigns for Social and Economic Justice

A significant part of the repertoire of nonviolent resistance, such as pickets, strikes and boycotts, derives from movements for economic justice in the past. Strikes became widespread in the evolving trade union movements of the nineteenth and early twentieth centuries, although there are much earlier examples of workers' striking for their rights.

Strikes have also often been used to win political goals, such as the right to vote, or as part of nationwide struggles against repressive government – for many examples see Volume I of this Guide (available at: http://civilresistance.info). But in industrialized and highly unionized countries economic strikes (sometimes supported by sympathetic action by other workers), became a part of the bargaining between unions and employers, though right wing governments have succeeded in imposing restrictions on the legal right to strike. Very many strikes since 1945 have not been either of central political significance or important examples of civil resistance. One exception has been strikes by those suffering discrimination, who are non-unionized or not well supported by trade union leaders. A number of strikes by women workers in the 1960s and 1970s in Britain (by cleaners, non-unionized Asian workers and the Ford Dagenham women's strike for equal pay) fall into this category. These are covered under Feminist Movements (F.1.b.).

As a result, however, of the move away from heavy industry and the dominance of neoliberal ideology and policies since the 1980s, trade unionism has been weakened in the west – especially in Britain and the USA. So strikes and protests by low paid workers, who may not be guaranteed a fixed minimum of hours at work, have become a new arena for struggle. As a result of the processes of globalization workers in developing countries forced to accept low pay and bad conditions can potentially be supported in their protests by transnational action. Because the economic and movement context changed, this kind of concerted action became more widespread from the 1990s (see sub-section A.5.).

The unemployed cannot exert pressure by withdrawing their labour, but in various times and places they have responded by extended protests demanding government action (or opposing government policies promoting unemployment) – for example during the 1930s Depression the 'Hooverville' tent city of the unemployed in Washington DC and the Hunger Marches in Britain. Sometimes those without work have attempted creative solutions, such as occupying factories which have been closed down and running them under the control of the workers (see A.1.b.ii.)

Refusal to pay high rents has long been a tactic of both the rural and urban poor. Recent campaigns against high rents are covered in sub-section A.2. Struggles against forced evictions of the poor in cities are shaped by national circumstances but also in more recent years reflect a global trend towards 'slum clearance' to give scope to developers and/or to build facilities for international sporting events (A.2.b). The problem of landlessness, and organized campaigns to extend land ownership are particularly associated with dynamic movements in Latin America, but movements confronting the same problem have arisen also in Asia and Africa (the theme of A.3.).

Local struggles for economic justice have been increasingly affected by economic globalization. Global forces can be the target of urban and land campaigns, but the impact of globalization is even more clearly related to local campaigns against multinational corporations engaged in logging, mining and oil extraction, or selling products which have harmful consequences (examined in sub-section A.4). Globalization does, however, open up possibilities for transnational action to provide solidarity for those most oppressed – campaigns related to the garment industry are a key example (A.5.)

Concerted resistance in many parts of the world marked the 'Anti-Globalization' or 'Global Justice' Movement which was widely publicized by the demonstrations in Seattle in December 1999 against a meeting of the World Trade Organization. Transnational protests at summits of international bodies promoting a neoliberal global economic order – such as the WTO, IMF, G8, North American Free Trade Agreement – highlighted the scale of this resistance. The Multilateral Agreement on Investment, which promoted stringent policies on debt repayment on the poorest countries, also prompted summit protests (Jubilee 2000 in London), and the World Bank, which provided finance for controversial projects such as dams, has been another target. But the most important resistance to neoliberal policies, such as privatization of water and energy and other key state services, occurred at local and national levels in Africa, Asia, and most dramatically in Latin America. The Global Justice Movement (sub-section A.6) prompted a large literature and became associated with movements for land and against multinationals in many parts of the world. There have also been significant struggles in Africa, Asia and in Latin America against policies of privatization, encouraged by 'free trade' agreements and often a condition of IMF and other international financial support (sub-section A.7.) But in its specific organizational form of contesting summits of prominent neoliberal bodies, and annual conferences of its own counter-international, the World Social Forum (and regional bodies) it lost some of its momentum after 2005, especially in the west.

The next wave of western protests against global economic policy was precipitated by the banking crisis of 2008 and resulting deep economic depression. Although sparked by national disasters, these movements – the Indignados and Occupy were prominent – also had a transnational dimension, influencing campaigners elsewhere and infused with awareness of the global nature of the crisis and its causes. Sub-section A.8. covers these protests..

A.1. Campaigns by Workers

Introduction

The move towards a global neoliberal economy from the 1970s has created new problems for trade unions. One logical response has been to try to maintain and extend international solidarity between unions (though sometimes national economic interests may be in conflict) and to extend transnational cooperation between trade unions and social movements. A second important response has been to focus on creating local solidarity: in the move towards 'community unionism' workers have cooperated with local civil society groups, and often other unions, to support activism by a vulnerable workforce. For analyses of both responses see:

17. Banks, Andy, 'The Power and Promise of Community Unionism', *Labor Research Review*, no. 18 (1991). Online at :http://digitalcommons.ilr. cornell.edu

Discusses the 'Justice for Janitors' campaign in Los Angeles from 1986-1990 and success in reaching out to the immigrant community.

18. Bieler, Andreas and Ingemar Lindberg, eds., *Global Restructuring, Labour and the Challenges for Transnational Solidarity*, London, Routledge, 2011, pp. 280.

A range of transnational case studies, including cooperation between unions in developing and developed countries, illustrate problems and possibilities of solidarity.

19. Fine, Janice, 'Community Unions and the Revival of the American Labor Movement', *Politics and Society*, vol. 33 no. 1 (2005), pp. 153-99.

20. Greenwood, Ian and Jo McBride, eds., *Community Unionism: A Comparative Analysis of Concepts and Contexts*, Basingstoke, Palgrave/Macmillan, 2009, pp. 264.

Explores the diverse meanings of community unionism, provides case studies from the UK – the 'London's living wage' campaign, and activism by black and minority workers and migrant workers – and from Japan, Australia and the US.

21. Woods, Alex, 'Winning at Walmart', *Red Pepper*, (Jun/Jul 2013), pp. 45-47.

On the campaign by OUR Walmart against the retail giant in USA in 2012, when non-unionized workers mobilized across the country with support from local communities, using blockades as well as brief strikes.

I.a. Selected Strikes

This sub-section concentrates on a few nationally significant strikes, starting with the strike by the Californian grape pickers for minimum economic justice and full union representation. It also covers a strike with major political implications, the 1984-85 British miners' strike to defend their industry and jobs against extensive pit closures. Strikes have occurred in many parts of the world resisting privatization (for example successive strikes by South Korean rail workers since the early 2000s) and other neoliberal economic policies; these fall under sub-section A.7.

One recent strike of national significance that qualifies for this section is the 2012 Marikana platinum mine workers' strike in South Africa. This was politically important because the wild cat strike for higher wages demonstrated disillusion with the National Union of Mineworkers (NUM), seen as too close to the ruling African National Congress (ANC) and accused of selling out to the mine owners. The strikers refused representation by the NUM. The strike led to an alternative union, the Association of Mineworkers and Construction Union. Above all Marikana made headlines round the world when on 16 August 2012 (after several days of demonstrations in which eight miners and two policemen were killed) police shot 34 striking miners – widely compared to the mass killings of the apartheid era.

1.a. i. California Grape Pickers' Strike and Boycott Campaign, 1965-1970

This was an important strike by the very poor and marginalized Chicano (Mexican American) workers, supported by wider union action to boycott handling grapes and by a consumer boycott, so it has attracted widespread interest on the left. Because of the emphasis on maintaining nonviolence, especially by the leading figure Cesar Chavez, it is also well covered in books on nonviolent action.

22. Bardacke, Frank, *Trampling Out the Vintage: Cesar Chavez and the Two Souls of the United Farm Workers Union*, London and New York, Verso, 2011, pp. 840.

Very detailed account and analysis by former civil rights activist who also worked in the fields for six seasons 1971 and 1979, charting contradictions within the movement and the role of Chavez, based on hundreds of field reports and first hand experience.

23.. Dalton, Frederick John, *The Moral Vision of Cesar Chavez and the Farm Worker Movement*, New York, Harcourt Brace, 1988, pp. 350.

24. Day, Mark, *Forty Acres: Cesar Chavez and the Farm Workers*, New York, Praeger, 1971, pp. 222.

25. Ferris, Susan and Ricardo Sandoval, *The Fight for the Fields: Cesar Chavez and the Farm Workers Movement*, New York, Harcourt Brace and Co, 1998, pp.352, pb. (Foreword by Gary Soto.)

Well documented and illustrated account of movement.

26. Ganz, Marshall, *Why D avid Sometimes Wins: Leadership, Organization and Strategy in the California Farm Worker Movement*, Oxford and New York, Oxford University Press, 2009, pp. 308.

Excellent insider study, emphasizing development of the United Farmworkers union, and 'strategic capacity' defined as a combination of motivation, understanding of the context and the ability to learn.

27. Jenkins, J. Craig, *The Politics of Insurgency: The Farm Workers Movement in the 1960s*, New York, Columbia University Press, 1985, pp. 131-74.

28. Levy, Jacques, *Cesar Chavez: Autobiography of La Causa*, New York, W.W. Norton, 1975, pp. 546.

29. Merriman , Hardy, 'Californian Grape Workers' Strike and Boycott 1965-1970' in Sharp et al., *Waging Nonviolent Struggle* (Introduction , 1.c.), pp.173-87.

30. Orosco, Jose-Antonio, *Cesar Chavez and the Commonsense of Nonviolence*, Albuquerque, NM, 2008, pp. 160.

31. Rosales, Francisco Arturo, *Chicano! The History of the Mexican American Civil Rights Movement*, Houston TX, Arte Publico, 1997, pp. 304.

32. Rose, Margaret, 'Women Power Will Stop these Grapes: Chicana Organizers and Middle Class Female Supporters in the Farmworkers' Grape Boycott in Philadelphia, 1969-70', *Journal of Women's History*, Winter 1995, pp. 8-33.

33. Taylor, Ronald B., *Chavez and the Farm Workers*, Boston, Beacon Press, 1975, pp. 342.

Includes assessment of impact of grape pickers' strike on immigrant labour in other industries.
A select bibliography on Chavez can be found at: http://www.colapublik. org/chavez/bibliography.htm

1.a.ii. British Miners' Strike 1984-85

The miners' strike to defend their industry against extensive pit closures was also a highly politicized conflict between the National Union of Mineworkers (under the leadership of Arthur Scargill) and the Conservative government under Margaret Thatcher. Scargill hoped to repeat the success of the NUM in the early 1970s in undermining the then Conservative government, and Mrs Thatcher was determined to force the miners into surrender. The strike, which the miners eventually lost, saw a government assault on civil liberties and high levels of tension, animosity, and sometimes violence between police and strikers, and was a turning point in industrial relations in Britain. The strike was in due course undermined by a breakaway regional miners' union who distrusted the NUM leadership, and the legitimacy of the strike was questioned because there had not been a national strike ballot. At the time the Coal Board and the Government stated that they only planned to close 20 pits, but Scargill claimed that the real goal was to close 70 pits: release of previously classified government information early in 2014 under the 30 year rule proves that Scargill was correct and the government lied at the time. The coal industry has been largely destroyed. The significance of the miners' strike, and the implications of the miners' defeat for British trade unionism, is suggested by the large number of books and pamphlets it generated, some of which are listed below. A documentary film, 'Still the Enemy Within', directed by Owen Gower, 113 minutes, was released in 2014. Another film released in 2014, 'Pride', was the fictionalized account of a true story: the links formed between the London-based group Lesbians and Gays Support the Miners and a Welsh mining community and local NUM between 1984-85.

One unexpected and more positive by product of the strike was that it mobilized many women in the mining communities (not previously active in industrial disputes) to organize support for the strikers and play a more prominent role locally (see section F.1.b).

The continuing significance of police methods during the strike was reflected in the 12 June 2015 Independent Police Complaints Commission (IPCC) Report on police tactics and alleged misconduct during the violent confontation with thousands of pickets at the Orgreave coking plant. The report accepted that mounted police charged without warning and miners threw missiles in response, and that some police used excessive violence. The report also found that some officers committed perjury (evidence of this led to the 1985 acquittal in court of 95 miners charged with riot and unlawful assembly). But despite criticism of senior police officers in South Yorkshire, the IPCC decided not to launch a formal investigation.

34. Beynon, Huw, ed., *Digging Deeper: Issues in the Miners' Strike*, London, Verso, 1985, pp. 280.

35. Callinicos, Alex and Mike Simons, *The Great Strike: The Miners' Strike of 1984-5 and its Lessons*, London, Socialist Worker, 1985, pp. 256.

36. Coulter, Jim, Susan Miller and Martin Walker, *State of Siege: Miners' Strike 1984: Politics of Policing in the Coal Fields*, London, Canary Press, 1984, pp. 240.
Critique of policing methods.

37. Francis, Hywel, *History on Our Side – Wales and the 1984-85 Miners' Strike*, Swansea, Parthian Books, 2009, pp. 96, pb. (new edition in preparation)
Account of how the strike developed differently in Wales from other parts of Britain, and grew into a national movement involving community groups, churches and Welsh nationalists and fostered a greater national consciousness with a lasting impact on Welsh politics.

38. Goodman, Geoffrey, *The Miners' Strike*, London, Pluto, 1985, pp. 224.
Examines why the strike failed and the role of key institutions and the pickets. Includes a chronology.

39. Kelliher, Diarmaid, 'Solidarity and Sexuality: Lesbians and Gays Support the Miners 1984-5', *History Workshop Journal*, vol 77 no. 1 (Spring 2014), pp.240-62. At: http://hjw/oxfordjournals.org.

Among the many groups that sprang up to offer financial support and solidarity to the miners was the London- based Lesbian and Gays Support the Miners. This article charts support offered by LGSM and discusses wider implications for the movement on the left.

40. McCabe, Sarah, et al, *The Police, Public Order and Civil Liberties: Legacies of the Miners' Strike*, London, Routledge, 1988, pp. 209.

41. Milne, Seumas, *The Enemy Within: The Secret War Against the Miners*, London, Verso, 1994 and Pan 1995, pp. 511.

42. Parker, Tony, *Red Hill: A Mining Community*, London, Faber and Faber, [1986] 2013, pp. 236.

Eyewitness accounts (from different perspectives) of impact of strike on community.

43. Samuel, Ralph, et al. ed., *The Enemy Within: Pit Villages and the Miners' Strike of 1984-5*, London, Routledge, Kegan and Paul, 1986, pp. 260.

Collection of first-hand accounts, interviews, letters, speeches etc.

44. Saunders, Jonathan, *Across Frontiers: International Support for the Miners' Strike*, London, Canary, 1989, pp. 288.

45. Winterton, Jonathan and Ruth Winterton, *Coal, Crisis and Conflict: The 1984-85 Miners' Strike in Yorkshire*, Manchester, Manchester University Press, 1989, pp. 360.

I.a.iii. Strike by Marikana Platinum Miners August 2012

The political significance of the Marikana strike was noted above. The miners' demonstrations from August 10 to August 16 led to increasing tension – on August 11 National Union of Mineworkers officials fired on the crowd, on August 12 the strikers were attacked by police with rubber bullets and on August 13 police fired on demonstrators who refused to hand over their own weapons, a clash that led to two deaths on each side. The miners tried to avoid violence spreading into the local community and the looting of shops by individuals taking advantage of the situation (as had happened in an earlier strike): when challenged by NUM officials on August 11 they moved to high ground some distance from their homes.

The police shooting of 34 miners occurred on August 16. The day after the shooting, wives of the miners demonstrated, claiming that the police shot first and demanding those responsible should be identified and punished. Civil society groups, for example Citizens 4 Marikana, have rallied to demand the police to be held to account, support the bereaved families and provide legal representation. An official enquiry, which did not include any civil society representatives, was launched in October 2012. The report, finally published in June 2015, absolved senior political figures, but did question the role of the national police chief, criticize police tactics and recommend that police involved in the shootings be investigated for criminal liability.

The Marikana strike, and the government's response, has been widely covered by the press and other media, but has not yet resulted in a large literature. But some references are listed below.

46. Alexander, Peter, Thapela Lekgonwo and others, *Marikana: A View from the Mountain and a Case to Answer*, Johannesburg, Jacana Media, 2013, pp. 144.

Interviews with strikers who took part in protests and written from their viewpoint.

47. Chinguno, Crispen, 'Marikana and the Post-Apartheid Workplace Order', Society, Work and Development Institute Working Paper, April 2013, pp. 40. Online at: http://www.academia.edu See also: Chinguro, Crispen, 'Marikana massacre and strike violence post-apartheid', *Global Labour Journal*, vol. 4 no. 2 (2013), pp. 160-66. Online at: http://digitalcommons.mcmaster.ca/globallabour/vol4/no2/

48. Pillay, Pearl, 'The Marikana Massacre: 'the sub-altern cannot speak', *Broken Rifle*, no. 98 (Dec. 2013). Online at:http://www.wri-irg.org/node/22772.

Brief article which details evolution of strike from 10-16 August.

49. Thanduxolo. Jika, et al., *We Are Going to Kill Each Other Today: The Marikana Story*, Cape Town, NB Publishers/Tafelberg, 2013, pp. 256, pb.

Account by City Press reporters and photographers, supplemented by edited evidence from official Enquiry, and including analyses of labour migration.

50. Twala, Chitja, 'The Marikana Massacre: A Historical overview of the Labour Unrest in the Mining Sector in South Africa', *Southern African Peace and Security Studies*, vol. 1 no. 2 (2013) pp. 61-67.

A.I.b. Protests by the Unemployed

I.b.i. Dolci and the Reverse Strike

One unusual tactic, associated with the prominent nonviolent activist Danilo Dolci, is the 'reverse strike'. Thus tactic was used in Sicily as part of a series of campaigns between 1952 and 1965 to relieve the extreme local poverty. When unemployed men started to repair a road outside Partinico in 1956, appealing to their constitutional right and duty to work, the police sent them home, and banned a second attempt to repair the road, arresting Dolci and six others. Gene Sharp records in *The Politics of Nonviolent Action*, Part Two under 'Reverse Strike' that the Congress of Racial Equality used a similar tactic in Chicago, mobilizing unemployed young men to engage in slum clearance, and leaving a bill for the work at City Hall.

51. Dolci, Danilo, *The Outlaws of Partinico*, London, MacGibbon and Kee, 1960, pp. 316.

Describes context of his campaigns – not much detail on the campaigns themselves.

52. McNeish, James, *Fire Under the Ashes: The Life of Danilo Dolci*, London, Hodder and Stoughton, 1965, pp. 256.

I.b.ii Factory Occupations

A nationwide movement of workers' seizing and running factories may be part of a wider revolution, as in Russia in 1917, or potentially revolutionary movement, as in Italy 1918-1920. A recent example is the occupation of factories in Argentina as part of the popular resistance and organization from below in response to the collapse of the Argentine economy in November 2001 (covered in detail in Volume I of this bibliography, Section E. 2.b.). As the economy recovered the popular movement tended to wane, but left a legacy of a significant number of worker owned factories.

Occupation of work places occurs during sit-in strikes, when the workers may takeover for weeks (there was, for example, a 77 day occupation in South Korea in 2009) in order to bring pressure on employers and/or governments. But this is distinct from workers taking over closing factories in order to maintain jobs and to run them in the workers' interests, though some literature covers both.

There is a large literature on the theory and history of worker control and ownership and on noted contemporary examples, such as Mondragon in Spain. This section looks only at some examples of laid-off workers occupying their workplaces, either to prevent closure or to continue in operation under worker management.

53. Coates, Ken, *Work-ins, Sit-ins and Industrial Democracy*, Nottingham, Spokesman Books, 1981, pp. 175.

An account of sit-ins or work-ins to prevent workplace closures in Britain in early 1970s, and an examination of subsequent experiments in workers' control.

54. Greenwood, J. *Worker Sit-ins and Job Protection: Case Studies of Union Intervention*, Farnborough, Gower Press, 1977, pp.121.

Discusses sit-down strikes in Britain, the well-known occupation of the Lip factory in France in 1973 and West European sit-ins and work-ins protesting against redundancy.

55. McGill, Jack, *Crisis on the Clyde: The Story of the Upper Clyde Shipbuilders*, London, Davis-Poynter, 1973, pp. 143.

Account of the 1971 'work in' that took over shipyards threatened with redundancy and for a period maintained them under worker control and forced the government to delay closure.

56. Notes from Nowhere, ed., 'Forging Links in Ozarow', *We Are Everywhere* (163 A.6.a.), pp. 450-55.

On Polish worker occupation to prevent closure of a factory, supported by local community and anarchist groups.

57. Sherry, Dave, *Occupy! A Short History of Worker Occupations*, London, Bookmarks, 2010, pp. 157.

Covers campaigns in Argentina, Chicago (USA), France, Ukraine, Turkey, Egypt, South Korea and China.

A.2. Urban Campaigns against High Rents, Forced Evictions and Homelessness

Introduction

Having a home, like having a job, is a basic requirement, but in many cities the poor find that right threatened. Tenants may be faced with rents too high for them to pay, with the consequent threat of serious debt or eviction. Organized rent strikes have therefore been an important method of resistance. A famous example is the 1915 rent strike against landlords raising rents by women in Glasgow, whilst their men were engaged in the war. The refusal to pay the increase spread across the city and to other parts of Britain. When a landlord took some of his tenants to court, workers in the Clyde shipyards and munitions factories went on strike and others demonstrated in protest. The government was forced by this combined show of solidarity to legislate to prevent rent rises during the war. Rent strikes have also been used in many parts of the world since 1945.

Poor areas of cities are also quite often scheduled for drastic redevelopment, resulting in the eviction of thousands from their homes and destruction of their neighbourhoods; moreover 'slum' clearance does not always result in alternative provision of new housing. Redevelopment in many cities round the world may be part of a process of gentrification, but is also a strategy of governments hosting prestigious international exhibitions or sporting events, such as the Olympics, and has often been met by determined local resistance and wider protests.

Those who are homeless, for whatever reason, have quite often adopted a strategy of taking over empty houses or buildings, or seizing land to build on. Squatter movements have highlighted the lack of affordable housing and in some cases created new radical communities within cities.

Urban resistance movements may focus on other targets – for example protests and riots in response to police brutality, and in some cases have revolutionary aspirations and implications. Two theoretical analyses of urban revolt, which cover a wide range of urban movements in different parts of the world, are:

58. Castells, Manuel, *The City and the Grassroots: A Cross-Cultural Theory of Urban Social Movements*, Berkeley CA, University of California Press [1983] 1992, pp. 471.

59. Harvey, David, *Rebel Cities: From the Right to the City to the Urban Revolution*, London, Verso, 2012, pp. 208

2.a. Rent Strikes

Although rent strikes are normally against high or increased rents, the focus may also be on poor maintenance of housing, as in Harlem in the 1960s.

60. Brill, Harry, *Why Organizers Fail: The Story of a Rent Strike*, Berkeley CA, University of California Press, 1971, pp. 192.

Examines community action by the poor; (in Californian Studies of Urbanization and Environment series).

61. Jackson, Mandi Isaacs, 'Harlem's Rent Strike and Rat War: Representation, Housing Access and Tenant Resistance in New York 1938-1964', *American Studies*, University of Kansas, vol. 47, no. 1 (2006), pp. 53-71.

62. Lawson, Ronald and Mark Naison, eds., *The Tenant Movement in New York City, 1904-1984*, New Brunswick NJ, Rutgers University Press, 1986, pp. 289, pb.

See also article by Ronald Lawson: 'The Rent Strike in New York City 1904-1980: The End of a Social Movement Strategy', *Journal of Urban History*, vol. 10, no. 3 (May 1984), pp. 235-58.

63. Lipsky, Michael, *Protest in City Politics: Rent Strikes, Housing and the Power of the Poor*, Chicago, Rand McNally, 1970, pp. 214.

64. Moorhouse, Bert, Mary Wilson and Chris Chamberlain, 'Rent Strikes – Direct Action and the Working Class', in Ralph Miliband and John Saville, eds., *The Socialist Register, 1972*, London, Merlin Press, 1972, pp.133-56.

Starts with account of major rent strikes on the Clyde in 1915 and 1921-26, but includes materials on rent strikes in London 1959-61 and 1968-70 and their implications.

See also: Corr, *No Trespassing*: (73 2.c.).

2.b. Resisting Eviction

As noted in the Introduction to A.2., forced evictions, and often local or national resistance, have occurred around the world – for example in Shanghai before the 2008 Olympics and in Rio de Janeiro in preparation for the 2014 World Cup and 2016 Olympics. But often the poor are dispossessed to make way for urban development. This has occurred in many cities in South Africa, where about 10 percent of the population live in shacks in shanty towns, often with abysmal social facilities. An important movement campaigning for the rights of shack dwellers, Abahlali baseMjondolo (AbM) arose around Durban in 2005, and has since spread to settlements round South Africa, and has links to other African countries and internationally. It is a movement stressing participatory democracy which resists evictions, helps re-house the homeless, promotes better social services and opposes draconian provincial laws, such as the Kwa -Zulu Natal Slum Clearance Act, which AbM managed to overturn in the Constitutional Court. (Information about AbM available from War on Want (which provides support) and AbM's own website: http:// www.abahlali.org)

Another type of resistance to eviction is that by homeowners and their neighbours, when banks foreclose on mortgages and attempt to dispossess them. A significant movement has arisen in Spain since 2009 to prevent evictions in the context of the economic crisis that began in 2008. Since this is linked to the wider movement of the Indignados, it is covered under sub-section A.8.b.

65. Amnesty International Report, *Rights Razed: Forced Evictions in Cambodia*, 11 Feb 2008, Index No ASA 23/002/2008. Available as pdf.

Analysis of lack of proper consultation and of legal protection for those evicted.

66. Bhan, Gautam , 'This is No Longer the City I Once Knew. Evictions, the Urban Poor and the Right to the City in Millenial Delhi', *Environment and Urbanization*, vol. 21, no. 1 (April 2009), pp. 127-42. See also book co-authored by Bhan and Kalyani Menon-Sen: *Swept Off the Map: Surviving Eviction and Resettlement in Delhi*, New Delhi, Yoda Press, 2005.

67. Mason, Paul, 'We Will Barricade', chapter 10 in Mason, *Why It's Kicking Off Everywhere* (208 A.8.a).

Discusses resistance of slum dwellers in Philippines to eviction, but also their role in providing cheap workforce undermining organized labour.

68. Ockley, James, 'Weapons of the Urban Weak: Democracy and Resistance to Eviction in Bangkok Slum Communities', *Sojourn*, vol. 12, no. 1 (1997), pp. 1-25.

69. Olds, Kris, 'Urban Mega-Events, Evictions and Housing Rights: The Canadian Case', *Current Issues in Tourism*, vol. 1. no. 1 (1998)

Article covers responses by community and legal groups to: Expo '86 in Vancouver; 1988 Calgary Winter Olympics; and the rejected proposal for 1996 Summer Olympics in Toronto.

70. Schapiro Anjaria, Jonathan and Colin McFarlane, eds., *Urban Navigations: Politics, Space and the City in South Asia*, London, Routledge, 2001, pp. 347.

Focuses on conflicts over urban space, resources and housing in Cambodia, India, Nepal, Pakistan and Sri Lanka, and includes accounts of resistance in squatter settlements, e.g. in Kathmandu.

See also: Tyler, *Revolting Subjects*, on forced eviction 500 travelers in Britain in 2011 (14 Introduction, 1.b.).

2.c. Homeless Campaigns and Occupations

There have been two main types of movement to occupy empty buildings or land: action by the homeless to find somewhere to live, and counter-cultural initiatives to create new social spaces, forms of social activity and a model of society in miniature within modern cities. In the former category is the 2013 occupation of land in Cato Crest, Durban, by about 1,000 people, who had been illegally evicted by their municipality . They named their new settlement Marikana. In the latter category are the Kabouters (successors to the Dutch Provos) in the 1970s, and the independent community of Christiane founded on an old military base in Denmark in 1971 and continuing until today, though after state pressure in the 2000s there have been changes in its status. But this distinction is not absolute – some movements aim both to provide social housing and to offer a new model of society.

A third type of action was launched by the Occupy London campaign in 2011, involving widespread squatting in empty commercial property, partly to underline their anti-capitalist message (see A.8.)

Governments, especially right wing ones, have periodically evicted squatters and tried to make it more difficult. Parisian police evicted up to 1,000 West African immigrants living in a disused university residential block in August 2006 – a move criticized as a publicity stunt for presidential hopeful Nicolas Sarkozy (*Guardian*, 18 Aug 2006, p.25). The British Coalition government made squatting in residential buildings illegal in 2012 – members of the Squatters' Housing Action Group had earlier climbed onto the roof of the Justice Secretary's London home in protest against a criminalization of a solution to homelessness.

71. *Anarchy*, no 102 (vol. 9 no. 8), (August 1969)

Issue on 'Squatters' covering London campaign starting in 1968, including extract from Kropotkin on 'The expropriation of dwellings'.

72. Bailey, Ron, *The Squatters*, Harmondsworth, Penguin, 1973, pp. 206.

Covers the London Squatters Campaign 1968-71, but notes background of the mass movement by homeless people in Britain at the end of the Second World War to occupy military bases, and later luxury flats, in 1945-46.

73. Corr, Anders, *No Trespassing: Squatting, Rent Strikes and Land Struggles Worldwide*, Cambridge MA, Southend Press, 1999, pp. 256.

Discusses the success of squatter movements by the homeless, addresses issues such as 'direct action and the law' and 'tactics and mobilization' and includes case studies of squatter settlements and rent strikes.

74. Cress, Daniel M. and David A. Snow, 'The Outcomes of Homeless Mobilization: The Influence of Organization, Disruption, Political Mediation and Framing', *American Journal of Sociology*, vol. 105 (2000), pp. 1063-104.

Analysis of how organization, tactics, political context and 'framing' of the issue affect outcomes, based on 15 campaigns in 8 US cities.

75. Hinton, James, 'Self-help and Socialism: The Squatters Movement of 1946', *History Workshop Journal*, vol. 25 no. 1 (1988), pp. 100-26.

Covers a significant movement in post-war Britain when many houses had been destroyed by bombing.

76. Katz, S. and M. Mayer, 'Gimme shelter: Self-help Housing Struggles within and against the State in New York City and West Berlin', *International Journal of Urban and Regional Research*, vol. 9 no.1 (1985), pp. 15-47.

77. Klein, Naomi, 'Italy's Social Centres' in *Fences and Windows* (Introduction 1.c.), pp. 224-27.

78. Martinez Lopez, Miguel A., 'The Squatters' Movement in Europe: A durable struggle for social autonomy in urban politics', *Antipolitik: A Radical Journal of Geography*, vol. 45, no 4 (Sept 2013), pp. 866-87.

Examines squatting in empty properties in European cities over three decades, and argues squatting has promoted a mode of citizen participation, protest and self-management.

79. Neuwirth, R., *Shadow Cities: A Billion Squatters: A New Urban World*, London, Routledge, 2006, pp. 335.

Author lived in squatter communities in Rio, Bombay, Nairobi (where squatting was linked to building new homes) and Istanbul.

80. Priemus, H., 'Squatters in Amsterdam: Urban Social Movements, Urban Managers or Something Else?', *International Journal of Urban and Regional Research*, vol. 7 no. 3 (1983), pp. 417-27.

81. Pruijst, Hans, 'Squatting in Europe', Erasmus Universisteit Rotterdam, Faculteit der Social Wetebschappen. English version of 2004 chapter available at: http:// www.eur.nl/fsw

82. Ruggiero, Vincenzo, 'New social movements and the "centri sociali" in Milan', *Sociological Review*, vol. 48, no. 3 (2000), pp.167-88.

83. Squatting Europe Kollektive: Cattaneo, Claudia and Miguel A. Martinez eds., *The Squatters' Movement in Europe: Commons and Autonomy as Alternatives to Capitalism*, London, Pluto Press, 2014, pp. 288, pb.

Case studies from most of Europe (excluding eastern Europe and Greece) covering direct action to create social housing and other community services over 30 year period.

84. Ward, Colin, *Housing: An Anarchist Approach*, London, Freedom Press, 1976, pp. 182.

Ward, a leading anarchist theorist and expert on housing, examines the post-1945 British squatters movement (pp. 13-27) and assesses the revival of squatting between 1968 and early 1970s.

85. Ward, Colin, *Cotters and Squatters: The Hidden History of Housing*, Nottingham, Five Leaves Publications, 2002, pp. 196.

A social history that goes up to end of 20th century, primarily discusses British examples, but has references to many other countries.

86. Wates, Nick, and Christian Wolmar, eds., *Squatting: The Real Story*, London, Bayleaf Books, 1983, pp.240.

Written and produced by squatters, focusing primarily on history in Britain, but some reference to squatting round the world.

A.3. Struggles over Land

3.a. Land Occupations and Demands for Land Reform

The urban poor may seize land to create homes, but land seizures both historically and today are primarily a strategy by struggling farmers and landless agricultural workers to enable them to cultivate the land. In Europe peasant seizure of land has often been part of a wider revolutionary upsurge, as in France in 1789, Russia 1905 and 1919, Italy 1919 and Spain in 1936-37, but today (unlike urban forms of resistance) is not central to Western protest movements. There is a particularly strong tradition in Latin America of peasant farmers seizing land (with varying degree of nonviolence or violence) from absentee or large landowners and planting crops on the land. Sometimes land seizures were retrospectively legalized by government laws or by sale of land, or even encouraged by leftist politicians, Peasant leagues in Colombia in the 1930s created an independent communist republic in the mountains based on land seized. In the 1950s and 1960s peasants seized land in Colombia, Bolivia, Brazil, Peru and Venezuela.

More recently the best known landless movement has been Movimento Sem Terra (MST) in Brazil, founded in 1984, but arising out of the rural and industrial militancy of the 1970s when there were many land seizures. It has continued to organize the landless and unemployed in taking over land from large landowners and multinationals and setting up cooperative farms, as well as organizing slum dwellers in large cities in the southeast, providing them with allotments. But hunger for land, and resistance to its use by large corporations, extends to other parts of Latin America (for example Honduras) and many countries in Africa and Asia.

87. Borras, Saturnino M. Jr, Mark Edelman and Cristobal Kay, eds., *Transnational Agrarian Movements: Confronting Globalization*, Oxford, Wiley Blackwell, 2008, pp. 376.

Covers transnational farmer resistance to WTO and other global institutions and high profile global alliances such as the small farmer organization Via Campesina. Case studies include Indonesian forest dwellers chopping down rubber plants to grow rice to eat, and Mexican migrants returning home to transform their communities. Also includes information on early 20th century agrarian movements.

88. Branford, Sue and Oriel Glock, *The Last Frontier: Fighting over Land in the Amazon*, London, Zed Press, 1985, pp. 336.

89. Branford Sue and Jan Rocha, *Cutting the Wire*, London, Latin American Bureau, 2002, pp. 305.

Well researched account of MST.

90. Carter, Miguel, *The Origin of Brazil's Landless Workers Movement MST: the Natalino Episode in Rio Grande do Sul (1981-84) – a case of ideal interest mobilization*, University of Oxford Centre of Brazil Studies, Working Paper Series CBS-43-2003, 2003, pp. 71,. Online at: http;//www.brazil.ox.ac.uk/Carter 43.pdf

91. Chabot, Sean and Stellan Vinthagen, 'Rethinking Nonviolent Action and Contentious Politics: Political Cultures of Nonviolent Opposition in the Indian Independence Movement and Brazil's Landless Workers' Movement', *Research in Social Movements. Conflict and Change*, vol. 27, 2007, pp. 91-121.

92. Desmarais, Annette Aurelie, *La Via Campesina: Globalization and the Power of Peasants*, London, Pluto, 2007, pp. 254.

Examines impact of modernization and globalization on agriculture and explores alternative forms of development and the evolution of an international peasant voice in Via Campesina, formed in 1993 to challenge the neoliberal economic agenda.

93. Hammond, J.L., 'Law and Disorder: The Brazilian Landless Farmworkers Movement', *Bulletin of Latin American Research*, vol. 18, no. 4 (1991), pp. 269-89. See also Hammond, John L. 'The MST and the media: Competing images of the Brazilian Landless Farmworkers' Movement', *Latin American Politics and Society*, vol. 4, no. 4 (Winter 2004), pp. 61-90.

94. Hurley, Judith, 'Brazil: A Troubled Journey to the Promised Land' in McManus and Schlabach, eds., *Relentless Persistence* (Introduction 1.c.) pp. 174-96.

The author, who founded a US support group for the landless, provides excerpts from her journal of visiting sites of land struggle in 1987. She notes intensified confrontations in 1980s between the landed elite and the landless, who resorted to lawsuits, demonstrations, fasts, vigils, marches, mock funerals and, above all, land occupations.

95. *Latin American Perspectives*, vol. 30, no. 4 (issue 167) (July 2009).

The whole issue is dedicated to 'Peasant Movements in Latin America' including 2 articles on MST.

96. Rosset, Peter M, Roy Patel and Michael Courville, eds., *Promised Land: Competing Visions of Agrarian Reform*, Oakland CA, Food First, 2006, pp. 380.

Includes chapters on Brazil, Colombia, Cuba, Guatemala, India, Mexico, South Africa and Zimbabwe (the latter refrains from discussing the human rights issues of the government sponsored post 1996 land occupations). Not all chapters discuss social movements, but the book does cover gender and indigenous issues.

97. Schlabach, Gerald, 'The nonviolence of desperation: Peasant land action in Honduras' in McManus and Schlabach, eds., *Relentless Persistence* (see Introduction 1.c.), pp.48-62.

Examines 200 peasant occupations in 1972 (assertion of a tradition of 'les recuparaciones') in context of developing forms of protest since the 'great strike' against United Fruit Company in 1954.

98. Schock, Kurt, 'Land Struggles in the Global South: Strategic Innovations in Brazil and India' in Gregory M. Maney, Rachel V. Kutz-Flamenbaum, Deana A. Rothlinger and Jeff Goodwin, eds., *Strategies for Social Change*, Minneapolis MN, University of Minnesota Press, 2012, pp. 221-44.

99. Schock, Kurt, 'People Power and Alternative Politics' in Peter Barnell and Vicky Randall, eds., *Politics in the Developing World*, Oxford, Oxford University Press, 2008, pp. 186-207.

Pays special attention to Ekta Parishad (an Indian land rights organization), the Assembly of the Poor in Thailand and MST in Brazil.

100. Stedile, Joao Pedro, 'Landless Battalions', *New Left Review*, no 15 (May/June 2002), pp.77-104.

Account by participant in evolution of land seizures and of how MST eventually achieved legal possession.

101, Welch, Cliff, 'Movement Histories: A Preliminary Historiography of the Brazil Landless Laborers Movement (MST)', *Latin American Research Review*, vol. 41, no. 1 (2006), pp. 198-210.

102. Wright, Angus and Wendy Wolford, *To Inherit the Earth: The Landless Movement and the Struggle for a New Brazil*, Oakland CA, Food First Books, 2003, pp. 357.

Situates MST in the broader context of Brazilian history but also based on first hand research at MST settlements.

3.b. Resisting Land Grabs in the 21st Century

Ownership and use of land is becoming an increasingly contested issue in recent years. Apart from multinational corporations claiming land to exploit its resources – minerals, oil or coal (see A.5.) – companies are also taking over land for biofuels or fast growing trees to be used as timber, some governments are buying up land in other parts of the world to ensure against future lack of food or for investment, and financiers and oligarchs are also involved in taking land from local small farmers. Although some of these land deals are undertaken officially and authorized by governments, others occur secretly and the precise number of land deals since 2000 is not known. Oxfam has estimated that over two million square hectares were taken over in the first decade of the 21st century, two thirds in Africa (where Chinese state corporations have been especially active). This extensive land grab has generated local resistance in Africa, Asia and Latin America – sometimes in an attempt to defeat the project and keep their land, and sometimes demanding better terms for local people being incorporated into these vast projects. There are, for example, impressive examples from India, where in December 1999 the Adivasi indigenous movement organized a 1,7000 mile march to launch a Land Entitlement Satyagraha (Starr, *Naming the*

Enemy, p. 59 (114 A.4)). Sunitra Narain noted numerous campaigns (some successful) to resist takeover of land or water for hydro-electric projects and dams in India ('A Million Mutinies', *New Internationalist* (Jan/Fen 2009), pp. 10-11).

103. *Canadian Journal of Development Studies*, Issue on 'Land Grabbing in Latin America', vol. 33, no. 4 (2012).

104. Hall, Derek, *Land*, Cambridge, Polity, 2012, pp. 176.

Analyzes conflicts over land in terms of its role as territory (leading to inter-state claims or wars), its status as property, and ways in which its use is regulated. The book examines the attempts of NGOs to protect property rights and environments in the Global South and the land grabs by corporations and governments, drawing on wide range of examples, including China and Honduras.

105. *Journal of Peasant Studies*, Special Issue on 'Green Grabbing – a New Appropriation of Nature?', vol. 39. no. 2 (2012).

Prints papers from international conference: The Land Deal Politics Initiative, (convenor of) 'The Second International Academic Conference on Land Grabbing' , Cornell University, 17-19 October 2012.

106. Kerssen, Tanya, *Grabbing Power: The New Struggles for Land, Food and Democracy in Northern Honduras*, Oakland CA, Food First Books, 2013, pp. 188.

This book covers the popular resistance that has developed in the towns since the coup in 2009, but especially in the Bajo Aguan valley, where peasants who are contesting their dispossession from their land since 1992 by the Dinant Corporation and other large landowners promoting palm oil plantations, are staging large scale occupations of land. The area has a large military presence and special forces are implicated in killing local activists.

107. Mazgaonkar, Moses (Anand), 'India – Macro Violence, Micro Resistance: Development Violence and Grassroots Unarmed Resistance', in Clark, ed., *People Power* (Introduction, 1.c.), pp. 76-85.

Include two brief accounts of struggles to retain land, by Adivasi (indigenous) people in Gujarat against dispossession from traditional lands by the Forest Department, and the 'Save Our Lands' campaign in Gujerat for common lands held by villages and often used by the landless for herding animals, plant collecting, etc, who were threatened by corporate agriculture.

108. Pearce, Fred, *The Landgrabbers: The Fight Over Who Owns the Earth*, London, Transworld, Eden Project Books, 2012, pp. 400.

Examination of how land is being taken from subsistence farmers round the world, for example across Africa, South-East Asia and parts of Eastern Europe.

109. Schneider, Alison Elizabeth, 'What Shall We Do without Land? Land Grabs and Resistance in Rural Cambodia', paper at International Conference on Global Land Grabbing, 6-8 April 2011, organized by Land Deals Politics Initiative with Journal of Peasant Studies at Sussex University, 6-8 April 2011.

Covers three different types of land grab (one by military) and types of peasant resistance, from overt protests and petitions to 'everyday resistance' such as sleeping on threatened land and organizing road blocks.

110. Vergara-Camus, Leandro, 'The Legacy of Social Conflicts over Property Rights in Rural Brazil and Mexico: Current Land Struggles in Historical Perspective', *Journal of Peasant Studies*, vol. 39 no. 5, 2012, pp. 1133-58.

A.4. Resistance to Multinationals

Campaigns against powerful multinational companies are quite often undertaken by indigenous peoples seeking to protect their land and way of life; some of these specific campaigns are included in this section. There is also often an overlap between anti-corporate and environmentalist struggles, but resistance to specific corporations is covered here. Thirdly an upsurge of protest against multinationals was part of the Global Justice (or Anti-Globalization) Movement, but often preceded protests directed specifically against international economic institutions and neoliberal policies (see A.7. below).

Supermarket chains are a good example of extensive corporate power – driving smaller shops and traders out of business, imposing their requirements on farmers, able to exploit suppliers from poorer countries and dictate unfavourable terms to their workforce. The US retail giant Walmart has been particularly strongly criticized, evoking strong resistance in South Africa in 2011 to its planned takeover of Massmart, and a protest by farmers and retailers in Delhi in 2007, organized by the Movement for Retail Democracy. Inside the USA a campaign in Chicago in October 2004 opposed the setting up of the first Walmart store inside the city (*Guardian* (4 Oct 2004), pp. 6-7). Supermarkets in Britain have also been criticized, by War on Want, Action Aid and others, for driving down wages of overseas workers, for example those picking tea, fruit and flowers in countries such as Kenya and South Africa. One source of information on ongoing struggles is Corporation Watch , based in San Francisco: http:// www.corpwatch.org

There have been numerous protests at shareholders' annual meetings of large corporations, focusing on a range of peace, environmental, economic justice and human rights issues. Protests range from questions by nominal shareholders to the platform to protest banners and disruption of proceedings.

Some general theoretical studies which include information on a range of anti-corporate campaigns are:

111. Crossley, N., 'Global Anti-Corporate Struggle: A Preliminary Analysis', *British Journal of Sociology*, vol. 53 no. 4 (2002), pp. 667-91.

A preliminary sociological analysis of the 'recent wave of anti-corporate protest' seeking to provide a framework and highlight important themes.

112. Klein, Naomi, *No Logo*, London, Flamingo, 2001, pp. 490.

Now a classic analysis of the role of brands and sources of leverage on corporations, including extensive information on a range of campaigns, many including direct action.

113. Newell, Peter, 'Campaigning for Corporate Change: Global citizen action on the environment', in Edwards and Gaventa, eds., *Global Citizen Action* (3 Introduction 1.a.), pp. 189-201.

114. Starr, Amory, *Naming the Enemy: Anti-Corporate Movements Confront Globalization*, London, Zed Books, 1999, pp. 268.

Both documents and theorizes the growing transnational resistance to multinationals and neoliberal globalization.

115. Stolle, Dietland, Marah Hooghe and Michele Micheletti, 'Politics in the Supermarket: Political consumerism as a form of political participation', *International Political Science Review*, vol. 26 no. 3 (2005), pp. 245-69.

a. Logging and Mining

As reserves of natural resources run out, corporations try to find new resources on remote lands which often belong to indigenous peoples. As a result there are a growing number of struggles by local people against mining and timber companies.

116. Achterberg, Emily, 'Resistance to Mining in El Salvador: A Battle for Water, Life and National Sovereignty', *Revista* (Winter 2014): http://revista. drclas.harvard.edu/book/resistance-mining-el-salvador

117. Evans, Geoff, James Goodman and Nina Lansbury, eds., *Moving Mountains: Communities Confront Mining and Globalisation*, London, Zed Books, 2002, pp. 284.

Discusses role of corporations and governments in different parts of the world. Chapters 8-12 focus on resistance in Bougainville, the Philippines and Australia. Chapter 12 (pp. 195-206) covers the resistance to the Jabiluka uranium mine by the local Aboriginal people, supported by environmentalists.

118. Gedicks, Al, *The New Resource Wars: Native and Environmental Struggles against Multinational Corporations*, Boston MA, South End Press, 1993, pp. 270.

Examines campaigns by the Ojibwa Indians against mining and over land tenure and the role of multinationals in Wisconsin.

119. Magnusson, Warren and Karena Shaw, eds., *A Political Space: Reading the Global through Clayoquot Sound*, Minneapolis MN, University of Minnesota Press, 2002, pp. 320, pb.

Campaign on Vancouver Island, Canada, against corporate loggers trying to take over indigenous land. Protesters blocked roads against logging. Both men and women took part, but cited as a protest organized on feminist principles.

120. Moody, Roger, *Rocks and Hard Places: The Globalisation of Mining*, London, Zed Books, 2007, pp. 213.

Detailed analysis by committed campaigner. Chapter 8 'No Means No' discusses strategy against mining, calling for more emphasis on nonviolent direct action and greater scepticism about certification.

121. Moody, Roger, ed., *The Risks We Run: Mining Communities and Political Risk Insurance*, Utrecht, International Books, 2005, pp. 342.

Part 1 investigates the shadowy world of international mining finances, while Part 2 has case study chapters on mining projects and local resistance in West Papua, Papua New Guinea, Guyana, Kyrgyzstan, Tanzania and Peru.

122. Ozkan, Kemal, 'Rio Tinto's "Sustainable Mining" Claims Exposed', *Ecologist*. 30 July 2014, pp. 3. Online: http://www.theecologist.org

Ozkan, Associate General Secretary of IndustriALL Global Union, comments critically on Rio Tinto's record and notes his union's commitment to campaign for changes in corporate policies. IndustriALL has produced reports on Rio Tinto, for example 'Rio Tinto in Africa: Global Citizen or Corporate Shame', available from: www.industrial-union.org

123. Wilton, Jen, 'Touch the Earth ', *New Internationalist,* (March 2014), pp. 24-5.

Provides snapshots of struggles by local people against chromite, bauxite, copper, silver and gold mining in Canada, Guinea, Burma, Mexico, Papua New Guinea and Mozambique, and notes movement in northern Peru, beginning 2008 and erupting into mass blockades in 2009, against logging and oil drilling.

See also: Keck and Sikkink, *Activists Beyond Borders,* pp. 150-60 on campaign against deforestation in Sarawak by Dayaks, who barricaded logging roads (Introduction, 1.c.)

For additional references see also: B.2.a. and 2.b. and C. 2.b. and 2.d.

4.b. Oil Companies

124. Bowman, Andy, 'Shell to Sea', *Red Pepper* (Dec/Jan 2009), pp. 40-41.

Discusses community campaign in County Mayo on west coast of Ireland against a planned gas pipeline and refinery. The campaign involved fasting, blockades and civil disobedience by five men who defied compulsory purchase orders and went to jail. (See also Rossport 5 and Siggins below)

125. Clark, Howard, 'An Obstacle to Progress', *Peace News,* (Dec. 2002-Feb.2003), pp. 12-13.

Campaign of the U'wa people of Colombia to prevent oil drilling.

126. Cooper, Joshua, 'The Ogoni Struggle for Human Rights and Civil Society' in Nigeria' in Zunes, et al. eds., *Nonviolent Social Movements* (Introduction, 1.c.), pp. 189-202.

Account of one of the best known and documented campaigns against oil drilling which damages the local environment and communities, by the Ogoni people of Nigeria against Shell.

127. George-Williams, Desmond, 'The Ogoni Struggle' in George-Williams, Desmond, *Bite Not One Another: Selected Accounts of Nonviolent Struggle in Africa,* Addis Ababa, University of Peace Africa Development Programme, 2006, pp. 68-74. (available online at http:// www.upeace.org)

128. Hunt, Timothy J., *The Politics of Bones: Dr Owens Wiwa and the Struggle for Nigeria's Oil*, Toronto, McClelland and Stewart, 2005, pp. 400.

Focuses on the brother of the executed leader of the Ogoni movement, Kenule Sarowiwa, and his efforts to carry on the campaign.

129. Obi, Cyril I., 'Globalization and Local Resistance: The Case of Shell versus the Ogoni' in Barry K. Gills, ed., *Globalization and the Politics of Resistance*, Basing stoke, Macmillan, 2000; Palgrave (paperback) 2001, pp. 280-94.

130. Rossport 5, *Rossport 5 – Our Story*, Small World Media, 2007, pp. 208, pb. Introduction by Mark Garavan.

Accounts by five farmers (and wives) jailed for resisting Shell high-pressure gas pipeline in County Mayo, Ireland. This campaign against Shell's gas refinery gained national and transnational attention and support, and involved reciprocal solidarity actions with the Ogoni people.

131. Saro-Wiwa, Ken, *A Month and a Day: A Detention Diary*, London, Penguin, 1995, pp. 237. Republished as: *A Month and a Day and Letters*, Ayebia Clarke Publishing, 2005, with Foreword by Wole Soyinka.

132. Sawyer, Suzana, *Crude Chronicles: Indigenous Politics, Multinational Oil and Neoliberalism in Ecuador*, Durham NC, Duke University Press, 2004, pp. 294.

Shows how neoliberal policies led to a crisis of accountability and representation that spurred one of 20th century Latin America's strongest indigenous movements.

133. Siggins, Lorna, *Once Upon a Time in the West: The Corrib Gas Controversy*, Dublin, Transworld, 2010, pp. 448.

Account by *Irish Times* reporter of the 'Shell to Sea' struggle and civil disobedience by locals in Rossport County Mayo against gas pipeline, but with emphasis on planning process and legal issues.

134. Turner, Terisa E. and M.O. Oshare, 'Women's Uprisings against the Nigerian Oil Industry in the 1980s', revised version of paper presented to Canadian African Studies Association in May 1992, online at: http://uoguelph.ca

135. Wokoma, Iyenemi Norman, 'Assessing accomplishments of women's nonviolent direct action in the Niger Delta' in Edith Natuku da-Togboa and Dina Rodriguez Mintero, eds., *Gender and Peace Building in Africa*, Costa Rica, University of Peace, 2005, pp. 167-85. A shorter account by Wokoma also available in George-Williams, *Bite Not One Another* (127 A.4.b.).

136. Yearley, Steve and John Forrester, 'Shell, a Target for Global Campaigning?' in Cohen and Rai, *Global Social Movements* (Introduction 1.c.) pp. 134-45.

4.c. Food and Drink Multinationals

McDonald's has been one focus for resistance, for example through a well-publicized libel trial of two members of London Greenpeace from 1992-97, with the judge finding for McDonald's on 5 issues, but for the defendants on three; and in February 2005 the European Court of Human Rights ruled that their rights were violated when they were refused legal aid. Nestle's has been targeted by an extended boycott because of its misleading marketing of baby milk in Africa.

Local resistance to Coca Cola, and to Nestle's bottled water plants. for their excessive and sometimes illegal use of water supplies is covered under 'water privatization ', A.7.a.

137. Bove, Jose, 'A Farmers' International?' *New Left Review*, no. 12 (Nov/ Dec 2001), pp. 89-101.

Discusses the Confederation Paysanne and the farmers' international Via Campesina, but also gives account of French farmer resistance to McDonald's.

138. Fazal, Anwar and Radha Holla, *The Boycott Book: Two Steps Forward and One Step Back: Lessons from the Nestle Boycott (1977-1984)*. Available at: http://www.theboycottbook.com

139. Gill, Lesley, '"Right There With You": Coca-Cola Labor Restructuring and Political Violence in Colombia', *Critique of Anthropology*, vol. 27 (Sept. 2007), pp. 235-60.

140. Johnson, Douglas A. 'Confronting Corporate Power: Strategies and Phases of the Nestle Boycott', *Research in Corporate Social Policy and Performance*, vol. 8 (1986), pp. 323-44.

141. Vidal, John, *McLibel: Burger Culture on Trial*, Basingstoke, Macmillan, 1997, pp. 354.

Detailed account of the trial of two members of London Greenpeace, who refused to withdraw a leaflet denouncing McDonald's.

See also: Klein, *No Logo* (112 A.4. Introduction), pp.387-96 on anti-McDonald's campaign.

A.5. Transnational Solidarity with Exploited Workers: Campaigns against Sweatshops

Resistance to multinationals quite often prompts transnational supporting action, for example at the headquarters of a corporation or at its shareholders' meetings, and may also (if local resistance is suppressed) invoke protests from human rights bodies. Opposition to multinationals and their activities may also take the form of consumer boycotts. Factories run by multinationals in the developing world take advantage of cheap and often non-unionized labour. But poor pay, long hours of work, dangerous working conditions and violations of workers' rights may be even more likely to result when smaller scale local companies are under pressure to reduce the prices of their goods by marketing companies and chain stores in the west. The garment industry has historically been subject to low pay and dangerous workplaces, and still is so today in parts of the world, as the deaths of over 1,000 Bangladeshi workers trapped in collapsing factory buildings in 2013 dramatically illustrated. Sweatshop conditions (including dangerous workplaces) can also exist in other forms of production, such as shoes (Nike was the target of a significant campaign in the USA in the 1990s) or toys. One result of these campaigns is that major companies in the west have become (at least temporarily) more concerned to monitor conditions under which the goods they buy are produced.

142. Ambruster-Sandoval, Ralph, *Globalization and Cross-Border Labor Solidarity in the Americas: The Anti-Sweatshop Movement and the Struggle for Social Justice*, New York, Routledge, 2005, pp. 224.

143. Brooks, Ethel C., *Unraveling the Garment Industry: Transnational Organizing and Women's Work*, Minneapolis MN, University of Minneapolis Press, 2007, pp. 304.

Contrasts the necessity of local resistance – e.g. the right to unionize – with the transnational emphasis on consumer boycotts that, she argues, can unintentionally reinforce the global forces they denounce.

144. Carty, Victoria, 'Transnational Mobilizing in Two Mexican Maquiladoras: The Struggle for Democratic Globalization', *Mobilization: An International Quarterly*, vol. 9 no. 3, (Oct. 2004), pp. 295-310.

145. Hale, Angela and Linda M. Shaw, 'Women Workers and the Promise of Ethical Trade in the Globalised Garment Industry: A Serious Beginning?' in Peter Waterman and Jane Wills, eds., *Place, Space and the New Labour Internationalism*, Oxford, Blackwell, 2001, pp. 206-26.

Discusses company codes of conduct introduced in response to ethical trade boycotts in west of products made with sweatshop labour, and analyzes the global economic conditions undercutting such codes and the right to union organization.

146.. Johns, R. and L. Vural, 'Class, Geography and the Consumerist Turn: UNITE and the Stop Sweatshops Campaign', *Economic Geography*, vol. 74 (2000), pp. 252-71.

147. Ross, Andrew, ed., *No Sweat: Fashion, Free Trade and the Rights of Garment Workers*, New York, Verso, 1997, pp. 256.

148. Taylor, Julie, 'Leveraging the Global to Empower Local Struggles: Resistance and Efficacy in Transnational Feminist Networks', *St Antony's International Review*, vol. 1 no. 2 (Nov. 2005), pp. 102-17. Also at: http://www.sant.ox.ac.uk

Three case studies of networks based in Latin America and Caribbean supporting garment workers (the Maquilla network created 1996) and domestic workers in Trinidad and Tobago; and promoting women's health in rural and urban Brazil.

149. Young, Iris, 'From Guilt to Solidarity: Sweatshops and Political Responsibility', *Dissent*, (Winter 2003), pp. 39-44.

On US movement.

See also: Klein, *No Logo* (112 A.4. Introduction) pp. 325-77, covering sweatshop campaigns and especially opposition to Nike.

A.6. Global Justice Movement

The demonstrations at the December 1999 WTO summit at Seattle launched the 'Anti-Globalization', 'Anti-Capitalist' or 'Global Justice' Movement into the western media (resistance had been taking place much earlier in the Global South). Although this movement was publicized in particular through its demonstrations at summit meeting of key international financial and economic institutions (see Introduction to A), it was also directed against the neoliberal international policies imposed by these institutions, in particular privatization of national resources and services. As noted under A.4., resistance to specific projects by multinational corporations was also seen as part of the broad movement, and internationally endorsed neoliberal policies strongly favoured these companies and weakened the power of national governments to restrict their activities.

After December 1999 there was an explosion of publications both by participants in the movement and by mainstream publishers. A lively theoretical debate also ensued between critics and proponents of neoliberalism, which is not covered here. Well known critics include Benjamin Barber, Walden Bello, Alex Callinicos, Susan George, Naomi Klein and George Monbiot. An important contributor to the general debate was former World Bank chief economist Joseph Stiglitz , who became very critical of aspects of neoliberal policies, and who published *Globalization and its Discontents* (2002) and *Making Globalization Work,* (2006) (both published by Penguin).

The Global Justice Movement brought together many from other social movements, who saw their own goals threatened by neoliberal policies. It also embraced the struggles of many indigenous peoples and exploited workers and poor communities round the world. Although the focus is social justice, the World Social Forum, and its European branch the European Social Forum, which provide a platform for participating groups, also played a role in coordinating protests against the 2003 Iraq War. But diversity of groups and campaigns has also meant diversity of ideologies and attitudes to nonviolence. For counter-summit protests there has been an agreement on tactical diversity, which meant respecting nonviolent actions but not imposing an overall nonviolent discipline.

a. General Titles

150. Bircham, Emma and John Charlton, eds., *Anti-Capitalism: A Guide to the Movement,* London, Bookmarks Publications, 2000, pp. 407.

Collection of brief articles on key issues, protest by regions, key actors, and assessments by actors within the movement.

151. Conway, Janet, 'Civil Resistance and the "Diversity of Tactics" in the Anti-Globalization Movement: Problems of Violence, Silence and Solidarity in Activist Politics', *Osgoode Hall Law Journal*, vol. 41 (2003), pp. 505-29; online at: http://www.ohlj,ca/archive/articles/41_23_conway.pdf

152. De Sousa Santos, Boaventura, *The Rise of the Global Left: The World Social Forum and Beyond* , London, Zed Books , 2006, pp. 240.

Examines history and organization of WSF and argues need to move beyond acting as platform for diverse movements.

153. *Development*, Issue on 'The Movement of Movements', vol. 48 no. 2 (June 2005), pp.1-121.

Analysis of Social Forum processes, the nature of the global justice movement and the Zapatista experience. NB: *Development*, vol. 47 no 3 (2004) is on 'Corporate Social Responsibility'.

154. Drainville, Andre C., *A History of World Order and Resistance: The Making and Unmaking of Global Subjects*, London, Routledge, 2011, pp. 216.

Looks at Global Justice Movement in a broad historical framework and relates it to case studies of earlier struggles in the USA, UK, France, South Africa, Algeria, the Philippines and Jamaica.

155. Eschle, Catherine and Bice Maiguascha, eds., *Critical Theories, International Politics and the 'Anti-Globalization Movement': The Politics of Global Resistance*, London and New York, Routledge, 2005, pp. 264, pb.
156. *Essays in Philosophy: A Biannual Journal*, vol. 8 no. 2 (June 2007).

Includes essays related to the anti-globalization movement and on civil disobedience in context of transnational mobilization.

157. George, Susan, *Another World Is Possible If …* London, Verso, 2004, pp. 268.

Committed political and economic analysis of the injustices and dangers of neoliberal globalization by a leading thinker and activist in the Global Justice Movement. Includes brief discussion of campaigns (Jubilee 2000, opposition to the Multilateral Agreement on Investment, summit protests) and ends with chapter on why the movement should be nonviolent.

158. Goodman, James, ed., *Protest and Globalisation: Prospects for Transnational Solidarity*, Annandale NSW, Pluto Press, 2002, pp. 276.

Analyses by both Australian and international contributors of problems posed by globalization.

159. Graeber, David, 'The New Anarchists', *New Left Review*, II no.13 (Jan/Feb 2002), pp.61-73.

160. Kingsnorth, Paul, *One No, Many Yeses: A Journey to the Heart of the Global Resistance Movement*, London, Free Press, 2003, pp. 355.

Wide ranging exploration of campaigns in all parts of the world seen at first hand. Includes coverage of Sem Terra in Brazil, Cochabamba in Bolivia, township resistance to privatization in South Africa, the Zapatistas, opposition to mining in West Papua, and campaigning groups in the USA.

See also his: 'Protest still matters'. *New Statesman,* 8 May, 2006, discussing why the Global Justice Movement has dropped out of the news, the turn away from street demonstrations to social forums, and stressing that struggles still continue, especially in the Global South.

161. Klein, Naomi, 'Farewell to the "End of History": Organization and Vision in Anti-Corporate Movements', in Leo Panitch and Colin Leys, eds., *A World of Contradictions: Socialist Register 2002.* London, Merlin Press, 2001, pp. 3-14.

162. Monbiot, George, *Anticapitalism: A Guide to the Movement.* London, Bookmarks, 2001, pp. 416.

163. Notes from Nowhere, ed., *We Are Everywhere,* London, Verso, 2003, pp. 521.
Extensive collection of brief articles on campaigns round the world using different tactics and approaches.

164. O'Nions, James, 'New Turn in Tunis', *Red Pepper* (June/July 2013), pp. 30-32.
Assessment of World Social Forum conference in Tunisia March 2013, attempting to link the 'alter-globalization' movement and the 'Arab Spring'.

165. Polet, Francois, ed., *The State of Resistance: Popular Struggles in the Global South,* London, Zed Books, 2007, pp. 176.
Over 40 contributions from writers and activists on resistance to neoliberal globalization, including material on anti-privatization campaigns in South Africa and Indian peasants opposing the WTO.

166. Prokosh, Mike and Laura Raymond, *The Global Activists Manual: Local Ways to Change the World,* New York, Thunder Mouth Press/Nation Books, 2002, pp. 324.
Accounts of campaigns illustrating movement building and different types of action. Final section on 'practical tips' and list of organizations.

167. Sellers, John, 'Raising a Ruckus', *New Left Review,* II no. 10 (July/Aug 2001), pp. 71-85.
On the evolution of Ruckus out of Greenpeace.

168. Solnit, David, ed., *Globalize Liberation: How to Uproot the System and Build a Better World,* San Francisco, City Lights, 2004, pp. 451.
Thirty three essays, mainly by US-based activists, on the new radicalism and direct action in the Global Justice Movement.

169. Starhawk, *Webs of Power: Notes from the Global Uprising* , Gabriola Island BC, New Society Publishers, 2003; New Catalyst Books, 2008, pp. 288.

Part 1: the author, an activist and ecofeminist, chronicles the global justice movement from Seattle to Genoa. Part 2 explores the future of the movement and debates between advocates of violent and nonviolent tactics.

170. Starr, Amory, *Global Revolt: A Guide to the Movements Against Globalization*, London, Zed Books, 2005, pp. 272.

171. Vinthagen, Stellan, 'Global Movements and Local Struggles: The Case of World Social Forum'. in Clark, ed., *People Power*, pp. 184-90 (Introduction, 1.c.).

172. Wainwright, Hilary, 'The WSF on Trial', *Red Pepper* (March 2005). Online :http://www.redpepper.org.uk/social-forums/
On the fifth World Social Forum gathering in Porto Alegre.

173. Welton, Neva and Linda Wolf, eds., *Global Uprising: Confronting the Tyrannies of the 21st Century*, Gabriola Island BC, New Society Publishers, 2001, pp. 273.

b) Resistance to International Economic Organizations

i. Demonstrating at Global Summits

The demonstrations at summits of international economic and financial bodies, which began at the WTO Seattle summit in December 1999, involved various forms of nonviolent direct action (and more violent forms promoted primarily by the Black Bloc anarchists), and quite often violent retaliation against protesters by the police. Police violence was particularly extreme at Genoa in 2003 where almost 100 were injured in a police raid. Summits began to avoid confrontation with protesters by choosing remote venues and requiring extensive security measures. When the G.8 went to a small village in Perth in July 2005, campaigners converged instead on Edinburgh. Striking forms of nonviolent protest at summits included Korean farmers jumping into the harbour at Hong Kong during the December 2005 WTO summit and two Greenpeace dinghies attempting to deliver a petition to G8 leaders meeting in June 2007 at Heligendamm from the Baltic sea.

174. Della Porta, Donatella, Massimiliano Andretta, Lorenzo Mosca and Herbert Reiter, *Globalization from Below: Transnational Activists and Protest Networks*, Minneapolis MN, University of Minnesota Press, 2006, pp. 338.

An in depth look at the Genoa G.8 summit in 2001, and European Social Forum, from protesters' point of view, based on survey of 800 activists at Genoa and 2,400 participants in 2002 Florence European Social Forum.

175. Donson, Fiona, Graeme Chesters, Ian Welsh and Andrew Tickle, 'Rebels with a Cause: Folk Devils without a Panic: Press Jingoism and Policing Tactics and Anticapitalist Protest London and Prague', *Internet Journal of Criminology*, 2004, pp. 34: http://www.internetjournalofcriminology.com

176. Drainville, Andre C., 'Quebec City 2001 and the Making of Transnational Subjects' in Leo Panitch and Colin Leys, eds., *A World of Contradictions: Socialist Register 2002*, London, Merlin, 2001, pp.15-42.

177. Epstein, Barbara 'Not your Parents' Protest', *Dissent*, vol. 47 (Spring 2000), pp. 8-11.
On Seattle.

178. Graeber, David, *Direct Action: An Ethnography*, Edinburgh and Oakland CA, A.K. Press, 2009, pp.592.
Participant observation study of Global Justice Movement, centred on case study of Summit of the Americas in Quebec City 2001.

179. Hilary, John, 'Anti-Capitalism Alive and Well', *Red Pepper*, (Dec/Jan 2010), pp. 14-15.
On 10th anniversary of closing down WTO summit at Seattle, author celebrates the setbacks of the WTO since. He notes broadening of movement, illustrated by role of migrant workers and women's rights groups from across Asia leading protests at WTO 2005 Hong Kong summit.

180. Morse, David, 'Beyond the Myths of Seattle', *Dissent*, vol. 48 (Summer 2001), pp. 39-43.

181. Neale, Jonathan, *You Are G 8. We Are 6 Billion: The Truth Behind the Genoa Protests*, London, Vision Paperbacks, 2002, pp. 275.

182. Starr, Amory, Luis A. Fernandez and Christian Scholl, *Shutting Down the Streets*, New York University Press, 2011, pp. 224.
The authors, who took part in protests at summits, from the 1999 WTO demonstrations in Seattle to the 2007 G.8. protests in Heiligendamm (Germany), analyze direct action at 20 summits and how government social control (including a Berlin-type wall at Heiligendamm) limits space for dissent.

See also: Kingsnorth, *One No, Many Yeses*, pp.51-62 (Genoa and Seattle) and Sellers 'Raising a Ruckus' on role of Ruckus at Seattle (160 & 167 A.6.a.).

ii. Opposing World Bank Policies and Projects

World Bank loans for projects with major environmental consequences often prove controversial. For example it was under pressure from human rights organizations to withdraw a loan from the Bajo Aguan valley palm oil project in Honduras which had led to serious conflict: http://popularresistance.org 'World Bank's Lending Arm Linked to Deadly Honduras Conflict' 11 Jan., 2014.

183. Brown, L. David and Jonathan Fox, *The Struggle for Accountability: NGOs, Social Movements and the World Bank*, Cambridge MA, MIT Press, 1998, pp. 570.

See also: Brown and Fox, 'Transnational Civil Society Coalitions and the World Bank: Lessons from Project and Policy Influence Campaigns' in Edwards and Gaventa, eds., *Global Citizen Action*, pp. 43-58 (3 Introduction, 1.a.).

184. Palit, Chitaroopa, 'Monsoon Risings: Megadam Resistance in the Narmada Valley', *New Left Review*, II no. 21(May/June 2003), pp. 80-100.

Anti-dam resistance persuaded the World Bank to withdraw from funding one of the dams, but did not change Indian government policy.

See also Keck and Sikkink, *Activists Beyond Borders*, (Introduction 1.c.) on opposition to World Bank loans to projects affecting indigenous peoples, pp. 135-47; and Kerssen, *Grabbing Power* (106 A.3.b.) which focuses on Bajo Aguan valley peasant resistance and government repression in Honduras.

7. Opposing IMF Policies and Privatization
Introduction

Movements round the world have mounted resistance to IMF conditions for financial assistance, and their government's endorsement of these neoliberal policies of privatizing large sectors of the economy, and opening them up to multinational corporations. These struggles were viewed as part of the Global Justice Movement after 1999, but predated the protests at global summits, and have continued after such protests have waned, since they have roots in community opposition. Some of the most significant movements have occurred in Latin America – the successful resistance to the water privatization (and the Bechtel Company) in Cochabamba, Bolivia is often cited. There were widespread demonstrations by most sections of society in Peru in 2003 when protesters blocked the roads into Lima; in 2008 unions called a nationwide strike against high food prices seen as a consequence of neoliberal policies, and indigenous people marched in the old capital of Cuzco, which was hosting the Asia-Pacific Economic Cooperation annual summit (*Red Pepper* (July 2003), p. 16 and *New Internationalist* (December 2008), pp.10-11). Moreover in three Latin American countries the scale of popular resistance to privatization and/or other neoliberal policies forced changes in national policy and led to immediate (or subsequent) changes of government: Argentina 2001-2002, Bolivia 2003 and Ecuador 2005. These national movements are included in Volume 1 of the *Guide to Civil Resistance*, E.IV. 2b, 3b and 7. The Bolivia entries include several studies of the Cochabamba struggle. These titles are not repeated here – though an additional Cochabamba reference is listed.

Many trade unions in other parts of the world have opposed the terms of IMF and other loans and 'free trade' agreements requiring privatization. For example South Korean unions called strikes 1996-97 against plans for a more 'flexible' labour market and in 1998 calling for renegotiation of an IMF loan, and Indian unions called a general strike in 2003 against privatization and changes to the labour laws. Indian trade unions also brought one million onto the streets in a one day strike against neoliberal policies on 28 Feb. 2012, and even larger numbers in a two-day strike in Feb. 2013 (*Red Pepper* (Jun/Jul 2013) p. 40. Unionists have often been joined by students and women's groups: *New Internationalist* in a March 2004 issue focusing on the IMF and World Bank provides snapshots of demonstrations and strikes in Indonesia, Zambia and Romania among others.

Resisting privatization includes opposition to handing over state services, such as railways and the post office, and social services, such as the health care and education, to large corporations. There are examples of trade unions and others resisting these policies: health workers in San Salvador in 2002, teachers in Guatemala and Peru in 2003. More recently health care workers in Colombia were in 2013 resisting effective privatization as part of a wider resistance to the US-Colombia Free Trade Agreement: http://commondreams.org, 25 Aug 2013.

The best documented struggles are, however, those against energy and water privatization: some references are listed below.

a. Resistance to Energy and Water Privatization

Opposition to privatization continues in many parts of the world. For example the *The Times of India* reported in January 2014 a threatened strike by power engineers in the state of Uttar Pradesh opposing state plans to privatize power supplies in four cities. It is impossible to provide solid references for all these struggles, but those cited below give an impression of the breadth of resistance.

185. Abramsky, Kolya, ed., *Sparking a Worldwide Energy Revolution: Social Struggles in Transition to a Post-Petrol World*, Edinburgh and Oakland CA, A.K. Press, 2010, pp. 480.
Chapters by authors from 20 countries on developments in energy sector and struggles.

186. Bakker, Karen, 'The "Commons" versus the "Commodity": Alter-Globalization, Anti-Privatization and the Human Right to Water in the Global South', *Antipode*, vol. 39 no. 3 (June 2007), pp. 430-55.
Examines different (though overlapping) alternatives to privatization developed through North-South and red-green alliances and argues concept of the 'commons' most effective basis for a strategy of action.
187. Balanya, Belen et al, eds., *Reclaiming Public Water: Achievements, Struggles and Visions from around the World*, Amsterdam, Transnational Institute and Corporate Europe Observatory, 2005, pp. 284. Downloadable at:http://www.tni.org

188, Davidson-Harden, Adam, Anil Naidoo and Andi Harden, 'The Geopolitics of the Water Justice Movement', *Peace, Conflict and Development*, issue 11 (Nov 2007), pp. 34. Online: http://www.peacestudiesjournal.org.uk

189. Food Empowerment Project, 'Water Usage and Privatization': http://foodspower.org
Useful summary analysis including brief case studies of corporate misuse of water and resistance to them (and further references): Nestle in US, Vivendi and Suez in Mexico, Bechtel in Bolivia and Coca Cola in India.

190. Hall, David, Emanuele Lobina and Robin de la Motte, 'Public Resistance to Privatisation in Water and Energy', *Development in Practice*, vol. 15 nos. 3-4 (June 2005). Online: http://www.psiru.org/reports/2005-06-W-E-resist,pdf
Examines role of different types of opposition in 'delaying, cancelling or reversing the privatization of water and energy', including success in Nkondobe (South Africa), Paraguay where parliament voted in 2002 to suspend indefinitely privatization of state-owned water and Poznan in Poland in 2002, and failure of campaigns in UK, Chile and Philippines.

191. Kumar, Rahul, 'Indian Water Activists Launch Anti-Privatization Campaign', OneWorld, 7 Feb. 2006 ": http://www.commondreams.org

192. Olivera, Oscar (with Tom Lewis), *Cochabamba: Water War in Bolivia*, Cambridge MA, South End Press, 2004, pp. 224.

193. Romano, Sarah, 'From Protest to Proposal: The Contentious Politics of the Nicaraguan Anti-Water Privatization Social Movement', *Bulletin of Latin American Research*, vol. 31 no. 4 (2012), pp. 499-514.

194. Spigarelli, Gina, 'Water Festival of El Carmen de Vibore: Communities Resist Water Privatization and Multinational Mining in Colombia', Upside Down World, 13 November 2013. On line at: http://upsidedownworld.org

195. Shiva, Vandana *Water Wars: Privatization, Pollution and Profit*, Cambridge MA, Southend Press, 2002, pp. 156.
Outlines 9 principles of 'water democracy ' and highlights activism against corporations claiming water supplies.

196. Shiva, Vandana, 'Resisting Water Privatisation, Building Water Democracy', Paper for the World Water Forum, 2006. Online at: http://globalternative.org
Includes information on successful local campaigns: 1. against Coca Cola bottling plant, closed in 2004, leading to national campaign "Coca-Cola-Pepsi Quit India Campaign'; 2. resistance to water diversion in Uttar Pradesh; 3. campaign in Delhi against raised tariffs and proposed privatization.

b. South Africa: Resistance to Privatization

Post-apartheid South Africa has seen widespread resistance to privatization, which has also been well documented, so these struggles are listed in a separate subsection.

197. Barchiesi, Franco, 'Transnational Capital, Urban Globalisation and Cross-Border Solidarity: The Case of the South African Municipal Workers', in Peter Waterman and Jane Wills, eds. *Place, Space and the New Labour Internationalisms*, Oxford, Blackwell, 2001, pp.80-102.
Discusses problems faced by union in new global context of neoliberal economic dominance and its resistance to water privatization.

198. Bond, Patrick with Trevor Ngwane, 'Community Resistance to Energy Privatization in South Africa' in Abramsky, ed., *Sparking a Worldwide Energy Revolution* (185 A.7.a.)

199. Buhlungu, Sakhela, 'The Anti-Privatisation Forum: A Profile of a Post-Apartheid Social Movement', 2004, pp. 22, at http://www.africanafrican.com

A case study for the University of KwaZulu-Natal project Globalisation, Marginalisation and new Social Movements in post-Apartheid South Africa.

200. Desai, Ashwin, *We Are the Poors: Community Struggles in Post-Apartheid South Africa*, New York, Monthly Review Press, 2002, pp. 153.

On struggles against neoliberal policies and privatization in the townships, strikes, and the Durban Social Forum.

201. Mayekiso, Mzwanele, *Township Politics: Civic Struggles in the New South Africa*, New York, Monthly Review Press, 1996, pp.288.

202. McKinley, Dale T., 'Lessons of Struggle: The Rise and Fall of the Anti-Privatisation Forum', South African Civil Society Information Service, 8 Feb 2012. Online at: http://www.sacsis.org.za

Critical analysis of failings of Forum, which was set up in 2000 and active for 10 years, but also noting its positive role as voice for marginalised and promoter of grass roots activism.

203. Ngwane, Trevor, 'Sparks in the township', *New Left Review*, II no. 22 (July/Aug 2003), pp. 37-56.

See also: Kingsnorth, *One No, Many Yeses*, (160 A.6.a.) pp. 89-123: Polet, *The State of Resistance* (165 A.6.a.)

8. Resistance since Financial Crisis of 2008

Introduction

The disastrous impact of the threatened collapse of the banks in 2008 on western economies led to widespread protests in both North America and much of Europe. To some extent these denoted a revival in the west of the Global Justice Movement and of an awareness of the abuses of global capitalism: the financial crisis exposed the greed and irresponsibility of many of those involved and publicized the enormous salaries and bonuses they received. But the scale of protests were also a direct response to the wide scale poverty and unemployment triggered by the financial crisis, especially in countries most deeply affected. Outside of the west, struggles over homelessness and evictions, land, multinational corporations, international neoliberalism and privatization (some documented earlier in Section A) had never abated, and continued after 2008.

Anger at the role of the banks in the crisis of 2008, suspicion of large corporations, resistance to neoliberal government policies and calls for greater economic justice were manifested in varying degrees in many countries from 2008. One of the countries to suffer disastrously from collapsing banks was Iceland, where protests broke out in January 2009 on a scale not seen since 1949, and where the goal was to topple the government. Naomi Klein compared the crowds in the streets banging pots and pans to Argentina a decade earlier. She also noted the spread of protest to Latvia, where people were resisting an IMF emergency loan requiring stringent austerity measures, and to Greece, as well as South Korea.('Que se vayan todos! – That's the Global Backlash Talking' (*Guardian*, 6 Feb. 2009 taken from similar version in the *Nation*.)

The response to the crisis was dramatized by the imaginative, radical direct action groups like the Indignados, Occupy and UK Uncut, but it also evoked a response from the trade unions, especially in countries where they were still relatively strong. In France unions mobilized over one million in a general strike in January 2009 and an estimated two million demonstrated in March that year against President Sarkozy's response to the recession (*Guardian*, 30 Jan. 2009, p. 27 and *Independent*, 20 Mar. 2009, p. 10).

The European Trades Union Confederation organised Europe-wide strikes and demonstrations on 29 September 2010 – workers from many parts of Europe paralysed Brussels, in Spain a general strike was called, Portuguese protesters marched in Lisbon and Porto, Greek unions also demonstrated and protests took place in Ireland (hit hard by the banking crisis). Lithuania, Slovenia and other countries (*Guardian*, 30 Sep. 2010, p. 28).

The literature in English available so far on the movements is quite strong for some countries and limited to press reports for others.

a. General Titles (including Iceland)

204. Fillmore-Patrick, Hannah, 'The Iceland Experiment (2009-2013): A Participatory Approach to Constitutional Reform', *Democratization Policy Council Policy Note*. New Series 02, (2013), pp. 21. Available as pdf at:http://www.democratizationpolicy.org

Examines the financial collapse and the popular protests in 'the Kitchenware Revolution' (which included banging pots and pans), which led to widespread popular involvement in changing the constitution to prevent a future financial collapse and betrayal of trust.

205. Hilary, John, *The Poverty of Capitalism: Economic Meltdown and the Struggle for What Comes Next*, London, Pluto Press, 2013, pp. 240.

Analysis by War on Want director of how neoliberal elite is using the 2008 crisis to entrench its own power and impose neoliberal policies on Greece, Spain, Portugal and Ireland. The book ends with a sketch of the growing worldwide struggle against neoliberalism and suggesting how alternatives might be strengthened.

206. Hosseini, Sayed Abdolhamed, *Alternative Globalizations: An Integrative Approach to Studying Dissident Knowledge in the Global Justice Movement*, London and New York, Routledge, 2010, pp. 288.

Discusses whether growing popular opposition to neoliberalism, especially since 2008, can develop coherent alternative ideologies.

207. Jackson, Ross, *Occupy World Street: A Global Roadmap of Radical Economic and Political Reform*, Vermont VT, Chelsea Green Publishing, 2012, pp.336.

The chair of the Danish-based Gaia Trust advocates return to smaller decentralised communities with a more sustainable life style.

208. Mason, Paul, *Why Its Kicking Off Everywhere: The New Global Revolutions*, London, Verso, 2012, pp.237.

Wide-ranging exploration, by BBC economics journalist, of campaigns round the world since 2008, including the Arab uprisings of 2011, but mainly focused on resistance to economic policies and including accounts of protest in UK, USA and Greece. Discusses economic and social causes of unrest and role of new communications.

209. Mirowski, Philip, *Never Let a Serious Crisis Go to Waste: How Neoliberalism Survived the Financial Meltdown*, London, Verso, 2014, pp. 384, pb.

Economic historian's caustic analysis of self-validating nature of neoliberal thought among economists and politicians and suggested bases for an alternative analysis of economic crisis and future possibilities.

210. Sitrin, Marina and Dario Azzellini, *They Can't Represent Us! Reinventing Democracy from Greece to Occupy*, London, Verso, 2014, pp. 192, pb.

Combines history of direct democracy from classical Greece to the Indignados, drawing on interviews with activists in contemporary movements, including Occupy, that are based on forms of participatory democracy and reject liberal parliamentary democracy.

8.b. The Indignados: Spain and Greece

The financial crisis of 2008 had a disastrous effect on the scale of national debt in Spain and Greece, leading to governments accepting bailouts from the European Bank and IMF in return for stringent austerity programmes cutting jobs and welfare, and privatization of public facilities. Widespread public resistance to austerity measures was launched on 15 May, 2011 in Spain, where the Real Democracy Now! campaign organized marches in cities and an impromptu protest camp was set up in the Puerta del Sol in Madrid. Thousands more came to the camp and it lasted 78 days; other camps were set up in towns and cities round the country, and the 15M movement (named after the date of the first protest) was launched. Within the broad resistance to the austerity programmes other initiatives have developed: for example to tackle the social crisis of mass evictions in Spain of people defaulting on their mortgages (the Platform of People Affected by Mortgage (PAH). The multiple crises of food and welfare in Greece have prompted numerous solidarity networks.

The political position in Greece has been particularly unstable, with widespread public anger about the corruption and incompetence of politicians, and demonstrations have quite often become violent. The growth of the Golden Dawn extreme right anti-immigrant party has also been an ominous sign. On the left Syriza, a new radical coalition of small parties, emerged as the party close to popular protest and strongly opposed to the austerity programmes. Syriza was elected in January 2015 with a mandate to renegotiate the terms of continuing IMF/EU financial aid to avoid even harsher austerity measures. Crisis point was reached in June/July 2015. Syriza called a snap referendum on the bail out terms on 5 July, and 61 per cent supported the government in voting 'No'.

Portugal received a large EU/IMF loan in 2011. The victory of a centre-right coalition in elections ensured that the government pressed ahead with austerity measures, leading to high unemployment and widespread privatization. Public sector workers went on strike in protest, but there was not a major popular movement comparable to the Indignados in Spain and Greece.

The linking of privatization measures to austerity programmes has also prompted specific campaigns, for example against water privatization in Greece and a Portuguese strike by postal workers in November 2013 against privatization of the postal service..

In addition to protest there have been positive local and democratic alternatives arising from the crisis, such as the neighbourhood assemblies in Spain and imaginative experiments in Greece, for example to bypass use of money through local exchange schemes.

All these issues are briefly covered in the references below, although some of these are fairly brief articles from journals sympathetic to the Indignados, such as the UK-based *Red Pepper*, *New Internationalist* and *Peace News;* and the *Progressive* in the USA.

211. Carriou, Maria, 'Spaniards Take On the Banks', *The Progresive* (Nov. 2012). Online: http://www.progressive.org

Examines campaign against the banks' ruthless treatment of those unable to pay mortgages and other campaigns such as defiance by doctors and health care workers of law requiring them to refuse treatment to immigrants.

212. Castaneda, Ernesto, 'The Indignados of Spain: A Precedent to Occupy Wall Street', *Social Movement Studies: Journal of Social and Cultural Political Protest*, vol. 11 nos.3-4 (2012), pp. 309-19. Online: http://www.tandfonline. com

Builds on participant observation in Barcelon in summer of 2011.

213. Clark, Howard, 'No More Mortgage Suicides! Spain's Social Movements Struggle for Housing Justice', *Peace News*, Issue 2552-2553 (Dec 2012-Jan 2013), online at: http://peacenews.info

On the vigorous campaign to support mortgage defaulters and the wider 15M movement.

214. Dhaliwal, Puneet, 'Public Squares and Resistance: The Politics of Space in the Indignados Movement', *Interface: A Journal for and about Social Movements*, vol. 4 no. 1 (May 2012), pp.251-73.

215. Flesher Fominaya, Cristina, 'Debunking Spontaneity: Spain's 15-M/ Indignados as Autonomous Movement', *Social Movement Studies*. Published online 19 Aug. 2013: http://www/tandfonline

Argues emergence of movement not 'new' and 'spontaneous' but product of evolution of a collective identity and culture stressing deliberative democracy since the 1980s.

See also her blog on the LSE website: 'Spain is Different: Podemos and 15-M' on the rise of the leftist but non-ideological Podemos party in the European Parliamentary elections of June 2014, and influence of 15-M movement on the nature of the new party: http://blogs.lse.ac.uk/ eurocrisispress/20140604/spain-is-different-podemos -and-15-m/

216. Garcia Lamarca, Melissa, 'Sparks from the Spanish Crucible', *New Internationalist* (Apr. 2013), pp.16-17.

On the Platform for Mortgage Affected People (PAH) set up in February2009 to campaign about the hundreds of thousands of foreclosures and evictions of people unable to keep up mortgages on their homes, and often faced with a huge debt to the banks even after eviction. The group organized mass resistance to evictions, occupied foreclosed flats and houses to provide shelter for those made homeless, and to lobby Parliament to end evictions, promote affordable rents and changes to the mortgage law.

217. Garcia, Ter, 'A Year of Small Victories for the Spanish Foreclosure Movement', Waging Nonviolence, 28 Dec 2011, 3pp. Online: http://www.wagingnonviolence.org

Survey of first year of PAH.

218. Gerbaudo, Paolo, 'Los Indignados', *Red Pepper* (Aug/Sept 2011), pp. 33-35.

On launch of movement by Real Democracy Now! on 15 May 2011 with marches and protest camp in Madrid, its spread across Spain and to Greece.

219. Hancox, Dan, *The Village Against the World*, London, Verso, 2013, pp. 252, pb. (Successor to author's ebook *Utopia and the Valley of Tears*, 2012, on same topic.)

Discusses the small village, Marinaleda, in southern Spain that has battled for decades with the state and capitalist policies, but gained international attention in 2012 when its mayor (and farmers union leader) organized the filling of ten shopping trolleys, refused to pay, and distributed them to the poor from a military base and mansion of a local large landowner.

220. Katerini, Tonia, 'Organising to Survive', *Red Pepper* (Dec/Jan 2013), pp. 43-45.

Examines scale of crisis created in Greece by austerity programme and the growing movement Solidarity for All (promoted by the left coalition Syriza) creating support networks supplying food, health, education, cultural activity and legal advice, and setting up informal exchanges of goods and services.

221. Prentoulis, Marina and Lasse Thomassen,'The Legacy of the Indignados', openDemocracy, 13 August 2013: http://www.opendemocracy.net

Discusses impact two years later of Spanish and Greek movements: their new form of political activism and extended definition of politics.

222. Reyes, Oscar. 'Rooted in the Neighbourhood', *Red Pepper* (Oct/Nov. 2012), pp. 36-37.

Comments on decline in the neighbourhood assemblies that arose in 2011, but argues widespread willingness to take part in local initiatives survives, and is (for example) strengthening the campaign against eviction of those unable to pay their mortgage.

223. Romanos, Eduardo, 'Evictions, Petitions and Escraches: Contentious Housing in Austerity Spain', *Social Movement Studies*, vol. 13 no. 2 (2013), pp. 296-302. Online: http://www.tandfonline.com

Examines different types of action used by movement against evictions and how a range of people drawn into movement.

224. Vradis, Antonis and Dimitris Dalakoglu, eds., *Revolt and Crisis in Greece: Between a Present Yet to Pass and a Future Still to Come*, Edinburgh and London, A.K. Press/Occupied London, 2011, pp. 378.

Wide range of contributors, including David Graeber, on economic meltdown in Greece and popular responses to government's extreme austerity programme.

See also Mason, *Why Its Kicking Off Everywhere* (208 8.a), pp. 87-104 on Greece.

8.c. Occupy, USA

The Occupy movement in the USA was launched on September 17, 2011, when a march on Wall Street developed into the occupation of Zuccotti Park nearby. Support for the 'Occupy Wall Street' protest camp increased, especially after the police arrested 700 people for blocking Brooklyn Bridge two weeks later, and spread to other parts of New York City and many other cities in the USA. The movement was characterised by lively debates about the injustices of the economic and financial system, coined the slogan 'we are the 99%' (opposed to the inordinate wealth and power of the 1%) and initiated various blockades, for example of the New York Stock Exchange. After two months police closed down the Zuccotti Park encampment, making 200 arrests, and several other cities did the same. By March 2012 there had been 6,700 arrests in 112 cities. The energy generated by the movement spread into related activities – as in Spain some activists engaged with the mortgage crisis, occupied foreclosed homes and undertook dramatic protests at courts and auctions of seized houses and apartments. Occupy activists also turned to foreign policy issues and other social causes.

In the radical environment of Oakland (an ethnically diverse working class city, where the unionised workers at the port are unusually militant, and the students at the nearby Berkeley campus have a tradition of activism) the Occupy movement gained strong support and called a general strike in November 2011. It also became the radical wing of the wider US movement, but by mid-2012 was in danger of alienating local support, particularly through its provocative demonstrations against the city police.

The early achievements of the Occupy movement were to influence the terms of national debate (polls suggested strong public sympathy for the basic message of economic injustice), demonstrate a participatory democracy in action and to have an international impact. The euphoria generated by the movement generated an immediate literature, referenced below. The longer term implications of the movement, as economic conditions begin to improve in the USA, are more uncertain.

225. Byrne, Janet, ed., *The Occupy Handbook*, New York City, Back Bay Books, 2012, pp. 560, pb.

Includes discussion of why the 1% have such a dominant economic position.

Calhoun, Craig, 'Occupy Wall Street in Perspective', *British Journal of Sociology*, vol. 64 (2013), pp. 26-38. Avaialable as pdf at: http://eprints.lse.ac.uk

Argues Occupy Wall Street was 'less an organized effective movement' than a dramatic performance.

226. Chomsky, Noam, *Occupy*, London, Penguin Books, and Brooklyn, Zucotti Park Books, 2012, pp. 120, pb.

This book comprises five sections: 1. Chomsky's Howard Zinn Memorial Lecture given to Occupy Boston in Oct.2011; 2.an interview with a student in Jan 2012; 3. a question and answer session with 'InterOccupy'; 4. a question and answer session partly on foreign policy; and 5. Chomsky's brief appreciation of the life and work of radical historian Howard Zinn. There is a short introductory note by the editor, Greg Ruggiero.

227. Gitlin, Todd, *Occupy Nation, the Roots: The Spirit and the Promise of Occupy Wall Street*, New York, Harper Collins, 2012, pp. 320

Book by former radical student leader in the 1960s, providing a portrait of the movement.

228. Graeber, David, *The Democracy Project: A History, a Crisis, a Movement*, London, Allen Lane, 2013, pp. 352, pb.

Reflections on Occupy Wall Street movement and its beginning in the occupation of Zucotti Park, September 2011, from standpoint of an anarchist theorist.

229. Healey, Josh, 'Whose Streets? Our Streets!', *Red Pepper* (Apr/May 2012), pp. 41-43.
Examines Occupy Oakland, its potential and downside.

230. *Social Movement Studies: Journal of Social Cultural and Political Protest*, vol. 11 issue 3-4 (2012). This issue has several articles on Occupy. See:
Kerton, S. 'Tahrir Here? The influence of the Arab Uprisings on the emergence of Occupy', pp.302-308;.
Pickerill, J. and J. Krinksy, 'Why does Occupy matter?', pp. 279-87;
Smith, J. and B. Gidden, 'Occupy Pittsburgh and the challenges of participatory democracy', pp. 288-94.

231. Taylor, Astra, Keith Gessen et al, *Occupy! Scenes from Occupied America*, New York and London, Verso, 2012, pp. 224.
Collection of brief accounts of events at Zuccotti Park encampment and initial assessments by writers from leftist New York media, plus extracts from speeches of visiting intellectuals and activists – Judith Butler, Slavoj Zizek, Angela Davis and Rebecca Solnit.

232. Van Gelder, Sarah, ed., *This Changes Everything: Occupy Wall Street and the 99% Movement*, Bainbridge Isle WA, Yes! Magazine, 2012, pp. 96.
Contributors include Naomi Klein, David Korten, Ralph Nader and Rebecca Solnit.

233.. Writers for the 99%, *Occupying Wall Street: The Inside Story of an Action that Changed America*, Chicago IL, Haymarket Books, 2012, pp. 217. (Initially published by OR Books New York on print-on-demand and ebook basis.)
Detailed account of daily life at the camp by figures on the left.

8.d. UK

In Britain the campaigning group UK Uncut was launched in October 2010 to use direct action against tax avoidance by large corporations and to oppose austerity cuts to public services. It dramatized its demands with a number of sit-ins in stores and a sit-down at Westminster Bridge, London to oppose the Health and Social Care Bill going through parliament. It inspired US Uncut and Portugal Uncut.

In early 2011 the TUC initiated a series of protests against austerity – notably the 'March for the Alternative' mobilizing about 500,000 in London on 26 March 2011. UK Uncut protesters took part, occupying Fortnum and Mason and blockading Boots. Many were arrested – they were easier targets for the police than the Black Bloc anarchists who were smashing up shops. Subsequently there was strong pressure from MPs and other public figures for charges against the nonviolent Uncut activists to be dropped.

The Occupy movement was launched in London in October 2011: protesters tried to occupy the financial centre of the City, but finally established their camp the precinct of St Paul's cathedral, where it highlighted the moral ambiguity of the Church of England participating in an unjust financial system. Three more camps were set up in London: in Finsbury Square just north of the City, in disused offices owned by UBS and in the (disused) Old Street Magistrates Court. The high profile St Paul's camp was not dismantled by police until the end of February 2012 (*Guardian*, 29 Feb. 2012, pp. 1-2, 30 and 32). Occupy London then turned to other forms of campaigning.

Although protests did not alter the Conservative-Liberal Coalition austerity policies, the government was more responsive on the issue of tax – the Treasury announced changes to UK rules on legal tax avoidance on 6 December 2010, and the Parliamentary Public Accounts Committee has pursued this and related issues vigorously. There has been a real shift in public debate, with much greater awareness of the need to justify bankers' rewards – shareholders at Barclays annual meeting in 2011 criticised 'obscene bonuses', criticism of tax avoidance by large companies and protests (including by churches) against exploitation of the poor by loan companies and the misery created by some welfare reforms. Local credit unions and food banks have been constructive responses. Exploitation of workers by offering 'zero hours contracts' (i.e. no guarantee of a minimum number of paid hours' work a week) became an issue in 2013 – McDonald's was identified as the biggest such employer, admitting that 90% of its workforce was on these contracts.

234. Hancox, Dan, ed., *Fight Back! A Reader on the Winter of Protest*, OpenDemocracy, 2011, pp.350: http:// openDemocracy.net

Covers both student protests in late 2010 (e.g against high tuition fees) and wider demonstrations against cuts. Edited by young protesters, but includes essay by Anthony Barnett, founder of openDemocracy reflecting on potential significance of new activism.

See also: Mason, *Why Its Kicking Off Everywhere* (208 A.8.a.) pp.57-63 on UK Uncut.

B. Indigenous Movements

Indigenous peoples round the world have suffered centuries of violence and repression as a result of colonialism and colonization. Demands for recognition of the civil and political rights of indigenous peoples, and for respect for their cultures, only became a prominent political issue in the 1960s and 1970s, when other social movements provided inspiration, and changing social and political attitudes enabled indigenous peoples to be heard. The indigenous cause also benefited from the globalization of protest and the institutional possibilities offered by the United Nations. The World Council of Indigenous Peoples was created in 1975 and succeeded in getting recognition of their special rights from the UN Human Rights Commission, and 1993 was designated the UN Year of Indigenous Peoples. The UN General Assembly adopted the 'Declaration on the Rights of Indigenous Peoples' in 2007 – the governments of the US, Canada, Australia and New Zealand all voted against it, arguing it went too far. The Unrepresented Nations and Peoples Organization based at the Hague has also offered support to indigenous struggles. Survival International, based in London, campaigns for tribal peoples' rights globally, and their website provides a guide to today's struggles, see: http:// www.survivalinternational.org

Indigenous movements have campaigned for changes in the public recognition of their history – for example the abolition of 'Columbus Day' in the United States. They have also demanded cultural rights, including changes in the way their artefacts and history are presented in museums, respect for sacred sites and return of sacred objects. At a political level indigenous peoples have demonstrated for basic civil and political rights, protesting against economic, social and political discrimination. In Australia Aborigines and Torres Straits Islanders still did not have the right to vote in all elections until the mid-1960s; in 1972 the Aboriginal Tent Embassy was set up outside the Commonwealth parliament to symbolize the fact that Aborigines were effectively foreigners in their own country.

In several countries indigenous peoples, often suffering from extreme poverty and social discrimination, as well as loss of their traditions and identity, began in the 1970s to reject the goal of assimilation into mainstream society, and to give priority to demands for land and political and economic autonomy within it. In Canada the Inuit gained the self-governing territory of Nunavit in 1999; other aboriginal groups were granted autonomy (within the framework of the Canadian Constitution), or devolution under Treaty Land Entitlement to members of the Cree Nation living on reserves, who may be able to acquire additional territory. In Australia the creation of the Australian and Torres Straits Islanders Commission in 1989 was a contentious and much more limited gesture towards indigenous autonomy. In the USA the lands and status of Native Americans rest on numerous treaties (frequently broken by the Federal Government) and on later Congressional laws. The 1934 Indian Reorganization Act did attempt to halt privatization of communal lands and promote self-government, but did not restore lost land. The legal rights of tribal groups have increased since the evolution from the 1960s of both protest and resistance and legal action.

The semi-nomadic Saami living in northern Scandinavia and parts of Russia were politically mobilized in the 1970s, when the Norwegian government launched a project to build a dam and hydroelectric power station, which would encroach on the pastures for reindeer, central to the Saami lifestyle. The Saami occupied the site and began a protest fast outside the Norwegian parliament. Despite only partial success, in reducing rather than ending the dam project, the Saami went on to demand educational and political autonomy and achieved separate parliaments in Norway, Finland and Sweden, which cooperate across boundaries in a Saami Parliamentary Council created in 2000.

Although political and cultural claims have been extremely important, indigenous peoples have also been, and are increasingly, engaged in bitter struggles to preserve their local livelihood and environment from national governments and multinational corporations seeking to exploit their natural resources and use their land. Occasionally indigenous people may be divided over the possible economic advantages of mining or other projects, as against preservation of their natural and cultural milieu. But the general picture is one in which the global economy and giant corporations within it pose a fundamental threat to indigenous survival.

Resistance to economic exploitation often involves forms of nonviolent (or sometimes violent) forms of defiance or obstruction, which may be accompanied by political advocacy or use of the courts by the protesters or national and international supporters. Campaigning for political change by indigenous minorities has included important symbolic demonstrations, such as the Native American protest caravan in 1972, and forms of disobedience, such as 'freedom rides' against segregation in New South Wales in 1965. But it has often focused on petitions, lobbying and rallies. An important stage in the campaign by Australian Aborigines was a referendum in 1967 on whether to include Aborigines in the census, when both Aborigines and white supporters campaigned for a 'yes' vote. Resort to the courts has also been very important as means of claiming rights to land: in Canada it has led to constitutional entrenchment of entitlement to land in 1982, and in Australia to the Mabo Judgment in the High Court in 1992, which based Aboriginal entitlement on continuing connection to land and waters before and after white settlement to the present. The Maoris in New Zealand campaigned in the 1960s and 1970s for official legal recognition of the Treaty of Waitangi, signed in 1840 between Maori chiefs and the British Crown, and subsequently largely ignored. In 1975 the Treaty of Waitingi Act was passed and set up a tribunal to examine complaints, but its limited powers led to disillusion among Maoris (and there are additional problems arising from discrepancies between the Maori and English versions of the original treaty).

Where indigenous groups form a significant proportion of the whole population, it may be possible for them to achieve a government supportive of their goals through elections, as has happened in Bolivia with the election of Morales. In Latin America indigenous goals are very closely linked to resistance to the ideology and practice of neo-liberal globalization and the international economic treaties and institutions that enshrine these doctrines, and remove restrictions on multinationals. In Bolivia the election of Morales was preceded by the 2003 national rebellion, opposing gas exports and the Free Trade Agreement of the Americas, which toppled the President (Guide to Civil Resistance, vol. 1, E.IV. 3.b).

B.1. Campaigns for Civil, Political and Cultural Rights

Introduction

This section focuses primarily on four countries in which European colonization led to indigenous peoples losing their lands and way of life (and in some cases their almost total destruction): Australia, New Zealand and Canada and the USA. In all four there have been vigorous campaigns for indigenous rights since the 1960s. Some Native American organizations span the USA and Canada, and the US Civil Rights Movement as well as its subsequent Black Power phase, influenced indigenous groups both in North America and in New Zealand and Australia. This section also briefly covers the struggle of the only European indigenous people, the Saami, in northern Scandinavia.

For an overview of the political and legal position of indigenous peoples within these countries and comparative assessments see:

235. Chesterman, John and Brian Galligan, *Citizens Without Rights*, Cambridge, Cambridge University Press [1997] 1998, pp. 288, pb.

On Australia. It includes some references to protests.

236. Dyck, Noel, ed. *Indigenous Peoples and the Nation State: 'Fourth World' Politics in Canada, Australia and Norway*, St John's Nfld, Institute of Social and Economic Research, Memorial University of Newfoundland, 1985, pp. 263, pb.

237. Fleras, Augie and Jean Leonard Elliott, *The Nations Within*, Oxford, Oxford University Press, 1992 pp. 267.

Covers Canada, New Zealand and the USA.

238. Ivanitz, Michele, 'Democracy and Indigenous Self-Determination' in April Carter and Geoffrey Stokes, eds., *Democratic Theory Today*, Cambridge, Polity, 2002, pp. 121-48 (compares Australia and Canada).

239. Macklem, Patrick, 'Distributing Sovereignty: Indian Nations and Equality of Peoples', *Stanford Law Review*, vol. 45 no 5 (May 1993), pp. 1311-67 Compares Canada and USA from a legal perspective.

I.a. Australia

240. Bennett, Scott, *Aborigines and Political Power*, Sydney, NSW, Allen and Unwin, 1989, pp. 167.

General analysis, includes some references to protest.

241. Burgmann, Verity, *Power and Protest: Movements for Change in Australian Society*, St Leonards NSW, Allen and Unwin, 1993, pp. 302.

Chapter 1 'Black Movement, White Stubbornness' covers land occupations, freedom rides, 'black power' and the tent embassy.

242. Mandle, W.F., *Going It Alone: Australia's National Identity in the Twentieth Century*, Ringwood VIC, Penguin, 1980.

Chapter on 'Donald Macleod and Australia's Aboriginal Problem', pp. 174-89 covers Pilbara strike and Pindan movement of late 1940s.

243. Read, Peter, *Charles Perkins: A Biography*, Melbourne VIC, Penguin 2001, pp. 392.

Perkins has been one of the leading activists in New South Wales and his role in leading protests is described in some detail.

I. b. New Zealand

244. Hazelhurst, Kayleen M., *Political Expression and Ethnicity: Statecraft and Mobilization in the Maori World*, Westport CT, Praeger, 1993, pp. 222.

Includes information on demonstrations, but focus on the Mana Motukhake political party founded at beginning of 1980s which contested several elections and by-elections in that decade.

245. Poata-Smith, Evan Te Ahu, 'The Evolution of Contemporary Maori Protest' in Paul Spoonley, Cluny Macpherson and David Pearce, eds., *Nga Patai: Racism and Ethnic Relations in Aotearoa*, Palmerston N.Z., Dunmore Press, 1996, pp. 97-116. Also posted online in the tino-rangatiratanga news group as: Te Ahu, 'The Evolution of Contemporary Maori Protest',19pp. available at: maorinews.com

Account by Maori activist and academic which covers links to other movements, 'brown power', the Maori Land Rights movement of 1975-84, cultural campaigns, claims to the Waitangi Tribunal and responses by the Labour Government.

246. Walker, Ranginui, *Ka Whawhai Tonu Motu: Struggle Without End*, Auckland NZ, Penguin Books, [1990] 2004, pp. 334.

History of the Maori, including resistance to white occupation in 19th century: chapters 11-12 cover recent political protest, for example to protect land and fishing rights, and other forms of political activism.

247. Williams, David V., 'Seeking Justice for the Historical Claims of Indigenous People in Aotearoa New Zealand', chap. 6 in Yash Ghal and Jill Cotterell, eds. *Marginalised Communities and Access to Justice*, London, Routledge, 2010, pp. 270.

I.c. Canada

248. Boldt, Menno, Anthony Long and Leroy Little Bear, eds., *The Quest for Justice*, Toronto, Toronto University Press, 1988, pp. 406

Over 20 contributions from a wide range of aboriginal peoples and organizations, academics and government representatives, discussing land rights and other contentious issues in an historical, legal and political framework, and from regional and international perspectives.

249. Cody Cooper, Karen, *Spirited Encounters: American Indians Protest Museum Policies and Practices*, Walnut Creek CA, Alta Mira Press, 2007, pp. 224, pb.

Covers cultural protests relating to presentation in museums, returning sacred objects and naming of national days in both USA and Canada. Includes discussion of call by Lubicon Lake Band of Cree in Northern Alberta for a boycott of the 1998 Winter Olympics in Canada over land claim and related boycott of exhibition on Canada's First People.

250. Robertson, Heather, *Reservations are for Indians*, Toronto, James Lewis and Samuel, 1970, pp. 303. 2nd edition with new preface 1991.

Account of life on four reservations, the impact of government and emergence of new more radical leaders. Includes material on a protest march and 'drink-in' in 1960s.

251. Shadian, Jessica M. *The Politics of Arctic Sovereignty: Oil, Ice and Inuit Government*, New York, Routledge, 2013, pp. 272.

A political history of the Inuit Circumpolar Council.

I.d. USA

The primary focus of this sub-section is on political protest and legal claims, but for a guide to the legal rights of Native Americans see Pever (254) below. One notable victory was achieved by the Navajo in September 2014, when the Obama Administration agreed to pay $554 million in compensation for federal government mismanagement of Navajo resources for nearly 60 years, settling a lawsuit filed in 2006.

252. Cohen, Fay G., *Treaties on Trial: The Continuing Controversy over Northwest Indian Fishing Rights*, Seattle, University of Washington Press, 1986, pp. 229.

Includes protest 'fish-ins'

253. Deloria, Vine Jr., *Behind the Trail of Broken Treaties: An American Indian Declaration of Independence*, Austin TX, University of Texas Press, 1985, pp. 296.pb.

Covers developing activism in the 1960s, the protest caravan of 1972 culminating in the occupation of the Bureau of Indian Affairs, and site occupations, including the 71 day occupation and siege at Wounded Knee, South Dakota in 1973.

254. Pever, Stephen L., *The Rights of Indians and Tribes: The Basic ACLU Guide to Indian Tribal Rights*, New York, Oxford University Press, 2012, pp. 540, 4th edn. (first edition of this American Civil Liberties Union Guide published 1985 and 2nd 1992 by Southern Illinois University Press).

255. Schragg, James L. 'Report from Wounded Knee' in Hare and Blumberg eds., *Liberation Without Violence*, (Introduction 1.c.), pp. 117-24.

On the spot account by pacifist during the occupation, noting the demands of the American Indian Movement protesters, that they had been invited by organizations representing many of the Sioux on the Pine Ridge Reservation angry about the conduct of the reservation government, and commenting on disparity between the light rifles of the protesters and the full military arsenal being deployed by the FBI.

256. Smith, Paul Chaat and Robert Allen Warrior, *Like a Hurricane: The Indian Movement from Alcatraz to Wounded Knee*, New York, New Press 1996, pp. 384.

Examines the militant American Indian Movement (AIM). from the seizure of Alcatraz in 1969 to Wounded Knee in 1973, assessing failures as well as successes.

257. Steiner, Stan, *The New Indians*, New York, Harper Row, 1968, pp. 220.

On the development of the 'Red Power' movement rejecting white culture.

258. Weyler, Rex, *Blood of the Land: The Government and Corporate War Against the American Indian Movement*, New York, Random House/ Vintage, [1982] 1984, pp. 304, pb.

259. Wilkinson, Charles, *Blood Struggle: The Rise of Modern Indian Nations*, New York, W.W. Norton, 2006, pp. 560, pb.

Part 1 'the Abyss' examines the socio-economic conditions of many Native Americans in the 1950s, Part 2 the development of a movement, leadership on the reservations and 'Red Power', whilst Part 3 explores 'the Foundations of Self-determination'.

I.e. The Saami: Norway, Sweden and Finland

260. Ingold, Tim, *The Skolt Lapps Today*, Cambridge, Cambridge University Press, 1976, pp. 290, pb.

Primary focus on Saami in Finland. Study of reservation resettled due to boundary changes with USSR after 1945, looking at ecological imbalances, links to government and debates about future. But also notes influence of broader Nordic movement and its different approaches (conservative defence of Lapp culture, or left focus on neocolonialism). Chapter 21 examines the evolution of the wider Saami movement and inter-Nordic conferences (pp. 235-44).

261. Paine, Robert, 'Ethnodrama and the "Fourth World": The Saami Action Group in Norway 1979-81', in Dyck, ed., *Indigenous Peoples and the Nation-state* (236 Introduction to B).

Analysis by social anthropologist of campaign against the Alta Hydropower Dam, and its impact in promoting cultural and political rights.

262. 'Saami and Norwegians protest construction of Alta Dam, Norway, 1979-81', Global Nonviolent Action Database (30 Jan. 2011), pp. 3. Online: http://nvdatabase.swarthmore.edu

Useful summary with references.

263. Thuen, T., *Quest for Equity: Norway and the Saami Challenge*, St John's Nfld, Institute of Social and Economic Research Books, 1995, pp. 300.

(NB Saami is sometimes spelled Sami in the literature)

B.2. Indigenous Resistance to Government and Corporate Threats to their Environment

2.a. In West

Resistance to national and corporate projects threatening water rights and their natural environment has been part of the indigenous movements in the countries listed under B.1 above. Opposition to hydro-electric projects in Norway and Canada, resistance to uranium mining in Australia and the USA, and protests against mineral extraction in Sweden are important in relation to land and water rights and genuine political autonomy. Threats to first peoples' environments still constitute a major issue and source of political conflict.

264. Banerjee, Subhankar, *Arctic Voices: Resistance at the Tipping Point*, New York, Seven Stories Press, 2012, pp. 560.

Narratives and assessments by 30 activists and researchers of struggle by indigenous peoples and environmentalists to prevent proposed exploitation of oil, gas and coal in Arctic Alaska.

265. Dekar, Paul, 'The Australian No Uranium Mining Campaign', *Peace Magazine* (Jul. – Sep. 2000), p. 27. Online: http://peacemagazine.org

See also: Milburn, Caroline, 'Australia: Women at Forefront of Jabiluka Resistance', *The Age* (13 Mar 1999). Online at: WISE: World Information Service on Energy: http://www.wiseinternational.org

266. Gedicks, Al, 'International Native Resistance to the New Resource Wars' in Bron Raymond Taylor, ed., *Ecological Resistance Movements*, pp. 89-108 (299 C.1.a.)
Covers resistance by Cree and Inuit, supported by Kayapo Indians in Brazil and transnational green groups, to major hydro-electric project in Quebec.

267. Grenfell, Damian, 'Environmentalism, State Power and "National Interests"' in James Goodman, ed., *Protest and Globalisation*, pp. 111-15 (158 A.6.a)
Covers 'Stop Jabiluka' campaign by Aborigines and environmentalists in Kakadu National Park.

268. Jarvis, Brooke, 'Idle No More: Native-led Protest Movement Takes on Canadian Government: First nations groups organize to oppose controversial tar sands pipelines' *Rolling Stone* (14 Feb. 2013). Online at: http://www.rollingstone.com

269. La Duke, Winona, 'Uranium Mines on Native Land' *The Harvard Crimson* (2 May 1979). Online at: http://www.thecrimson.com
On struggle in late 1970s by Navajos against proposed uranium and coal mining, stressing dangers of uranium mining.
See also her article: 'Uranium Mining, Native Resistance and the Greener Path: The impact of uranium mining on indigenous communities', *Orion Magazine* (Jan/Feb 2009). Online at: http://www.orionmagazine.org On Navajo resistance in past and new threat from revived stress on nuclear power. (Includes references to Kakadu.)

270. Norrell, Brenda, 'Indigenous Peoples Call for Global Ban on Uranium Mining' (1 Feb. 2007). Online at: http://www.cipamericas.org
On 30 Nov. 30- 2 Dec. 2006 Indigenous World Uranium summit in Arizona

271. Risong, Malin and David MacDougall, 'Sweden's Indigenous Sami in Fight against Miners' , Associated Press (29 Aug. 2013); published by MAC: Mines and Communities (01-09-2013) online:
http://www.mines and communities.org
Saami in Sweden have right to use land for herding but no ownership rights. The dispute over iron ore mining has prompted calls for Swedish government to give legal recognition to Saami ownership rights.

272. Schwartz, Daniel and Mark Gollom, 'N.B. Fracking Protests and the Fight for Aboriginal Rights: Duty to Consult at Core of Conflict over Shale Gas development', *CBC News* (posted 19 Oct. 2013, updated 13 Apr. 2014). Online: http://www.cbc.ca/news/canada/

On New Brunswick protest blockade by Elsipogtog First Nation and supporters.

273. Tanner, Adrian, 'Culture, Social Change and Cree Opposition to the James Bay Hydroelectric Development' in James P. Hornig, ed., *Social and Environmental Impacts of the James Bay Hydroelectric Project*, Montreal, McGill-Queens University Press, 1999, pp. 121-40.

274. Wilkinson, Charles, 'Indian Water Rights in Conflict with State Water Rights: The Case of the Pyramid Lake Paieiten Tribe in Nevada, US', in Boelens et al eds., *Out of the Mainstream*, pp. 213-22 (276 B.2.b.).

Focuses on legal struggle.

See also: Katona, Jacqui, 'Mining Uranium and the Indigenous Australians: The fight for Jabiluka' in Evans et al, eds., *Moving Mountains* (117 A.4.a.), pp. 195-206.

2.b. Global Indigenous Resistance to Environmental Threats

Threats to indigenous peoples' land and rights from corporations and government around the world are growing as the search for resources becomes more desperate. This sub-section cannot provide a comprehensive bibliography – it aims simply to indicate some relevant sources.

275. Anderson, Robert S. and Walter Huber, *The Hour of the Fox: Tropical Forests, the World Bank and Indigenous People in Central India*, Seattle, University of Washington Press, 1988, pp. 173.

276. Boelens, Rutgerd, David Getches and Armando Guevara Gil, eds., *Out of the Mainstream: Water Rights, Politics and Identity*, New York, Routledge, 2011, pp. 384.

Compares struggles over water in Andean communities of Peru, Chile, Ecuador and Bolivia and Native American communities in S .W. USA noting the combined goals of cultural justice and socio-economic justice.

277. Gandhi, Ajay, 'Indigenous Resistance to New Colonialism', *Cultural Survival Quarterly*, issue 25.3 (Fall 2001), pp. 4. Online: http://www.culturalsurvival.org

Notes opposition by indigenous activists (at 'People's Summit' in Quebec City April 2001) to Free Trade Agreement of the Americas debated at official government Summit of the Americas elsewhere in the city, and reports some of speeches.

278. Mander, Jerry and Victoria Tauli-Corpuz, eds., *Paradigm Wars: Indigenous Peoples' Resistance to Globalization*, Los Angeles CA, University of California Press, 2007, pp. 272, pb. (new expanded edition).

Documents how multinationals are targeting resources in indigenous lands and strong indigenous resistance. Section V discusses activism and social movements and what can be done.

279. Palma, Lillian. 'A Struggle for Sacred Land: The Case of Wirikuta': *openDemocracy* (26 Sep. 2013), pp. 5. At: http://www.opendemocracy.net

Examines resistance by indigenous people in desert of Central Mexico to government granting mining concessions to Canadian First Majestic Silver in their protected zone, and wider support in Mexico for their cause.

280. Sawyer, Suzana, and Edmund Terence Gomez, eds., *The Politics of Resource Extraction: Indigenous Peoples, Multinational Corporations and the State*, New York, Palgrave Macmillan, 2012, pp. 336.

Studies cover Peru, India (Orissa), Philippines, Nigeria (the Niger Basin), Chad and Cameroon, as well as Australia and Canada.

See also: Gedicks, *The New Resource Wars* (118 A.4.a.); and Clark, 'An Obstacle to Progress' (on U'wa in Colombia) and Sawyer, *Crude Chronicles: Indigenous Politics, Multinational Oil and Neoliberalism in Ecuador* (125 & 132 A.4.b.).

Environmental struggles involving indigenous peoples are also listed under C.2.b., C.2.c. and C.2.d.

C. Green Campaigns and Protests

The most dynamic social protest in the west in the later 1970s tended to be environmental campaigns, which mounted some major direct action protests against nuclear power. By the 1980s environmental groups like Greenpeace were also taking direct action against nuclear tests, and green protests often overlapped with peace activism. These protests also developed new styles of informal democratic organization for mass demonstrations. Green resistance to logging, dams, motorways, toxic dumps and other environmental hazards mounted during the 1980s and 1990s and continues today in various contexts. Uprooting genetically modified crops was widespread in the early 2000s. Opposition to 'fracking' (releasing gas from shale) has become a key issue in the second decade of the 21st century. An overarching threat to the global environment is the impact of climate change, and promoting means of limiting change and resisting economic activities which accelerate climate change has become central to green thinking and campaigning.

Green activists have taken up nonviolent direct action with daring and imagination, greatly extending the range of tactics used. Some greens have also used forms of sabotage (ecotage), raising questions about the limits of nonviolence. But, alongside direct action, environmental campaigners have also developed sophisticated lobbying techniques, some have moved towards closer cooperation with corporations and governments, and others have developed green political parties to fight local, national and (where relevant) EU elections. As in many movements, greens are divided over strategy, so moderate ('realistic') approaches are opposed by the more radical groups. The ideological range stretches from 'deep ecologists' to people protecting local neighbourhoods. Direct action against roads and airports, for example, is often undertaken by committed environmentalists, but many may also be supported by local residents trying to minimise disruption to their locality. Opposition to nuclear energy and the dangers of radiation leaks was a focus for many green s in the 1970s, but growing concern about climate change has meant that some green advocates now see nuclear energy as less dangerous than more immediately destructive forms of energy releasing CFCs. However, the destructive impact of the earthquake and tsunami on the Fukushima Dalichi reactor in March 2011 aroused widespread fears about the extent of radioactive fallout inside Japan, and reminded others of the potential hazards of nuclear power. The Japanese government's decision in March 2014 to restart two nuclear reactors (all had been closed down in the aftermath of the accident) led to protests.

Environmental concerns have not of course been confined to developed states. Many countries in the Global South have been exposed to devastating pollution through the activities of irresponsible corporations – oil pollution created by Shell in the Niger delta over decades, and the release of poisonous gas from the explosion of the United Carbide Bhopal chemical plant in India with deadly results – are two well known examples. There are many others, for example pollution of the Peruvian Amazon by oil companies for over 40 years, a danger increased since the Peruvian government made three quarters of the rain forest available to corporations for drilling in 2008. Many local and indigenous communities are engaged in bitter struggles to preserve their land, livelihood and way of life from logging, mining, oil drilling or, more recently, widespread commercial planting for biofuels. (For references to resistance to multinationals engaged in mining, logging and oil drilling see A.4.a. and A.4.b, and for some indigenous campaigns see B.2.a. and B.2.b.)

Development of environmental protest can sometimes be a prelude to more widespread resistance in politically repressive regimes, both because individuals may be mobilized by specific environmental issues and because focusing on pollution etc. is a less direct challenge to the regime than specific political opposition. There was a rise in environmental awareness and protest in the Soviet bloc during the 1970s and 1980s, sometimes linked to nationalist discontent (as in the Baltic states); and green protest is one strand in the opposition to Putin today (see Vol. 1). There have also been many environmental protests in China since the 1990s, where the regime has gradually become more responsive to environmental concerns, increasing penalties for industrial pollution in amendments to an environmental protection law in April 2014. Even in less authoritarian regimes, wider political dissatisfaction may be sparked by a specific green issue, as happened in Turkey in June 2013, when protest to save Gezi Park in Istanbul developed into a major movement (see H.1.c.).

Warnings and analyses of possible environmental disaster by scientists have become increasingly common since the ground-breaking book by Rachel Carson, *Silent Spring*, 1962. Green theorists and activists have also developed new interpretations of economics – exploring sustainable development, political thought, philosophy and spirituality. These literatures are not covered here.

Relevant periodicals: *The Ecologist* has long been a useful source of information on green issues and campaigns; in September 2014 it merged with *Resurgence*, which had adopted a nonviolent green agenda, to form: *Resurgence and Ecologist*. Environmental campaigns are also covered by movement periodicals such as *Peace News* and *New Internationalist*.

Online sources are now numerous: see for example, Earth Tribe Activist News, Reporting the Environmental Movement: http://www.earthtribe.co

For the many green campaigns involving indigenous peoples see: Survival International: http://www.survivalinternational.org

C.I. Green Movements

C.I.a. General and International Studies

281. Bahro, Rudolf, *Building the Green Movement*, Philadelphia PA, New Society Publishers, 1986, pp. 219.

Collection of writings (from Nov. 1982 to June 1985) by former East German dissident and radical ecologist. Covers issue such as North-South relations, the peace movement and the crucial role of communes in rebuilding an ecologically sound society. Includes his statement on resigning from the German Greens, claiming that they 'have identified themselves -critically- with the industrial system and its administration'.

282. Branagan, Marty, *Global Warming, Militarism and Nonviolence: The Art of Active Resistance*, Basingstoke, Palgrave, 2013, pp. 272.

Explores high carbon footprint of military defence, argues for an alternative nonviolent defence, and advocates 'active resistance' of kind pioneered by Australian environmentalists.

283. Carmin, JoAnn and Deborah B. Balser, 'Selecting Repertoires of Action in Environmental Movements: An Interpretative Approach', *Organization and Environment*, vol. 15 no. 4 (2002), pp. 365-86.

Compares North American Friends of the Earth and Greenpeace.

284. Carter Neil, *The Politics of the Environment: Ideas, Activism, Policy*, Cambridge, Cambridge University Press, 2007 (2nd edn), pp. 432.

Part I covers environmental philosophy and green political thought; Part II Green parties and NGOs; Part III policy making at international, national and local levels. This is a textbook, which gives guidance on other sources.

285. Dalton, Russell, *The Green Rainbow: Environmental Groups in Western Europe*, New Haven CT, Yale University Press, 1994, pp. 305.

Examines development of Green movement in Western democracies. Argues that environmental interest groups are important new participants in the contemporary political process and that, if the movement is politically successful 'it may at least partially reshape the style and structure of democratic processes in these countries'.

286. Doherty, Brian, 'Green Parties, Nonviolence and Political Obligation' in Brian Doherty and Marius de Geus, eds. *Democracy and Green Political Thought*, London, Routledge, 1996, pp. 36-55.

Discusses role of nonviolence in Green thought (and in original policy of German Greens) and case for nonviolent protest.

287. Dryzek, John et al., *Green States and Social Movements: Environmentalism in the United States, United Kingdom, Germany and Norway*, Oxford, Oxford University Press, 2003, pp. 238, pb.

Comparative study of successes and failures of four environmental movements since 1970, exploring implications of inclusion and exclusion from political process.

288. Flam, Helena, ed., *States and Anti-Nuclear Movements*, Edinburgh, Edinburgh University Press, 1994, pp. 427.

Deals with the anti-nuclear power movements and government responses to them and their demands in eight West European states – Austria, Britain, France, Italy, the Netherlands, Norway, Sweden and West Germany.

289. Hart, Lindsay, 'In Defence of Radical Direct Action: Reflections on Civil Disobedience, Sabotage and Nonviolence', in Jan Parkis and James Bowen, eds., *Twenty-First Century Anarchism: Unorthodox Ideas for a New Millennium*, London, Cassell, 1997, pp.41-59.

Defends new forms of radical direct action, including 'ecotage', arguing that violence should be measured by harm inflicted, not use of physical force.

290, Jancar-Webster, Barbara, ed., *Environmental Action in Eastern Europe: Response to Crisis*, Armonk NY, M.E. Sharpe, 1993, pp. 256, pb.

291. Jensen, Derrick and Lierre Keith, eds., *Earth at Risk: Building a Resistance Movement*, Crescent City C A, Flashpoint Press, 2012, pp. 288, pb.

292. Jimenz, Manuel, 'Southern European Environmental Movements in Comparative Perspective', *American Behavioral Scientist*, vol. 51 no. 1 (July 2008), pp. 1627-47.

293. Kalland, Arne and Gerard Persoon, eds., *Environmental Movements in Asia,* London and New York, Routledge, 1999, pp. 297, pb.

Includes campaigns against logging, tree plantations, factories and tourist facilities and in defence of nature reserves. Argues environmentalism in Asia has a local focus and is often a form of cultural and political protests where overt political opposition is too dangerous.

294. Kedzior, Sya Buryn and Liam Leonard, eds., *Occupy the Earth: Global Environmental Movements,* Bingley, Emerald Publishing Group, 2014, pp. 275.

Covers range of environmental campaigns in different parts of the world, including Ireland, France, Israel, Japan, India and Indonesia.

295. McCormick, John, *The Global Environmental Movement: Reclaiming Paradise,* London, Bellhaven, 1989, pp. 259. (US title: *Reclaiming Paradise: The Global Environmental Movement,* Bloomington IN, Indiana University Press, 1989.)

Despite its title, this is not primarily about protest, but the international / state context in which protest occurs, stressing the UN and international agreements.

296. Mauch, Christof, et al., *Shades of Green: Environmental Activism Round the Globe,* Lanham MD, Rowman and Littlefield, 2006, pp. 240.

Explores impact of political, economic, cultural and religious conditions on environmental activism.

297. Rootes, Christopher, ed., *Environmental Movements: Local, National and Global,* London, Routledge, 1999, pp.328, pb.

Primary emphasis on sociological analysis of how environmental movements change, with statistics on participation in them. Chapters on Germany, Spain and Southern Europe and the USA. Derek Wall writes on 'Mobilizing Earth First!' in Britain. Jeff Haynes, 'Power, Politics and Environmental Movements in the Third World' (pp. 222-42) includes specific references to the Chipko, Narmada and Ogoniland movements, as well as other forms of environmental action in Kenya and the role of the WTO.

298. Shiva, Vandana, *Staying Alive: Women, Ecology and Development,* London, Zed Press, 1988, pp. 244 (also Southgate Press 2010 and Kali/ Women Unlimited 2011).

An eco/feminist argument about the special role of women in preserving the environment.

299. Taylor, Bron Raymond, ed., *Ecological Resistance Movements: The Global Emergence of Radical and Popular Environmentalism*, Albany NY, State University of New York Press, 1995, pp. 422.

300. Wapner, Paul, *Environmental Activism and World Civic Politics*, Albany NY, State University of New York Press, 1996, pp. 252, pb.

Analysis of the roles of different types of transnational organizations and their impact on environmental 'discourse', including Friends of the Earth and the World Wildlife fund. Chapter 3 is specifically on Greenpeace, direct action and changing attitudes. See also: Wapner, 'Politics beyond the State: Environmental Action and World Civic Politics', *World Politics*, vol. 47 no. 3 (1995), pp. 311-40.

See also: AIDA (Environmental Law for the Americas), which reports on issues and protests relating to dam projects, marine pollution, climate change and other environmental threats, and promotes legal strategies which activists can adopt: http://aida-americas.org

C.1.b. Country Studies

301. Akula, Vikram, 'Grassroots Environmental Resistance in India', in Taylor, ed. *Ecological Resistance Movements* (299 C.1.a.), pp. 127-45.

Discusses early resistance in 19th and 20th centuries and contemporary campaigns against destruction of forests, dams, pollution and over-fishing of seas, and mining. Akula also describes Jharkand separatist 'tribal' struggle to own their historic land and promote sustainable use of resources.

302. Alonso, Angela, Valeriano Costa and Deborah Maciel, 'Environmental Activism in Brazil: The rise of a Social Movement', in L. Thompson and C. V. Tapscott, eds., *Citizenship and Social Movements: Perspectives from the Global South*, London, Zed Books, 2010, chapter 6.

303. Connors, Libby and Drew Hutton, *A History of the Australian Environmental Movement*, Cambridge, Cambridge University Press, 1999, pp. 324.

Survey from early concerns about conservation through the 'second wave' 1945-72, and the campaigns of 1973-83 up to the subsequent professionalization of the movement. Chapter 4 'Taking to the Streets' covers 'green bans' and the anti-uranium campaigns; 'Taking to the Bush' looks at direct action on a number of issues, culminating in the 1982 blockade of the Franklin Dam; and Chapter 6 'Fighting for Wilderness' assesses further protests around Australia. Chapter 8 considers the role of the Green Party.

304. Doyle, Timothy, 'Direct Action in Environmental Conflict in Australia: A Re-examination of Non-violent Action', *Regional Journal of Social Issues*, vol. 28 (1994), pp. 1-13.

305. Fagan, Adam, *Environment and Democracy in the Czech Republic: The Environmental Movement in the Transition Process*, Aldershot, Edward Elgar, 2004, pp.200.

General analysis of movement in 1990s and case studies of individual environmental organizations.

306. Gould, Kenneth, Allan Schnaiberg and Adam Weinberg, *Local Environmental Struggles: Citizen Activism in the Treadmill of Production*, Cambridge, Cambridge University Press, 1996, pp. 239.

A study of community power and regional planning on the environment, based on US case studies.

307. Hayes, Graeme, *Environmental Protest and the State in France*, Basingstoke, Palgrave, 2002, pp. 246.

308. Hicks, Barbara, *Environmental Politics in Poland: A Social Movement between Regime and Opposition*, New York, Columbia University Press, 1996, pp.263. pb.

309. Jiminez, Manuel, 'The Environmental Movement in Spain A Growing Source of Contention', *South European Society and Politics*, vol. 12 no. 3 (2007) (Special Issue on 'New and Alternative Movements in Spain), pp. 359-78.

310. Jun Jing, 'Environmental Protest in Rural China' in Perry and Selden, eds. *Chinese Society* (Introduction 1.c.) pp.198-214. Also available: http://facultywashington.edu

Discusses protest through letters, petitions, law suits and sometimes demonstrations and sabotage, against pollution, soil erosion, contaminated water, etc.

311. Kimber, Richard and J.J. Richardson, eds. *Campaigning for the Environment*, London, Routledge, 1974, pp. 238, pb.

Case studies of a range of environmental conflicts in Britain over urban development, water supply, power lines, M4 motorway, juggernaut lorries, the Cublington airport campaign, and the genesis of the Clean Air Act. Focus on pressure groups.

312. Seel, Benjamin, Matthew Patterson and Brian Doherty, eds., *Direct Action in British Environmentalism*, London, Routledge, 2000, pp. 223.

Essays include a survey of British environmentalism 1988-97 in the changing political context, assessments of different types of environmental activity and role of the media. Brian Doherty, 'Manufacturing Vulnerability: Protest Camp Tactics' looks at evolution of nonviolent direct action tactics and transnational influences. There is some discussion of the incidence of violence and media (mis)perceptions.

313. Shabecoff, Philip, *A Fierce Green Fire: The American Environmental Movement*, Washington DC, Island Press, 2003 (revised edn.), pp. 352.

History stretching back to origins of the republic, covering key individuals, NGOs and governmental responses.

314. Shiva, Vandana with J. Bandyopadhay, et al., *Politics and the Ecology of Survival*, London, Sage Publications (and Tokyo, UN University Press), 1991, pp. 365.

Analysis by expert on issues of ecology, development and the role of women in conflicts over natural resources in India; includes references to Appiko protests to save forests and satyagraha against mining.

315. Yang, Guobin, 'Environmental NGOs and Institutional Dynamics in China', *China Quarterly*, vol. 181 (March 2005), pp. 46-66.

Argues environmental NGOs becoming more visible in Chinese environmental politics and seizing opportunities offered by the media, internet and international NGOs. Author concludes environmental NGOs both sites and agents of democratic change.

See also: Weller, Robert P. and Michael Hsaio Hsin-Hung, 'Culture, Gender and Community in Taiwan's Environmental Movement' (chap. 4) and Tegbaru, Amare, 'Local Environmentalism in Northeast Thailand' (chap. 7) both in Kalland and Persoon, eds. *Environmental Movements in Asia* (293 C.1.a.).

I.c. Organizations and Individuals

316. Brown, Michael and John May, *The Greenpeace Story*, London, Dorling Kindersley, 1989, pp. 160.

Covers voyages to challenge nuclear testing at Amchitka Island, Alaska and at Mururoa Atoll, but also the voyages protesting against nuclear waste disposal and pollution, and to protect marine mammals.

317. Foreman, Dave, *Confessions of an Eco-Warrior*, New York, Crown Publications, Random House, 1993, pp. 95, pb.

By a founder of Earth First!

318. Hunter, Robert, *The Greenpeace Chronicle*, London, Pan Books, 1980, pp. 448. (Published in USA as *Warriors of the Rainbow: A Chronicle of the Greenpeace Movement*, New York, Rhinehart and Winston, 1978)

The story of Greenpeace from its emergence in the 1970s to the time of the book's publication. Autobiographical account by a founder member of Greenpeace International.

319. Lee, Martha F., *Earth First! Environmental Apocalypse*, Syracuse NJ, Syracuse University Press, 1995, pp. 221.

Study of the militant US movement founded in 1980, which split between what the author terms 'millenarian' and 'apocalyptic' wings, the former seeking to educate others and the latter trying to save biodiversity before it is too late.

320. 'London Greenpeace: A History of Ideas, Protests and Campaigns (1971-2005)', Radical History Network, Oct. 2009: http://radicalhistorynetwork. blogspot.co.uk/2009/10/London_greenpeace_history_of_ideas.html

Concise outline of campaigns by group distinct from the better known international organization. See also: Vidal, *McLibel* (141 A.4.c.) for their epic struggle against McDonald's.

321. Maathai, Wangari, *Unbowed: A Memoir*, Vintage, 2006, pp. 338; also published as: *Unbowed: My Autobiography*, Anchor 2008.

By prominent Kenyan woman who promoted mass planting of trees by women at grassroots level through the Green Belt Movement (founded in 1977) to reverse effects of deforestation. She also undertook vigils and fasts for human rights under the dictatorship of President Moi. See also her book: *The Green Belt Movement: Sharing the Approach and the Experiences*, New York, Lantern Books [1985] 2004, pp. 117.

322. McKibben, Bill, *The Bill McKibben Reader: Pieces from an Active Life*, New York, Henry Holt/Times Books, 2008, pp. 442, pb.

Anthology of 44 essays by noted writer and activist on green issues, including climate change (with some more personal reflections).

323. Weyler, Rex, *Greenpeace: An Insider's Account*, London, Pan Macmillan, 2004, pp. 600.

By a founder of Greenpeace International, focusing on the 1970s.

324. Zakin, Susan, *Coyotes and Town Dogs: Earth First and the Environmental Movement*, Tucson, Arizona University Press, 2002, pp. 483.

Account by sympathetic environmental journalist of evolution of Earth First! and its tactics of guerrilla theatre and direct action.

See also: McTaggart and Hunter, *Greenpeace III*,; Mitcalf, *Boy Roel*; and Robie, *Eyes of Fire*, on Greenpeace opposition to French nuclear tests (460, 461 & 463 D.3.c.).

2. Campaigns on Specific Issues

a. Campaigns Against Nuclear Power

325. Falk, Jim, *Global Fission: The Battle over Nuclear Power*, Melbourne, Oxford University Press, 1982, pp. 410.

Analyses anti-nuclear struggles globally, with particular attention to how each movement relates to the state promoting nuclear power.

326. Gyorgy, Anna and friends, *No Nukes: Everyone's Guide to Nuclear Power*, Cambridge MA, South End Press, 1979, pp. 478.

Includes large section on the transnational movement against nuclear power.

327. Joppke, Christian, *Mobilizing Against Nuclear Energy: A Comparison of Germany and the United States*, Berkeley, University of California Press, 1993, pp. 307.

328. Nelkin. Dorothy and Michael Pollak, *The Atom Besieged: Antinuclear Movements in France and Germany*, Cambridge MA, MIT Press, 1982, pp. 235.

Examines the political contexts, nature of the movements against nuclear power and their tactics, and government responses.

329. Newnham, Tom, *Peace Squadron: The Sharp end of Nuclear Protest in New Zealand*, Auckland, Graphic Publications, 1986, pp. 60.

Account of 'nuclear-free-zone' protesters who blocked nuclear-power vessels from entering port with ships, boats and canoes.

330. Opp, Karl-Dieter and Wolfgang Roehl, 'Repression, Micromobilization and Political Protest', *Social Forces*, vol. 69 no. 2 (Dec. 1990), pp. 521-47. Also available in: McAdam, Doug and David A. Snow, eds., *Social Movements: Readings on their Emergence, Mobilization and Dynamics*, Los Angeles CA, Roxburgh Press, 1997.

Uses experiences of West Germany anti-nuclear energy movement to discuss how repression impacts on protest.

331. Price, Jerome, *The Antinuclear Movement*, Boston MA, Twayne Publishers, 1982, pp. 207. (Revised edition 1989.)

General analysis of evolution of movement in the US and the groups and organizations involved. Chapter 4 examines direct action groups and their protests.

332. Rudig, Wolfgang, *Anti-Nuclear Movements: A World Survey of Opposition to Nuclear Energy*, Harlow, Longman, 1990, pp. 466.

333. Touraine, Alain, *Anti-Nuclear Protest: The Opposition to Nuclear Energy in France*, Cambridge, Cambridge University Press, 1983, pp. 202. Translation and abridgement of *La prophetie anti-nucleaire*.

334. Welsh, Ian, *Mobilising Modernity: The Nuclear Moment*, London, Routledge, 2000, pp. 256.

See especially chapter 6 'The Moment of Direct Action' and chapter 7 'Networking: Direct Action and Collective Refusal'.

335. Welsh, Ian, 'Anti-Nuclear Movements: Failed Projects or Heralds of a Direct Action Milieu?' Sociological Research Online, vol. 6 no. 3 (2001): http://www.socresonline.org.uk/6/3/welsh.html

Argues that these movements should be seen as a process of 'capacity building'.

See also: Epstein, *Political Protest and Cultural Revolution*, chapter 2 'The Clamshell Alliance' (Introduction 1.c.), pp. 58-91; Flam, ed. *States and Antinuclear Movements* (288 C.1.a.); Kolb, *Protest and Opportunities*, chapters 10-13 (Introduction 1.c.).

2.b. Campaigns Against Deforestation

336. Ramachandra, Guha, *The Unquiet Woods: Ecological Change and Peasant Resistance in the Himalayas*, Berkeley C A, University of California Press, 1989; expanded edition with Oxford University Press, 2000, pp. 244.

Emphasizes local roots of movement. including development of 'non-secessionist regionalism' in Uttarakhand. The epilogue, written in 1998, adds historical perspective on the movement's achievements and reports on-going struggles. Seeks to offer 'corrective' to romanticized western and ecofeminist interpretations.

337. Walter, Emily, 'From Disobedience to Obedient Consumerism: Influences of Market-based Activism and Eco-Certification on Forest Governance', *Osgoode Hall Law Journal* (York University Toronto) vol. 14 nos. 2-3 (2003), pp. 531-36. Online: http://digitalcommons.osgoode.yorku.ca/ohlj/vol41/iss2

Reports on anti-logging campaign in British Columbia, Canada, in 1980s and 1990s and discusses shift from pressurizing state to directly confronting lumber camps. Critiques approach leading to establishment of global regulatory body, the Forest Security Council, but supports offering 'carrot' of 'certification' in combination with 'stick' of campaigning for a boycott.

338. Weber, Thomas, *Hugging the Trees: The Story of the Chipko Movement*, New Delhi, Penguin, 1981 and 1989, pp. 175.

Traces development of the 'tree hugging' movement to protect Himalayan forests, stresses the importance of the Gandhian style legacy in the strategy and tactics of the movement, discusses the role of women and profiles the leading men.

See also: Keck and Sikkink, *Activists Beyond Borders* on resistance to deforestation in Sarawak (Introduction 1.c.), pp. 150-60; Knight, 'The Forest Grant Movement in Japan' (chapter 5) and Wong, 'The Anti-Tropical Timber Campaign in Japan' (chapter 6) in Kalland and Persoon, eds., *Environmental Movements in Asia* (293 C.1.a.); Maathai, *Unbowed* and *The Greenbelt Movement* (321 C.1.c.).

For information about the nonviolent direct action organization, San Francisco-based Rainforest Action Network (RAN) founded in 1985, see: http://ran.org

2.c. Campaigns Against Dams

339. Bratman, Eve Z., 'Contradictions of Green Development, Human Rights and Environmental Norms in light of Belo Monte Dam activities', *Journal of Latin American Studies*, vol. 46 no. 2 (May 2014), pp. 261-89.

340. Hirsch, Philip, 'The Politics of Environment: Opposition and Legitimacy' in Hewison, ed., *Political Change in Thailand* (Introduction, 1.c.), pp. 179-94.

Examines growing significance of environmental movement in Thailand since the success in stopping proposed dam in 1988.

341. Jumbala, Prudhisan and Maneerat Mitprasat, 'Non-governmental Development Organisations: Empowerment and the Environment', in Hewison, ed., *Political Change in Thailand* (Introduction, l.c.), pp. 195-216.

Analysis of two case studies in Thailand: the Raindrops Association encouraging villagers to resuscitate the natural environment; and the opposition to planned Kaeng Krung Dam.

342. Harbison, Rob, 'Cambodia: Growing Resistance by Indigenous People Slowing Dam Building', *The Ecologist* (28 July, 2014). Online at:http://www.nonviolent-conflict.org

343. Khagram, Sanjeev, *Dams and Development: Transnational Struggles for Water and Power*, Ithaca NY, Cornell University press, 2004, pp. 288.

Focused particularly on the controversy over the major Narmada River dam projects, but also provides comparative perspective by considering dam projects in Brazil, China, Indonesia, South Africa and Lesotho, where the World Bank and other lenders were persuaded to withdraw funding.

344. Khagram, Sanjeev, James V. Riker and Kathryn Sikkink, eds., *Restructuring World Politics: Transnational Social Movements, Networks and Norms*, Minneapolis, MN, University of Minnesota Press, 2002. See also: Khagram, 'Restructuring the Global Politics of Development: The Case of India's Narmada Valley Dams', pp. 206-30; and Smitu, Kothari, 'Globalization, Global Alliances and the Narmada Movement', pp. 231-44.

345. Routledge, Paul, 'Voices of the Dammed: Discourse Resistance amidst Erasure in the Narmada Valley, India', *Political Geography*, vol. 22 no. 3 (2002), pp. 343-70.

346. Roy, Arundhati, *The Greater Good*, Bombay, India Book Distributors, 1999, pp. 76.

Commentary by Booker-winning novelist and prominent Narvada Dam activist on struggle against the Sardar Sarovar Dam and the wider implications of government policy on building dams. Also available in various forms on the internet.

See also: Connors and Hutton, *History of the Australian Environmental Movement*, chapter 5 on resistance to Franklin dam (303 C.1.b.); Palit, 'Monsoon Risings: Megadam Resistance in the Narmada Valley' (184 A.6.b.ii).

2.d. Campaigns Against Mining and Pollution

Some major campaigns against mining or drilling for oil and its polluting effects (for example in the Niger Delta and on the west coast of Ireland) are covered in resistance to multinational corporations under A.4.a. and b. For brief articles on the impact of gold mining , see *New Internationalist* (Sept. 2014) 'Gold The Big Story', esp. Olivera, Roxana, 'Churning up the Cloud Forest', p. 17.

People living in large cities also often face various forms of pollution from industrial development and refineries. One example of sustained popular resistance to various threats is the South Durban Community Environment Alliance (SDCEA) founded in 1996: http://www/sdcea.co.za For an account of one of their campaigns, see: 'South African Environmental Justice Struggles against "Toxic" Petrochemical Industries in South Durban: The Enger Refinery Case': http://www.u.micg.edu

347. Beynon, Huw, Andrew Cox and Ray Hudson, *Digging Up Trouble: The Environment, Protest and Opencast Mining*, London, Rivers Oram, 1999, pp.288.

General analysis of impact of opencast (strip) mining which spread in Britain in the 1980s. Chapter 7 'Changing Patterns of Protest' (pp. 167-206) looks at the collaboration between the National Union of Miners' Support Groups and environmental groups to oppose mines creating pollution, and examines the turn from conventional protest to direct action.

348. Broadbent, Jeffrey, *Environmental Politics in Japan: Networks of Power and Protest.* Cambridge, Cambridge University Press, 1998, pp. 418.

Examines dilemma of growth versus environmentalism, and how Japan has resolved it, with focus on how anti-pollution protests 1960s-1973 changed government policy , using the movement in one prefecture as a case study.

349. Dekar Paul, 'The Australian No Uranium Mining Campaign', *Peace Magazine* (July-Sept. 2000), p. 27. Online: http://peacemagazine.org . See also: Milburn, Caroline, 'Australia: Women at the Forefront of Jabiluka Resistance' (11 May, WISE: World Information Service on Energy: http://www/wiseinternational.org (originally published in *The Age*, 13 March 1999).

The important Jabiluka campaign, which brought together aboriginal and environmental activists, is also referenced under B.2.a.

350. Dunlop, Tessa, 'Rosia Montana and Romania's Decade Long "Gold War"', BBC News, 3 Sept. 2012: http://www.bbc.co.uk See also: Earthhworks 'No Dirty Gold: Rosia Montana': http://nodirtygold.earth worksinaction. org; Solly, Richard 'Festival of Resistance to Romanian Gold Mine', London Mining Network, 18 Aug . 2014: http://londonminingnetwork.org

Sources for 15 year long local resistance in Romania to open-pit gold mine (which would use cyanide), proposed by Toronto-based Gabriel Resources, and for the evolution of government policy and legal challenges. The mine became a focus of national resistance in September 2013. The local opponents propose that the site should become a UNESCO heritage area (the open cast mine would destroy the original Roman gold mine) and a centre for farming.

351. McKean, Margaret A., *Environmental Protest and Citizen Politics*, Berkeley CA, University of California Press, 1981, pp. 291.

Study of 'Citizens' movements' against industrial pollution.

352. Strangio, Paul, *No Toxic Dump: A Triumph for Grassroots Democracy and Environmental Justice*, Sydney, NSW, Pluto Press, 2001, pp. 217.

An Australian case study.

353. Szasz, Andrew. *Ecopopulism: Toxic Waste and the Movement for Environmental Justice*, Minneapolis MN, University of Minnesota Press, 1994, pp. 216, pb.

Traces how a movement developed in the US out of official debate and television coverage into the formation of thousands of neighbourhood groups, and over a decade the establishment of strong civic organizations tackling different toxic threats.

See also: Bannerjee, *Arctic Voices* on resistance in Arctic Alaska (264 B.2.a.); and Grenfell, 'Environmentalism, State Power and "National Interests"' in Goodman, ed., *Protest and Globalisation* on Jabiluka (158 A.6.a..).

2.e. Campaigns Against Fracking

Many governments see the technology of fracking (releasing gas from shale) as a promising source of relatively cheap energy created within their own territories, and so reducing their dependence on importing oil or gas. Fracking has already made a considerable difference to energy supplies within the USA. However, many local communities are bitterly opposed to the potentially dangerous and polluting process of fracking taking place near where they live. Environmentalists are, in addition, deeply concerned about the impact of widespread fracking on climate change. So there has been a developing world wide resistance to fracking in 2013-14.

354. Castle, Ben, 'The Global Movement against Fracking : Lessons from Bulgaria, the UK and New York State', The Democracy Center, Climate Campaign Profiles, 2012, pp. 13. Online at: http://democracyctr.org/wp/wp-content/uploads/2013/01/Fracking.pdf

355. Chivers, Danny, 'The Frack Files', *New Internationalist* (Dec. 2013), pp. 12-28.
Report on development of fracking, its technology and implications, and the widespread resistance to it around the world. Larger coalitions of opposition listed at end.

356. Duhamel, Philippe, 'Civil Resistance as Deterrent to Fracking: Part I: 'The Shale Not Pass', 26 Sept. 2013; Part II: Shale 911', 26 Sept 2013, both at: *Open Democracy http://www.opendemocracy.net/civilresistance/philippe-duhamel/*

357. Lucian, Vesalon and Cretan Remus, '"We are not the Wild West...": Anti-Fracking Protests in Romania', *Environmental Politics*, vol. 24 no. 2 (2015).

358. Steger, Tamara and Milos Milicevic, 'One Global Movement, Many Local Voices: Discourse(s) of the Global Anti-Fracking Movement', in Kedzior and Leonard eds., *Occupy the Earth* (294 C.1.a.), pp. 1-35.

359. Sweeney, Sean and Lara Skinner, 'Global Shale Gas and the Anti-Fracking Movement. Developing Union Perspectives and Approaches', Trade Unions for Energy Democracy (TUEDF), in cooperation with the Rosa Luxemburg Stiftung and the Global Labor Institute at Cornell University, June 2014, pp. 28.
Online:http://www.rosalux-nyc.org/wp-content/files_mf /tuedworkingpapers1final.pdf

360. Willow, Anna J. and Sara Wylie, eds., 'Energy, Environment, Engagement: Encounters with Hydraulic Fracking', *Journal of Political Ecology*, vol. 21 nos. 12-17 (2014), special section, pp. 222-348. Free on line: http://jpe.library.arizona.edu/volume 21/voume_21.html

361. Wright, Marita, 'Making it Personal: How Anti-Fracking Organizations Frame Their Messages', *Columbia University Journal of Politics and Society*, vol. 24 (2013), pp.105-23. Online at: http://academiccommons.columbia.edu/catalog/ac%3A170829

See also: Schwarz and Gollon, 'N.B. Fracking Protests and the Fight for Aboriginal Rights' (272 B.2.a.)

2.f. Campaigning Against Roads, Airports, Redevelopment, etc.

362. Apter, David, E. and Nagayo Sawa, *Against the State: Politics and Social Protest in Japan*, Cambridge MA, Harvard University Press, 1984, pp. 271.

Analysis of major campaign by agricultural community against loss of land for Narita airport.

363. Burgmann, Verity and M. Burgmann, *Green Bans, Red Union: Environmentalism and the New South Wales Builders' Labourers Federation*, Sydney, University of New South Wales Press, 1998.

On the initiation of 'green bans' – work bans by unions to prevent redevelopment of working class neighbourhoods and destruction of historic buildings and urban green spaces in Sydney. Between 1971 and 1974 42 separate bans were imposed and linked unionists with middle class conservationists. See also: Mundey, Jack, *Green Bans and Beyond*, Sydney, Angus and Robertson , 1981.

364. Butler, Beverley, 'The Tree, the Tower and the Shaman: The Material Culture of Resistance of the No. M11 Link Roads Protest of Wanstead and Leytonstone, London', *Journal of Material Culture*, vol. 1 (Nov. 1996), pp. 337-63.

365. Doherty, Brian, 'Paving the Way: The Rise of Direct Action against British Road Building', *Political Studies*, vol 47 (1999), pp. 275-91.

366. Merrick [full name], *Battle for the Trees: Three Months of Responsible Ancestry*, Leeds, Godhaven Ink, 1996, pp. 132, pb.

Account of three months struggle against Newbury bypass.

367. Roddewig, Richard J., *Green Bans: The Birth of Australian Environmental Politics*, Montclair NJ, Allanheld, Osmun, 1976, pp. 180.

Compares Australian and US environmental activism in relation to their political and social context.

368. Wall, Derek, *Earth First! and the Anti-Roads Movement*, London, Routledge, 1999, pp. 219.

369. Welsh, Ian and Phil McLeish, 'The European Road to Nowhere: Anarchism and Direct Action against the UK Roads Programme', *Anarchist Studies*, vol. 4 no. 1 (1996), pp. 27-44.

2.g. Campaigning to Prevent Climate Change

370. Askanius, Tina and Julie Uldam, 'Online Social Media for Radical Politics: Climate Change Activism on You Tube', *International Journal of Electronic Governance*, vol. 4 no. 2 (2011). Available at: http://inderscience.metapress.com

Discusses evolution of alternative media campaigning from the 15th UN Climate Conference in December 2009.

371. Doyle, Julie, 'Climate Action and Environmental Activism: The Role of Environmental NGOs and Grassroots Movements in the Global Politics of Climate Change' in Tammy Boyce and Austin Lewis, eds., *Climate Change and the Media*, New York, Peter Lang, 2009, pp. 103-116.

372. Klein, Naomi, *This Changes Everything: Capitalism vs the Climate*, New York, Simon and Schuster and London, Allen Lane, 2014, pp. 566.

Well known critic of neoliberal globalization analyses its impact on climate change, argues against the adequacy of technical fixes and for fundamental social change. She also examines the developments in the environmental movement and suggests how campaigns against fracking and tar sands are front lines in the struggle against climate change.

373. Light, John, 'Five Groups Fighting Climate Change', Activism blog on Bill Moyers' website 7 Feb. 2014. Available at: http://billmoyers.com

Summary account of following organizations and their campaigns: 350.org (founded to combat climate change globally); the Sierra Club; Greenpeace; Idle No More (founded 2012 in Canada mostly by Native North Americans to combat government tar sands plan); and Union of Concerned Scientists.

374. Pearse, Guy, 'The Climate Movement: Australia's Patrons of Climate Change Activism', *The Monthly*, no. 7 (Sept. 2011), pp. 3. at: http://www.themonthly.com.au

375. Wheelan, James, 'Community Organising for Climate Action', *Social Alternatives*, vol. 31 no. 1 (Apr. 2012), edition on 'Community Climate Action', pp. 7. Online at: http://www.socialalternatives.com

Examines techniques of community organizing adopted by some environmental and climate change activists, and notes this approach alien to institutionalized and hierarchical NGOs.

See also: McKibben, *The Bill McKibben Reader,* by co-founder of 350.org (322 C.1.c.).

D. Peace Movements Since 1945

This section covers a wide range of campaigns against war, weapons and bases. It focuses particularly on protest in the west or countries allied to the west, but some issues such as nuclear testing, nuclear bases or military alliances have prompted opposition in many parts of the world. The campaign to ban landmines had particular importance for countries caught up in local conflicts. Conscientious objection to military service has also been a world-wide issue. Campaigns against specific wars receive some coverage under more general surveys, but for the more specialized literature see Section E.

1. General National and Transnational Movements

376.Bennett, Scott H., *Radical Pacifism: The War Resisters League and Gandhian Nonviolence in America, 1915-1963*, Syracuse NY, Syracuse University Press, 2003, pp.312.

Includes CO revolts in camps and prisons in World War Two against racial segregation, and role of League members in helping to found the Congress of Racial Equality and its nonviolent direct action strategy. Also covers relations of secular and radical WRL with other pacifist bodies, such as Christian Fellowship of Reconciliation.

377. Brock, Peter and Nigel Young, *Pacifism in the Twentieth Century*, Syracuse NY, Syracuse University Press, 1999, pp.434. (Revised and updated version of Peter Brock, *Twentieth Century Pacifism*, 1970, Van Nostrand Reinhold.)

History of opposition to war drawing primarily on US and British experience, but including material on Gandhi and the later Gandhian movement, assessments of the position of conscientious objectors in many parts of the world, and references to transnational organizations, e.g. the War Resisters' International. Although the focus is on pacifism, the book includes material on the role of pacifists in the nuclear disarmament and anti-Vietnam War movements.

378. Bussey, Gertrude and Margaret Tims, *Pioneers for Peace: Women's International League for Peace and Freedom 1915-1965*, London, WILPF British Section, 1980, pp. 255.

History of first 50 years of transnational body campaigning against war and for disarmament, which opposed NATO and nuclear weapons, was active (especially in the US) in resisting the Vietnam War and promotes social justice and reconciliation.

379. Carter, April, *Peace Movements: International Protest and World Politics Since 1945*, London, Longman, 1992, pp. 283.

Particular focus on European and North American movements against nuclear weapons in the 1950s-60s and 1980s and East European responses in the 1980s. But other nuclear disarmament protests, peace campaigns on other issues and nonviolent initiatives in other parts of the world are indicated more briefly.

380. Cockburn, Cynthia, *Anti-Militarism: Political and Gender Dynamics of Peace Movements*, London, Pluto Press, 2012, pp.320.

Feminist peace activist provides her theoretical perspective on cross-national case studies including UK peace movement, War Resisters' International, anti-militarist campaigns in Spain, Korea and Japan, and the anti-NATO demonstrations in Strasbourg 2009.

381. Cortright, David, *Peace: A History of Movements and Ideas*, Cambridge, Cambridge University Press, 2005, pp. 378.

Chapters 7 and 8 cover anti-nuclear weapon campaigns, opposition to Vietnam and Iraq wars, resistance in the military and also draft resistance and conscientious objection.

382. Flessati, Valerie, *Pax: The History of a Catholic Peace Society in Britain 1936-1971*, University of Bradford, PhD Thesis, 1991, pp. 535 (in 2 vols).

Detailed historical study of both Pax and the Catholic element in the British peace movement. Pax from the outset opposed war under modern conditions as contrary to traditional just war teaching, a stance underlined by the development of nuclear weapons. Influenced Catholic thinking about modern war and the decision of the Second Vatican Council to recognize the right to conscientious objection and to call upon states to make provision for it.

383. Gress, David, *Peace and Survival: West Germany, the Peace Movement and European Security*, Stanford CA, Hoover Institution Press, 1985, pp. 266.

384. Howorth, Jolyon and Patricia Chilton, eds., *Defence and Dissent in Contemporary France*, London, Croom Helm, 1984, pp. 264.

Part 1 covers France's defence policy since 1945 – including the wars in Indo-China and Algeria, and De Gaulle's decision (supported by the major political parties) to develop a French nuclear bomb. Part 2 focuses on anti-nuclear critiques and movements in the 1980s, including a military critique of French defence policy by Admiral Sanguinetti and Claude Bourdet on the 'The rebirth of the peace movement'.

385. Locke, Elsie, *Peace People – A History of Peace Activity in New Zealand*, Christchurch and Melbourne, Hazard Press, 1992, pp. 335.

Chronicles peace activities in New Zealand from Maori time and early colonial settlement to the anti-Vietnam war movement and anti-nuclear campaigns of the 1960s and 1970s. Includes accounts of the direct action protests against French nuclear tests in 1972.

386. Meaden, Bernadette, *Protesting for Peace*, Glasgow, Wild Goose Publications, 1999, pp. 151.

Sympathetic coverage of a wide range of campaigns in Britain – Greenham Common, Trident Ploughshares, the arms trade, British troops in Northern Ireland, US bases, the 'peace tax', and opposition to the (first) Gulf War.

387. Molin, Marian, *Radical Pacifism in Modern America: Egalitarianism and Protest*. Philadelphia PA, University of Pennsylvania Press, 2006, pp. 255.

388. Nepstad, Sharon Erickson, *Religion and War Resistance in the Plowshares Movement*, New York, Cambridge University Press, 2008, pp. 204, pb.

Study of radical nonviolent direct action movement initiated by Catholic left during Vietnam War (burning draft records and pouring blood on conscription papers), which developed into wider protests against nuclear weapons and unjust wars involving openly declared sabotage of missiles and planes. Compares movement in US with similar groups in UK, Australia, Germany, Netherlands and Sweden, and examines how a movement involving long prison sentences maintained itself over decades.

389. *Pacific Women Speak-Out for Independence and Denuclearisation*, Christchurch, Women's International League for Peace and Freedom, 1998, pp. 80.

Indigenous women from Australia, Aotearoa (New Zealand), Belau, Bougainville, East Timor, Ka Pa'aina (Hawaii), the Marshall Islands,

Te Ao Maohi (French Polynesia) and West Papua (Irian Jaya) condemn imperialism, war, 'nuclear imperialism' (in the form of nuclear tests) and military bases in the hope 'that when people around the world learn what is happening in the Pacific they will be inspired to stand beside them and to act'. The book is a contribution to the Hague Appeal for Peace, 1999.

390. Peace, Roger C., *A Just and Lasting Peace: The US Peace Movement from the Cold War to Desert Storm*, Chicago IL, The Noble Press, 1991, pp. 345.

Peace, a writer/activist, documents the growth of the peace and justice movement in the US, with particular focus on the 1980s. Areas covered include anti-nuclear campaigning and campaigns for justice in Latin America. Discusses also debates and controversies within the movement.

391. Prasad, Devi, *War is a Crime Against Humanity: The Story of War Resisters' International*, London, War Resisters' International, 2005, pp. 560.

A history of the first 50 plus years of the radical pacifist organization (1921-1973).

392. Taylor, Richard and Nigel Young, eds., *Campaigns for Peace: British Peace Movements in the Twentieth Century*, Manchester, Manchester University Press, 1987, pp. 308.

Collection of analytical and descriptive essays spanning period from late 19th century to 1980s, but the main focus is on post-World War Two movement against nuclear weapons. Michael Randle assesses 'Nonviolent direct action in the 1950s and 1960s', pp. 131-61.

Much of the information about peace protest and nonviolent direct action is to be found in movement newsletters or journals, though some of these are transient. Long-running peace periodicals are:

Peace News, London, which has transnational interests but particularly covers Britain; *Liberation, WIN Magazine* and *Fellowship* in the USA. *The Bulletin of the Atomic Scientists*, although primarily a socially concerned journal covering scientific and strategic issues has carried articles on peace campaigns. *Peace and Change* (published by Sage) is an academic journal which examines peace campaigns and activity.

2. Pacifist Protest, Conscientious Objection and Draft Resistance

Conscientious objection to taking part in or supporting war has for a long time been associated in the west with particular religious beliefs. Since the Reformation protestant groups such as the Quakers, Anabaptists,

Mennonites and Dukhobors have consistently refused military service. In past centuries some emigrated from Europe or Russia to North America to avoid conscription.

In the 20th century, although religious objectors to military service, such as Jehovah's Witnesses, have played a heroic role in resisting enforced military service in dictatorships, and a small but significant Catholic pacifist movement has also developed, there has been a growth of individual conscientious objection based on humanist beliefs. There have also been significant movements based on socialist or anarchist objections to capitalist wars, and major campaigns against participation in wars viewed as imperialist, racist, aggressive, illegal under international law or in any other way unjust. Many western states, especially since the end of the cold war, no longer require general conscription, but reservists or serving soldiers have also sometimes refused to take part in a particular war – as for example in the 1991 Gulf War.

Liberal democratic states have increasingly recognized the right to be a conscientious objector (CO) – and this has been reflected by many intergovernmental bodies, including the UN Human Rights Commission – and gradually extended the definition of conscience beyond religious beliefs. But militant resisters have rejected recognition of the state's right to demand alternative civilian service, and have committed themselves to total resistance. Open draft resistance has often occurred alongside draft evasion – many young US citizens crossed the border into Canada during the Vietnam War – and desertion from the forces. One important role for organized peace groups, nationally and transnationally, has been to provide legal information, advice and support.

Refusing military service is limited to those of military age and until very recently has been limited to young men, but some have also seen conscientious refusal to pay taxes for war as a relevant form of protest. Moreover, in national campaigns against particular wars, prominent individuals have encouraged defiance of the draft or even desertion by signing subversive manifestoes, or have taken direct action at recruitment offices. Some examples of conscientious objection and draft resistance in SouthAfrica and Israel have been covered in Volume I of this Guide (E.I.1.c.), but a few reference are listed under 2.b. See also Section E for resistance to specific wars, in particular Vietnam.

There is a large literature on pacifism, much of it not directly relevant here. Selective references dealing with pacifist beliefs, with transnational and national organizations and campaigns against conscription, with the experiences of COs and draft resisters, and analyses of the legal position are listed below. We also include a couple of references to just war theory, influential in opposition to many wars, but critical of pure pacifism.

2.a. Pacifist and Nonviolent Thought

393. American Friends Service Committee, *Speak Truth to Power: A Quaker Search for an Alternative to Violence*, Philadelphia PA, AFSC, 1955, pp. 71. Available as pdf at: http://www.afsc.document/speak_truth_power

Manifesto outlining a nonviolent approach to international politics and social change. Influenced the thinking of radical direct actionists in the US and Britain.

394. Ceadel, Martin, *Thinking about Peace and War*, Oxford, Oxford University Press, 1987, pp. 222.

A frequently cited analysis and classification of different ways of thinking about war, which examines 5 'ideal types' of 'militarism', 'crusading', 'defencism', 'pacific-ism' (representing many ideological and organizational strands within peace movements), and 'pacifism'.

395. Childress, James F., *Moral Responsibility in Conflicts: Essays on Nonviolence, War and Conflict*, Baton Rouge, Louisiana State University Press, 1982, pp. 224.

Includes chapters on conscientious objection and Reinhold Niebuhr on violent and nonviolent methods.

396. Hentoff, Nat, ed., *The Essays of A.J. Muste*, New York, Simon and Schuster, pp. 515.

Essays on revolution, nonviolence and pacifism by a key figure on US radical/pacifist left, from 1905 to 1966, commenting in later essays on conscientious objection, opposition to French nuclear tests in Africa, the Civil Rights movement and the opposition to the Vietnam War.

397. Mayer, Peter, ed., *The Pacifist Conscience*, Harmondsworth, Penguin, 1966, pp. 447.

Collection of writings on war, pacifism and nonviolence from 500 BC to 1960 AD, but emphasis on more modern figures, such as William Lloyd Garrison, Thoreau, Tolstoy, Gandhi, Simone Weil and Albert Camus. Includes also Martin Buber's criticism of Gandhi for advocating nonviolent resistance by Jews to Hitler, and Reinhold Niebuhr's reasons for leaving the (pacifist) Fellowship of Reconciliation.

398. Merton, Thomas, *The Nonviolent Alternative*, ed. Gordon C. Zahn, New York, Farrar Strauss Giroux, 1980, pp. 270.

Collection of essays by well-know Catholic thinker on war, peace and nonviolence.

399. Teichman, Jenny, *Pacifism and the Just War: A Study in Applied Philosophy*, Oxford, Blackwell, 1986, pp. 138.

Discussion of pacifist theory and major objections to it from a just war perspective.

400. Unnithan, T.K.N. and Yogendra Singh, *Traditions of Nonviolence*, New Delhi and London, Arnold-Heinemann, 1973, pp. 317.

Examines nonviolent traditions in Hindu, Chinese, Islamic and Judeo-Christian thought.

401. Walzer, Michael, *Just and Unjust Wars: A Moral Argument with Historical Illustrations*, Harmondsworth, Penguin, 1980, pp. 359.

Highly regarded interpretation of just war theory. See also his earlier essays on war and disobedience, including an essay on conscientious objection in: *Obligations: Essays on Disobedience, War and Citizenship*, Cambridge MA, Harvard University Press, 1970, pp. 244.

2.b. Conscientious Resistance and Legal Frameworks

402. Ajangiz, Rafa, 'The European Farewell to Conscription' in Lars Mjoset and Stephen Van Holde, eds., *The Comparative Study of Conscription in the Armed Forces*, Oxford, JAI/Elseveer, Comparative Social Research Series, vol. 22, 2002, pp. 307-33.

Discusses the relative impact of 'reasons of state' and 'social mobilization' (against conscription) as factors leading to the abandonment of conscription.

403. Amnesty International, *Out of the Margins: The Right to Conscientious Objection to Military Service in Europe*, London, Amnesty, 1997, pp. 61.

Surveys provisions for conscientious objection to military service, and expresses particular concerns in relation to treatment of COs in some countries. Recommends the release of all COs in prison, that all member states of EU and Council of Europe re-examine their legislation regarding conscientious objection, and that the EU include in the criteria for membership the recognition of conscientious objection and provisions for alternative service 'of non-punitive length'.

404. Biesemans, Sam, *The Right to Conscientious Objection and the European Parliament*, Brussels, European Board for Conscientious Objection, 1995, pp.109.

Urges incorporation of right to conscientious objection in national constitutions, and the European Convention of Human Rights and Fundamental Freedoms.

405. Blatt, Martin, Uri Davis and Paul Kleinbaum, eds., *Dissent and Ideology in Israel: Resistance to the Draft,1948-1973*, London, Ithaca Press for Housmans Bookshop, WRI, Middle East Research Group (MERAG) and Lansbury House Trust Fund, 1975, pp. 194.

Accounts by Israeli conscientious objectors of their experience and the reasons for their stance. Editors relate these to a critique of Zionism.

406. Braithwaite, Constance, with Geoffrey Braithwaite, *Conscientious Objection to Compulsions Under the Law*, York, William Sessions, 1995, pp. 421.

History of conscientious objection to compliance with various legal provisions involving compulsion of citizens, including taking of oaths, vaccination and religious education. Chapter on ethical and political problems related to conscientious objections takes the form of imaginary dialogue between author and a critic of her thesis.

407. Brock, Peter, *'These Strange Criminals': An Anthology of Prison Memoirs by Conscientious Objectors from the Great War to the Cold War*, Toronto, University of Toronto Press, 2004, pp. 505.

Anthology of prison memoirs by conscientious objectors from World War One to the Cold War. Contributions from Britain, Canada, New Zealand and the USA.

408. Casquette, Jesus, 'The Sociopolitical Context of Mobilization: The Case of the Anti-Militarist Movement in the Basque Country', *Mobilization: An International Quarterly*, vol. 1 no. 2 (Sept 1996), pp. 203-12.

409. Cinar, Ozgur Heval, *Conscientious Objection to Military Service in International Human Rights Law*, New York, Palgrave Macmillan, 2013, pp. 276.

An updated overview of the recognition of the right to conscientious objection in international human rights law, with a focus on the UN and Council of Europe.

410. Cinar, Ozgur Heval and Coskun Usterci, eds. *Conscientious Objection: Resisting Militarized Society*, London, Zed Press, 2009, pp. 272.

Collections of essays: Part 1 comprises Turkish experience and viewpoints; Part 2 examines conscientious objection from gender perspectives; Part 3 examines C.O. struggles in different parts of the world and Part 4 looks at conscientious objection and the law.

411, Ellner, Andrea, Paul Robinson and David Whetham, *When Soldiers Say No: Selective Conscientious Objection in the Modern Military*, Farnham, Ashgate, 2014, pp. 290.

Explores theoretical arguments for and against selective objection, together with case studies from US, Britain, Australia, Germany and Israel.

412. Elster, Ellen and Majken Jul Sorensen, eds., *Women Conscientious Objectors: An Anthology*, London, War Resisters International, 2010, pb. Also at: http://www.wri-org

A collection of essays by and about women COs in USA, Europe, Turkey, Israel, Eritrea, Korea, Paraguay and Colombia (also available in Spanish).

413. Evans, Cecil, *The Claims of Conscience: Quakers and Conscientious Objection to Taxation or Military Purposes*, London, Quaker Home Service, 1966, pp. 51.

414. *Fifth International Conference on War Tax Resistance and Peace Tax Campaigns and Founding Assembly of Conscience and Peace Tax International: Hondarribia, September 16-19 1994*, Pamplona-Irunea, Asamblea de Objecion Fiscal de Navarra, 1994, pp. 111.

Text of contributions, workshop reports and summaries of discussions. Conscience and Peace Tax International was established in Brussels as a non-profit association under Belgian law.

415. Flynn, Eileen P, *My Country Right or Wrong: Selective Conscientious Objection in the Nuclear Age*, Chicago, Loyola University Press, 1985, pp. 98.

Discusses varieties of conscientious objection, from pacifist objection to all wars, selective objection to particular wars considered unjust and objection to indiscriminate and, most notably, nuclear warfare. Includes a discussion of just war principles.

416. Horeman, Bart and Marc Stolwijk, *Refusing to Bear Arms: A World Survey of Conscription and Conscientious Objection to Military Service*, War Resisters International, 1998, pp. 310. (Ringbinder format for ease of update.) Foreword Devi Prasad.

The most authoritative country by country survey of the position on conscription and conscientious objection in all member states of the UN, following the same formula in each case and setting out legal possibilities for avoiding military service. Historical overview of the evolution of conscription and conscientious objection appended to many country reports. There are also often additional sections on forced recruitment by non-governmental armed groups. Each report is dated. The online version includes updates, especially 2008, on all the countries (and then candidate countries) in the Council of Europe, see http://www.wri-irg.org/co/rtba/index.html The 2008 update also published separately as:'Professional Soldiers and the Right to Conscientious Objection in the European Union', produced for Tobias Pfluger MEP, European Parliamentary Group European United Left/Nordic Green Left (GUE/NGL), 2008, http://wri-irg.org/pdf/eu-rtba2008update-en.pdf

417. Lainer-Vos, Dan, 'Social Movements and Citizenship: Conscientious Objection in France, the United States and Israel', *Mobilization: An International Quarterly.* Vol. 11 no. 3 (Oct. 2006), PP. 277-95.

Compares movements of objection to the French war in Algeria, the US War in Vietnam and Israel's invasion of Lebanon.

418, Moskos, Charles C and John Whiteclay Chambers, eds., *The New Conscientious Objection: From Sacred to Secular Resistance,* New York and Oxford, Oxford University Press, 1993, pp. 286.

Section 1 suggests 'the secularization of conscience and modern individualism have been the driving force' in the rise of conscientious objection. Section 2 looks at the historical record in the USA. Section 3 has articles on France, the Federal Republic of Germany, Denmark, Norway, Switzerland, the former Communist states in Eastern Europe, Israel and South Africa.

419. Office of the High Commissioner of Human Rights, *Conscientious Objection to Military Service,* Geneva, 2012. http://www.org.ohcr.org/documents/publications/conscientiousobjection.en.pdf, also available in Arabic, French, Russian, Spanish (pdf)

420. Pentikainen, Merja, ed., *The Right to Refuse Military Orders,* Geneva, International Peace Bureau in collaboration with International Association of Lawyers Against Nuclear Arms, Peace Union of Finland and Finnish Lawyers for Peace and Survival, 1994, pp. 110.

Contributions on various forms of refusal – to do military service, to fire at one's own people, to participate in torture, or to accept orders relating to nuclear weapons – together with summaries of relevant international law.

421. Quaker Council for European Affairs, *Conscientious Objection to Military Service in Europe*, Report for the Council of Europe, Parliamentary Assembly, Legal Affairs Committee, 1984, pp. 99.

Sets out the legal provision for COs in all the European states at that date. Notes the importance of resolutions in support of making provisions for COs adopted by the Council of Europe in 1967, the UN in 1978 and the European Parliament in 1983.

422, Quaker Peace and Service, *Taxes for Peace Not War: 6th International Conference on Peace Tax Campaigns and War Tax Resistance*, London, Quaker Peace and Service, 1997, pp. 51.

Assesses the impact of peace tax campaigns in the area of peacemaking and considers their possible future influence.

423. Rohr, John A, *Prophets Without Honor: Public Policy and the Selective Conscientious Objector*, Nashville and New York, Abingdon Press, 1971, pp. 191.

Examines lack of a constitutional right or political tolerance for selective refusal to take part in particular wars.

424. Schlissel, Lillian, *Conscience in America: A Documentary History of Conscientious Objection in America, 1757-1967*, New York, E.P. Dutton, 1968, pp. 444.

Documents and statements on conscientious objection, later sections cover COs in two world wars and Vietnam, and case for tax resistance.

425. Socknat, Thomas, 'Conscientious Objection in the Context of Canadian Peace Movements', *Journal of Mennonite Studies*, vol. 25 (2007), pp. 61-74.

426. Speck, Andreas, 'Refusal in the International War Resistance Movement: An Outline of Contemporary Refusal and Refusal Movements in Various Political Circumstances throughout the World', 5 Sep. 2007. Online at: http://www.wri-org/co/refusal-context.htm

427. Speck, Andreas, 'Transnational Solidarity and War Resistance: The Case of Turkey', in Clark, ed., *People Power* (Introduction 1.c.), pp. 164-70.

428. War Resisters' International, *A Conscientious Objector's Guide to the International Human Rights Systems*, London, 2013. At: http://co-guide.info (also downloadable as pdf).

A frequently updated overview of international human rights mechanisms available to conscientious objectors, including a wealth of case law.

429. Zemlinskaya, Yulia, 'Cultural Context and Social Movement Outcomes: Conscientious Objectors and Draft Resistance Movement Organizations in Israel', *Mobilization*, vol. 14 no. 4 (Dec. 2009), pp. 449-66.

Comparative analysis of two Israeli organizations supporting conscientious objection and draft resistance during the Second Palestinian Intifada, exploring impact of Israeli culture on tactics and how different tactics of two organizations have different impact in Israel.

See also: Brock and Young, *Pacifism in the Twentieth Century* (377 D.1.); Muste, A.J., 'Of holy disobedience', in Hentoff, ed., *Essays of A.J. Muste*, pp.355-77, on case for total resistance to conscription as opposed to alternative civilian service (396 D.2.a); and Kwon, *Gender, Feminism and Masculinity in Anti-Militarism*, and Natanel 'Resistance at the Limits'(637, 640 F.5.).

3. Opposition to Nuclear Weapons since the 1950s

After 1945 the invention of nuclear weapons created a new peril, dramatized by Hiroshima and Nagasaki, which gradually aroused widespread public concern. This concern was exacerbated from the mid-1950s by growing awareness of the dangers to health and the environment caused by the testing of nuclear bombs in the atmosphere.

But development of atomic and then hydrogen bombs, and later of nuclear missiles, was also a product of the arms race between the United States and the Soviet Union, and the deep distrust generated by the Cold War. Once both sides had nuclear weapons, developing strategic doctrines of the necessity of deterrence made opposition to US (or British) weapons more politically sensitive. The fact that the Soviet Union mobilized a worldwide 'peace campaign' against nuclear weapons in the early 1950s also meant that in the most frigid period of the cold war western peace protests were almost automatically seen by governments and the media as pro-Soviet. (How far these campaigns, which undoubtedly drew in many non-Communists concerned about the dangers of nuclear war, should be seen as part of the overall peace movement is disputed.)

A strong explicitly nonaligned movement against nuclear weapons, linked in Britain to the Campaign for Nuclear Disarmament (CND), did not therefore develop until 1957/58. The 'first wave' of the nuclear disarmament movement in the late 1950s and early 1960s resulted in mass marches and a wide variety of nonviolent direct action protests against nuclear testing sites, nuclear bases and installations and government buildings. In some cases (as in West Germany) protest originated on the organized left, in others popular protest impacted on trade unions and leftist political parties, leading for example to a unilateralist resolution being passed by the British Labour Party Conference in 1960. The debate also spread to the churches and raised the question whether nuclear weapons were compatible with the doctrine of just war. The 1963 Partial Test Ban Treaty, signed initially by the USA, Soviet Union and Britain, could be interpreted as a success for the movement, and the USA and USSR began to engage more seriously in a series of arms control negotiations.

By the late 1960s many campaigners had turned their energies to opposing the Vietnam War. During the 1970s environmental protests came to the fore, though concern about nuclear energy sometimes linked up with opposition to nuclear weapons. A second mobilization of mass opposition to nuclear weapons was sparked by US proposals to deploy the neutron bomb and by the NATO decision to deploy cruise and Pershing II missiles – Intermediate Nuclear Forces (INF) – in Western Europe. The campaigns of the 1980s had greater transnational reach, involved many more people than the 'first wave' of the movement, and influenced the policy of some local councils and regions. The role of the European Nuclear Disarmament (END) campaign in promoting a dialogue between western peace campaigners and East European and Soviet dissidents also opened up a new dimension.

The use of nonviolent direct action was even more widespread in the 1980s than in the 1950s/60s, and less controversial within the movement. There were, for example, many sit-downs and peace camps at bases. There was also widespread transnational cooperation, for example at the peace camp at the Comiso missile base in Sicily. The legality of nuclear weapons under international law was frequently raised in the courts. Some of the most militant actions, for example at the Greenham Common cruise missile base, are also associated with radical feminism and have been listed under the Feminist Movement (F.5.).

Although the nuclear disarmament movement has in general lost momentum since the break-up of the Soviet Union and the end of the cold war, the dangers from nuclear weapons and proliferation ensure that campaigning continues. There are still nonviolent direct action demonstrations in Britain, for example at nuclear bases and installations.

There is a large literature on the nuclear disarmament movement. The titles below include assessments from a range of ideological perspectives, but many of them have been chosen because they give some prominence to forms of direct action and civil disobedience.

3.a. Theoretical Debates about Nuclear Weapons

There is an immense literature on strategic thinking about nuclear weapons since the late 1950s, as theories of deterrence and arms control evolved and as missile deployments and strategic rationales altered over time. The titles selected here focus on moral, political and strategic arguments which influenced campaigners. But a well-regarded survey of official nuclear policies is: Mandelbaum, Michael, *The Nuclear Question: The United States and Nuclear Weapons 1946-1976*, Cambridge, Cambridge University Press, 1979.

430. Church of England, Board of Social Responsibility, *The Church and the Bomb: Nuclear Weapons and Christian Conscience. The Report of the Working Party under the Chairmanship of the Bishop of Salisbury*, London, Hodder and Stoughton, 1982, pp. 190.

Influential report which concluded that Just War principles forbid the use of nuclear weapons, and recommended that the UK should renounce its independent nuclear deterrent, followed by a phased withdrawal from other forms of reliance on nuclear weapons including, ultimately, the presence of US air and submarine bases.

431. Holroyd, Fred, ed., *Thinking about Nuclear Weapons: Analyses and Prescriptions*, London, Croom Helm in association with the Open University, 1985, pp. 409.

Covers a range of perspectives on nuclear weapons. Includes influential McGeorge Bundy/Kennan/McNamara/Smith article 'Nuclear weapons and the Atlantic Alliance', *Foreign Affairs*, vol. 60, 1982, arguing that NATO should not use nuclear weapons in response to a conventional attack. Also includes section from the Alternative Defence Commission report on 'The rationale for rejecting nuclear weapons', as well as an extract from Edward P. Thompson's 1980 pamphlet *Protest and Survive* (see below).

432. Schell, Jonathan, *The Abolition*, London, Picador in association with Jonathan Cape, 1984, pp. 170.

Definition of the nuclear predicament and radical proposals for the abolition of all nuclear weapons.

433. Stein, Walter, ed., *Nuclear Weapons and Christian Conscience*, London, Merlin Press, 1961 and 1981, pp. 163. With Foreword by Archbishop Roberts.

Essays by six leading Catholic thinkers on the moral issues raised by nuclear weapons. Had considerable influence in Christian and wider circles. The 1981 edition has a postscript by Anthony Kenny on Counterforce and Countervalue nuclear doctrines.

434. Thompson, Edward P., *Protest and Survive*, Campaign for Nuclear Disarmament and Bertrand Russell Peace Foundation, 1980, pp. 33.

This polemic, whose title was prompted by government civil defence advice 'Protect and Survive', provided considerable impetus to the rejuvenated nuclear disarmament movement of the 1980s, and the launch of the European Nuclear Disarmament (END) campaign in which Thompson played a leading role.

435. Urquhart, Clara, ed., *A Matter of Life*, London, Jonathan Cape, 1963; Praeger, 1973, pp. 255.

A collection of brief essays or speeches by eminent proponents of peace or nonviolence on dangers facing the world and role of civil disobedience. Contributors include Martin Buber, Danilo Dolci, Erich Fromm, Kenneth Kaunda, Jawaharlal Nehru and Albert Schweitzer. There are essays by founding members of the Committee of 100: Bertrand Russell, Michael Scott and Robert Bolt.

436. US Bishops, *The Challenge of Peace: God's Promise and our Response: The US Bishops' Pastoral Letter on War and Peace in the Nuclear Age*, London, CTS/SPCK, 1983, pp. 34.

Influential Catholic document. Argues that 'a justifiable use of force must be both discriminatory and proportionate' and that 'certain aspects of both US and Soviet strategies fail both tests'. Urged greater consideration of nonviolent means of resistance whilst upholding the right of governments to conscript (with provision for general or selective objection).

3.b. Comparative and General Studies

437. Evangelista, Matthew, *Unarmed Forces: The Transnational Movement to End the Cold War*, Ithaca NY, Columbia University Press, 1999, pp. 406.

Well-documented examination of the role of transnational civil movements in contributing to arms control and the ending of the Cold War. Includes assessment of the Pugwash Conference which brought together scientists from East and West, and also the wider anti-war movement.

438. Kaltefleiter, Werner and Robert L. Pfaltzgraff, eds., *Peace Movements in Europe and the United States*, London, Croom Helm, 1985, pp. 211.

Essays arising out of May 1984 conference at the Christian-Albrechts University, Kiel, on peace movements in Sweden, Norway, the Netherlands, West Germany, France, Italy, Britain and the US. Focus is on the anti-nuclear movements of the 1980s, though some contributors sketch the earlier history of movements in their countries.

439. Laqueur, Walter and Robert Edwards Hunter, eds., *European Peace Movements and the Future of the Western Alliance*, New Brunswick, Transaction Books in association with the Center for Strategic and International Studies, Georgetown University, Washington DC, 1985, pp. 450.

Generally critical contributions on the peace movements of the 1980s in various European countries and their impact on the Western alliance. Includes chapter on the US peace movement of the 1980s.

440. Nehring, Holger, *Politics of Security: British and West German Protest Movements in the Early Cold War 1945-1970*, Oxford, Oxford University Press, 2013, pp. 368.

Discusses cultural and social bases of protest against nuclear weapons, role of nationalism in the movements, and importance of British types of activism for German protest in light of experience in World War Two and the cold war. See also: Nehring, 'Demonstrating for "Peace" in the Cold War: The British and West German Easter Marches 1958-64', in Matthias Reiss, ed., *The Street as Stage: Protest Marches and Public Rallies since the Nineteenth Century*, Oxford, Oxford University Press, 2007, chap. 15; Nehring, 'National Internationalists: British and West German Protests Against Nuclear Weapons, the Politics of Transnational Communication and the Social Hisotry of the Cold War 1957-1964', *Contemporary European History*, vol. 14 no. 4 (2005), pp. 559-82.

441. Rochon, Thomas R., *Mobilizing for Peace*, Princeton NJ, Princeton University Press, 1988, pp. 232.

Wide-ranging analysis of West European anti-missile/nuclear disarmament campaigns 1979-1986, incorporating discussion of social movement theory and the wider political context. Focuses particularly on Britain, the Netherlands, West Germany and France. It includes great deal of information on organizations, campaigns and types of action, as well as many useful sources and references.

442.Wittner, Lawrence S., *Confronting the Bomb: A Short History of the World Nuclear Disarmament Movement*, Stanford CA, Stanford University Press, 2009, pp. 272.

A greatly condensed version of his three volume history (listed below).

443. Wittner, Lawrence S., *The Struggle Against the Bomb*, vol. 1, *One World or None: A History of the World Nuclear Disarmament Movement Through 1953*, Stanford CA, Stanford University Press, 1993, pp. 456.

Covers responses to the Bomb from 1945-1953, including by scientists and churches, but with emphasis on the Soviet-initiated protests under the World Peace Council.

444. Wittner, Lawrence S., *Resisting the Bomb: A History of the World Nuclear Disarmament Movement 1954-1970*, vol. 2, Stanford CA, Stanford University Press, 1997, pp. 641.

Extensive and thoroughly researched history of campaigns and governments responses, which includes quite a lot of material on nonviolent direct action.

445. Wittner, Lawrence S., *Towards Nuclear Abolition: A History of the World Nuclear Disarmament Movement 1971 to the Present*, vol. 3, Stanford CA, Stanford University Press, 2003, pp. 657.

Traces the development of the movement in the 1970s, the rise of a new activism in the 1980s, the 'breakthrough' of the Intermediate Range Nuclear Forces (INF) Agreement of 1987, and the end of the Cold War. While noting later more worrying trends, Wittner concludes that 'This study – like its predecessors – indicates that the nuclear arms control and disarmament measures of the modern era have resulted primarily from the efforts of a worldwide citizens' campaign, the biggest mass movement in modern history'.

3.c. Studies of Particular Countries, Campaigns or Actions

446. Baxendale, Martin, *Cruisewatch: Civil Resistance against American Nuclear Cruise Missile Convoys in the English Countryside: 1984-1990*, Stroud, Silent but Deadly, 1991, pp. 41.

447. Bigelow, Albert, *The Voyage of the Golden Rule: An Experiment with Truth*, Garden City NY, Doubleday, 1959, pp. 286.

Account by former Lieutenant in the US navy of an attempt by four people to sail a ketch into the US nuclear testing zone at Eniwetok in protest against the tests. Defying an injunction, the ketch sailed 5 miles into the zone before being stopped by US navy. Their example inspired a second attempt by Earle and Barbara Reynolds (see *The Forbidden Voyage* below).

448. Bradshaw, Ross, Dennis Gould and Chris Jones, *From Protest to Resistance*, Nottingham, Mushroom, 1981, pp. 64. (*Peace News* pamphlet)

Story of the rise of direct action against nuclear weapons in the British context. Includes diary of main protest in the 1957-1966 period, and interviews with those involved.

449. Breyman Steven, *Why Movements Matter: The West German Peace Movement and U.S, Arms Control Policy*, Albany NY, State University of New York Press, 2001, pp. 359.

Charts the evolution of the movement from 1979 to deployment of missiles in Germany at the end of 1983, linking accounts of major protests in West Germany to internal political developments and US/USSR negotiations. The final chapter assesses the impact of the movement and its relation to the INF Treaty.

450. Cairns, Brendan, 'Stop the Drop', in Verity Burgmann and Jenny Lee, eds., *Staining the Wattle*, Ringwood VIC, McPhee Gribble/Penguin Books, 1988, pp. 243-53.

On the 1980s revived movement against nuclear weapons, in particular Australia's People for Nuclear Disarmament.

451.Carter, April 'The Sahara Protest Team' in Hare and Blumberg, eds., *Liberation Without Violence* (Introduction 1.c.), 126-56.

On a transnational expedition in 1959-60 attempting to prevent French nuclear tests in the Algerian Sahara.

452. Clements, Kevin P, *Back from the Brink: The Creation of a Nuclear Free New Zealand*, Wellington NZ and HarperCollins NY, 1988, pp. 241 pb.

Account of significant popular movement in 1970s and 1980s (including local councils declaring themselves nuclear-free) that led to government action to turn New Zealand into a nuclear-free zone and to refuse to allow US warships carrying nuclear weapons to dock in its ports (although it did not remove US monitoring bases).

453. Deming, Barbara, 'Earle Reynolds: Stranger in This Country' in *Revolution and Equilibrium*, pp. 124-35 (Introduction, 1.c.)

On the transnational protests by the ship 'Everyman III' which sailed from London to Leningrad to protest against Soviet nuclear tests.

454. Driver, Christopher, *The Disarmers: A Study in Protest*, London, Hodder and Stoughton, 1964, pp. 256.

Account of the emergence of the Campaign for Nuclear Disarmament, Direct Action Committee Against Nuclear War and the Committee of 100 in Britain. Describes the main actions and internal debates within the movement.

455. Hinton, James, *Protests and Visions: Peace Politics in 20th Century Britain*, London, Hutchinson Radius, 1989, pp. 248.

Covers pacifist and anti-war campaigning in Britain from the 'imperialist pacifism' of the Victorian period, through both World Wars to the birth of the Campaign for Nuclear Disarmament and the New Left in the 1950s and 1960s. Written from a democratic socialist perspective. Final chapters cover CND's 'second wave' in the 1980s, the Gorbachev initiatives, and the role of the European Nuclear Disarmament campaign seeking to transcend the Cold War divide.

456. Hudson, Kate, *Now More than Ever*, London, Vision Paperbacks, Satin Publishers, Sheena Dewan, 2005, pp. 278.

Up to date account of British nuclear disarmament movement since the 1950s by chair of CND, giving some weight to direct action.

457. Jezer, Marty, *Where Do We Go From Here? Tactics and Strategies for the Peace Movement*, New York, A.J. Muste Institute, 1984, pp. 74.

Answers by range of peace activists to questions about the future of the movement, including whether it should focus on the arms race or more broadly on US foreign policy, its relationship to electoral politics, the role of civil disobedience and issues related to feminist separatism.

458. Katz, Milton, *Ban the Bomb: A History of SANE, the Committee for a Sane Nuclear Policy*, Westport CT, Greenwood Press, 1986, pp. 215

SANE was founded in the US in 1957 to campaign against nuclear tests, but also to draw attention to wider dangers of the arms race. Its emphasis was on public appeals, lobbying in Washington and backing peace candidates in the 1962 primaries, and its support was mainly from intellectuals and some business people; students tended to support more radical groups and nonviolent direct action against tests and bases was carried out by groups like the Committee for Nonviolent Action.

459. McCrea, Frances B. and Gerald E. Markle, *Minutes to Midnight: Nuclear Weapons Protest in America 1950s-80s*, Newbury Park CA, Sage, 1989, pp. 200.

460. McTaggart, David and Robert Hunter, *Greenpeace III: The Journey into the Bomb*, London, Collins, 1978, pp. 372.

Leading Greenpeace activists recount how their boat succeeded in sailing into the French nuclear testing zone near Muroroa Atoll in 1971, forcing the French government to halt one of its planned nuclear tests.

461. Mitcalfe, Barry, *Boy Roel: Voyage to Nowhere*, Auckland, New Zealand, Alister Taylor, 1972, pp. 154.

Diary of events aboard Boy Roel, one of the fleet of four ships, including Greenpeace III, which attempted to sail into French nuclear testing zone near Muroroa Atoll in 1972.

462. Reynolds, Earle, *The Forbidden Voyage*, Westport CT, Greenwood Press, 1975, pp. 281.

Earle and Barbara Reynolds lived in Hiroshima, where he was studying effects of atomic radiation, from 1951-1954. In 1958, whilst cruising on their yacht the Phoenix of Hiroshima, they heard about the arrest of Bigelow's Golden Rule protesting against US testing (see above) and later that year sailed 65 nautical miles inside the Bikini Atoll testing zone.

463. Robie, David, *Eyes of Fire: The Last Voyage of the Rainbow Warrior*, Philadelphia PA, New Society Publishers, [1986] 2005 2nd edition. pp.180.

Account of final voyage of Greenpeace ship the Rainbow Warrior, trying to sail into French nuclear testing area near Mururoa Atoll, before it was blown up by French secret service agents in Auckland Harbour July 1985. See also: Sunday Times Insight Team, *Rainbow Warrior: The French Attempt to Sink Greenpeace*, London, 1986, pp. 302.

464. Robson, Bridget Mary, *What Part did Nonviolence Play in the British Peace Movement 1979-1985?* MA Dissertation, Bradford, 1992, pp. 89.

Recounts debates surrounding the use of direct action and civil disobedience in anti-nuclear campaigns, noting the influence of New Left politics and feminism and the rise of nonviolence training, affinity groups and peace camps in the 1980s. Demonstrates that direct action was initiated at the grassroots level but in time accepted by CND leadership.

465. Rochon, Thomas and David Meyer, eds., *Coalitions and Political Movements: The Lessons of the Nuclear Freeze*, Boulder CO, Lynne Rienner, 1997, pp. 277.

Examines movement of the early 1980s which mobilized huge numbers in the US to protest against the dangers of nuclear weapons and strategies and demanding a US-Soviet agreement for a freeze on testing, production and deployment of nuclear weapons, bombers and missiles. The movement gained some support in Congress, organized a mass lobby in Washington and demonstrated throughout the country in 1983, and engaged in electoral activity. This book examines the successes and failures of the Freeze, and broader implications for other movements. See also: Meyer, *A Winter of Discontent: The Nuclear Freeze and American Politics*, New York, Praeger, 1990, pp. 320.

466. Sawyer, Steve, 'Rainbow Warrior: Nuclear War in the Pacific', *Third World Quarterly*, vol. 8 no. 4 (October 1986), pp. 1325-36.

Examines sinking of Rainbow Warrior, commenting on New Zealand's reactions and the heightened awareness of the dangers of nuclear testing in the Pacific.

467. Simpson, Tony, *No Bunkers Here: A Successful Nonviolent Action in a Welsh Community*, Merthyr Tydfil, Nottingham and Mid-Glamorgan CND and Peace News, 1982, pp. 47.

Account of direct action campaign against the building of a nuclear-blast-proof bunker.

468. Solnit, Rebecca, *Savage Dreams: A Journey into the Hidden Wars of the American West*, San Francisco Sierra Club Books, 1994, pp. 401.

Autobiographical account of radical campaigning activities against nuclear tests in Nevada. Author argues that policy of testing nuclear weapons in the American West is rooted in 19th century attitudes and policies towards native American peoples.

469. Taylor, Richard, *Against the Bomb: The British Peace Movement 1958-1965*, Oxford, Clarendon, 1988, pp. 368.

Well researched account of the first phase of the nuclear disarmament campaign in Britain, analysed and critiqued from a New Left/Marxist perspective.

470. Thompson, Ben, *Comiso*, London, Merlin Press jointly with END, 1982, pp. 17.

Account of transnational direct action against nuclear missile base in Sicily.

471. Vinthagen, Stellan, Justin Kennick and Kelvin Mason, eds., *Tackling Trident*, Sparsnas Sweden, Irene Publishing, 2012, pp. 362.

On two 'Academic Conference Blockades' at Faslane Trident missile base in Scotland in January and June 2007.

472. Zelter, Angie, *Trident on Trial: The Case of People's Disarmament*, Edinburgh, Luath Press, 2001, pp. 312.

Presents the legal case against nuclear weapons and for people's 'direct disarmament' actions against UK Trident missiles, and includes personal accounts by activists in Trident Ploughshares.

See also: Epstein, *Political Protest and Cultural Revolution*, chapter 4, 'the Livermore Action Group: Direct Action and the Arms Race' on protests against test launching of MX missile in California (Introduction 1.c.); Brown and May, *The Greenpeace Story*, Hunter, *The Greenpeace Chronicle* and Weyler, *Greenpeace* (316 318 & 323 C.1.c.); Muste, 'Africa Against the Bomb' in Hentoff, ed. *Essays of A.J. Muste* (396 D.2.a.) and Nepstad, *Religion and War Resistance in the Plowshares Movement* (388 D.1.).

4. Autonomous Peace Protest in the Soviet Bloc up to 1989

The significant movements against nuclear weapons in the west and in other parts of the world which suffered from nuclear testing, or had been drawn into the global network of nuclear bases and alliances, had no direct counterpart in the Soviet bloc in the 1950s and 1960s, where 'peace activity' was monopolised by the Communist regime sponsored 'Peace Committees', which focused on encouraging resistance to NATO nuclear policies (had their Communist-influenced western counterparts) and presented the Soviet nuclear arsenal and the Warsaw Pact as essentially defensive. By the 1980s, although the official Peace Committees were still prominent in the Soviet bloc, the nonaligned peace movement in the rest of the world was stronger than it had been in the first wave of anti-bomb protest and the European Nuclear Disarmament campaign initiated in 1980 made specific attempts to make links with dissident groups inside Eastern Europe, and other peace activists also promoted links across the East-West divide. The nature of Communist Party rule in the USSR and most of Eastern Europe was also somewhat less oppressive than in the 1950s, which meant that although open dissidents were still liable to harassment and imprisonment the space for protest had grown. Many opponents of some or all aspects of Communist Party rule in the Soviet bloc were primarily interested in internal political change, and greater national autonomy, rather than the dangers of nuclear weapons and were doubtful about western opposition to NATO policies. But there were a few autonomous peace initiatives and protests in both the USSR and Eastern Europe, as well as some conscientious objectors. Although the literature is limited, this autonomous peace activity was an important phenomenon.

473. *From Below: Independent Peace and Environmental Movements in Eastern Europe and the USSR*, New York, Helsinki Watch Report, 1987, pp.263.

474. Kavan, Jan and Zdena Tomin, *Voices from Prague: Documents on Czechoslovakia and the Peace Movement*, London, Palach Press, pp. 75.

See also: Sormova, Ruth, Michaela Neubarova and Jan Kavan, 'Czechoslovakia's Nonviolent Revolution' in Brian Martin et. al., *Nonviolent Struggle and Social Defence*, London, War Resisters International, 1991, pp. 36-41.

475. Klippenstein, Lawrence, 'Conscientious Objectors in Eastern Europe: the quest for free choice and Alternative Service' in Sabrina Petra Ramet, ed., *Protestantism and Politics in Eastern Europe and Russia: The Communist and Postcommunist Eras*, Durham, Duke University Press, 1992, pp. 276-309 and 393-404.

476. Koszegi, Ferenc and E.P. Thompson, *The New Hungarian Peace Movement*, London, Merlin Press/European Nuclear Disarmament, c.1983, pp. 53.

477. Ramet, Pedro, 'Church and Peace in the GDR', *Problems of Communism*, vol. 35 (Jul.–Aug. 1984), pp. 44-57.

478. Sandford, John, *The Sword and the Ploughshare: Autonomous Peace Initiatives in East Germany*, London, Merlin Press/European Nuclear Disarmament, 1983, pp.111.

479. Stead, Jean and Gabrielle Grunberg, eds., *END Special Report: Moscow Independent Peace Group*, London, Merlin Press, 1982, pp. 44.

See also Carter, *Peace Movements* (379 D.1.), pp.183-213.

5. Protests Against Militarism

Peace campaigners have also engaged in many activities which do not fall within either the categories of conscientious objection/draft resistance or opposition to nuclear weapons. There have for example been relatively successful campaigns to ban landmines and to achieve a treaty regulating the sale of arms, to prevent sales to repressive regimes or aggressors in wars. Much of this activity involves education and publicity or meetings, petitions and lobbying. But there is also a wide range of direct action, for example resistance to the siting or extension of military bases or firing ranges. A transnational movement against the arms trade includes both publicizing the extent and nature of the trade and regular demonstrations and blockades at arms fairs. In Britain the Campaign Against the Arms Trade publishes details of protests in *CAAT News,* and *Peace News* reports on demonstrations. The success of the international Stop the Shipments campaign in halting South Korean tear gas supplies to Bahrain (engaged in repressing internal protest) was celebrated in *Peace News.* No. 2566 (Feb. 2014), pp. 1 and 6.

480. Caldecott, Leonie, 'At the foot of the mountain: The Shibokusa women of Mount Fuji', in Jones, ed., *Keeping the Peace* (634 F.5.), pp. 98-107.

Account of prolonged struggle to recover agricultural land occupied by US forces in 1945 and later retained by Japanese armed forces.

481. Cameron, Maxwell A., Robert J. Lawson and Brian W. Tomlin, eds., *To Walk Without Fear: The Global Movement to Ban Landmines,* Oxford, Oxford University Press, 1998, pp. 512.

482. Deming, Barbara, 'San Francisco to Moscow: Why they walk' and 'San Francisco to Moscow: Why the Russians let them in' in *Revolution and Equilibrium* (Introduction 1.c.), pp. 51-59 and 60- 72. (Articles originally published in the *Nation* 15 July and 23 December 1961.)

483. Lyttle, Brad, *You Come with Naked Hands: The Story of the San Francisco to Moscow March for Peace,* Raymond NH, Greenleaf Books, 1966, pp. 246.

Participant's account of march for disarmament organized by the Committee for Nonviolent Action. After marching across the USA the participants walked in Britain, Belgium and West Germany (they were debarred from entering France). But they were allowed to enter the Soviet bloc to travel through parts of the GDR, Poland and the USSR.

484. Packard, George R., *Protest in Tokyo: The Security Treaty Crisis of 1960,* Princeton NJ, Princeton University Press, 1966, pp. 423.

Includes coverage of petitions, strikes and demonstrations of May June 1960 with emphasis on role of Zengakuren student organization.

485. Rawlinson, Roger, *Larzac: A Nonviolent Campaign of the 70s in Southern France,* York, William Sessions, 1996, pp. 202.

Story of the successful ten-year struggle of French farmers in Larzac to protect their land from military encroachment. The Gandhian pacifists at the Community of the Arch, and industrial and professional unions played a role in the struggle. An earlier account is: Rawlinson, *Larzac: A Victory for Nonviolence*, London, Quaker Peace and Service, 1983, pp. 43. See also: Rawlinson, 'The battle of Larzac' in Hare and Blumberg, eds., *Liberation Without Violence*, pp. 58-72 (Introduction, 1.c.)

486. Waldman, Sidney R., Susan Richards and Charles C. Walker, *The Edgewood Arsenal and Fort Detrick Projects: an Exchange Analysis*, Haverford PA, Center for Nonviolent Conflict Resolution, c. 1967, pp. 67.

'Exchange analysis' between organizers of two protests against Chemical and Biological Weapons (CBW) weapons production, the first a 21 month campaign at Fort Detrick from January 1960, the second planting a tree inside the base.

487. Walker, Charles C. 'Culebra: Nonviolent action and the US Navy', in Hare and Blumberg (eds.), *Liberation Without Violence*, (Introduction 1.c.), pp. 178-95.

Resistance to the use of Puerto Rican island as a US Navy bombing and gunnery range. Recounts direct action by Puerto Ricans and development of transnational action, involving US Quakers, to build chapel on the island.

488. Yeo, Andrew, *Activists, Alliances and Anti-US Base Protests*, New York, Cambridge University Press, 2011, pp. 240.

Examines the impact of anti-base movements on politics, and the role of bilateral military alliances influencing results of protest. Findings drawn from interviews with activists, politicians and US base officials in the Philippines, Japan (Okinawa), Ecudaor, Italy and South Korea. See also: Yeo, 'Anti-Base Movements in South Korea: Comparative Perspectives on the Asia-Pacific', *The Asia Pacific Journal*, vol. 24 no. 2 (14 June, 2010): online at: http://www.japanfocus.org 39-73.

See also: Routledge, *Terrains of Resistance* on 1980s resistance in Orissa, India, to Baliapal missile testing range (Introduction 1.c.), pp 39-73..

E. Resistance Movements Against Specific Wars Since 1945

Opposition to specific wars has quite often been spearheaded by pacifist and anti-militarist groups, and has usually included conscientious objection and draft resistance. But, depending on the political context and the war, opposition has often been much broader and involved a wide range of protests by those not subject to conscription. Moreover, significant resistance movements to specific wars has sometimes involved open conscientious refusal to obey orders by military personnel (either individual or collective) and/or desertion, as well as organized protest by veterans. Prolonged wars perceived by many as unjust, like the French war in Algeria 1954-62 and the US-led war in Vietnam, 1961-73, have evoked extensive and often radical forms of protest. There is a large literature on the Vietnam War (see E.1. below). But the English literature on French resistance to the Algerian war – in particular the nonviolent resistance to the draft and the military conduct of the war – is unfortunately limited. But perspectives on this important topic are:

489. Evans, Martin, *The Memory of Resistance: French Opposition to the Algerian War 1954-1962*, Oxford, Berg, 1997, pp. 250.

Focuses particularly on those who actively supported the Algerian guerrilla movement the FLN (the Jeanson network), but includes references to the September 1960 '121 Manifesto', in which intellectuals asserted the right to refuse to take up arms in the war. Not an overall history of opposition, but using oral reminiscences to show motivation for resistance.

490. Porter, David, *Eyes to the South: French Anarchists and Algeria*, Oakland CA, A.K. Press, 2011, pp. 550, pb.

Examines range of anarchist approaches in both France and Algeria and also covers period after independence.

Talbot, John, *The War Without a Name: France in Algeria 1954-1962* (Introduction 1.c.)

Clear account of the politics surrounding the war of liberation and French responses. Chapter 5 'Against Torture' describes resignation of General de Bollardiere in protest and criticisms by reservists, as well as opposition from intellectuals. Chapter 8 'Barricades and Manifestoes' covers French settler intransigence as well as draft resistance and desertions, the '121 Manifesto' and the Jeanson FLN-support network.

See also: Howarth and Chilton, eds., *Defences and Dissent in Contemporary France*, Part I (384 D.1.); and Lainer-Vos, 'Social Movements and Citizenship' (417 D.2.b.).

1. Resistance to the Vietnam War, 1961-73

Introduction

The evolution of the US-led War in Vietnam was complex. To understand events in Indo-China it is necessary to go back to 1945, when Japanese occupation of the area ended. The Communist-led guerrillas under Ho Chi Minh then established an independent state, whilst the French attempted to restore their former colonial empire and took control of South Vietnam. The French were decisively defeated by the Communist Vietminh forces in 1954 at the battle of Dien Bien Phu, and withdrew. But the US took over support for a South Vietnamese anti-communist state, and the international agreement, reached at the Geneva Conference of 1954, to create a unified Vietnam through elections, was ignored. As the South Vietnamese government struggled to resist internal guerrilla opposition by the National Liberation Front ('Vietcong'), and the increasing pressure from North Vietnam, the US government supplied military 'advisors', and from 1963 sent increasing numbers of US troops. The Australian government also agreed to send troops to Vietnam. In 1965 the US began to bomb North Vietnam.

Resistance to the US role in the war (initiated largely by pacifists from 1961) became widespread in 1965, when the first teach-ins were held, both in the US and around the world. Opposition was especially strong in Australia, where there was resistance to the draft, and in Japan, where US bases were used in prosecuting the war. Canadians became involved in offering refuge to US draft resisters. Protests against the war in countries not directly involved often took the form of marches and confrontations outside US embassies. In the US itself, in addition to frequent large demonstrations and student direct action against the military presence on campuses, there was also widespread draft resistance (eg. burning draft cards) and acts of solidarity with draft resisters. Resistance also grew significantly inside the armed forces, with the development of underground newsletters and organizations as well as public protest and acts of defiance, and also desertions. Vietnam veterans also became involved in militant opposition to the war.

US bombing, and dropping of chemicals to defoliate the Ho Chi Minh trail, spread beyond Vietnam to Laos. Even more controversially, the US under Nixon began in 1969 an undeclared war of bombing and military incursions against what it claimed were North Vietnamese/National Liberation Front bases in neutral Cambodia. This secret war destabilized Prince Sihanouk, who was eventually ousted in a military coup. After the US Administration launched an invasion of Cambodia in spring 1970, without consulting Congress, opposition increased dramatically – about a third of colleges and universities were closed down by mass protests. At Kent State university in Ohio confrontation between the students and the National Guard led to four students being shot dead.

Some books written at the time of the war or immediately afterwards are not now in print (though some have been republished). Many are, however, available second hand and will still be in libraries covering the history of the period. Some are excerpted or available in full online, as we have indicated in relation to some titles.

There is a large literature on the origins and development of the French and then American wars in Indo-China; only a few selective references are listed below:

491. Charlton, Michael and Anthony Moncrieff, *Many Reasons Why: The American Involvement in Vietnam*, London, Scolar Press, 1978, pp. 250; Hill and Wang, 1989, pp. 250, pb.

Based on BBC series of programmes and consisting primarily of interviews with wide range of those involved in first French and then US policy on Vietnam, and individuals prominent in opposition. Covers period 1945-1973. Chapters 7 and 8 discuss protests inside US and the leaking by Daniel Ellsberg of *The Pentagon Papers*, which revealed in detail secret internal policy making.

492. McCarthy, Mary, *Vietnam*, Harmondsworth, Penguin, 1968, pp. 119.

Influential account by US novelist of her visit to Vietnam, in which she argued that the US was fighting a war it could not win, and called for withdrawal.

493. Shawcross, William, *Side Show: Kissinger, Nixon an d the Destruction of Cambodia*, London, Andre Deutsch, 1979, Fontana 1980, pp. 467.

Detailed analysis of the evolution of the US war on Cambodia.

494. Sheehan, Neil, et al., *The Pentagon Papers as published by the New York Times*, New York, Bantam Books, 1971, pp. 677, pb.

Based on extensive Pentagon files on conduct of war and US role, leaked by Daniel Ellsberg, then an official in the Pentagon.

495. Wintle, Justin, *The Vietnam Wars*, London, Weidenfeld and Nicolson, 1991, pp. 202.

A brief history and analysis of the wars in Vietnam from the 1945 declaration of independence to the US withdrawal in 1973.

I.a. International Protest

496. Arrowsmith, Pat, *To Asia in Peace: The Story of a Non-Violent Action Mission to Indo-China*, London, Sidgwick and Jackson, 1972, pp. 188.

Account by participants in British team demonstrating opposition to US war in Vietnam and its extension to Cambodia. The team planned to share the hazards of US bombing in the hope of deterring it. They were received in Cambodia (but not North Vietnam); some later demonstrated at a US base in Thailand.

497. Dumbrell, John, ed., *Vietnam and the Antiwar Movement: An International Perspective*, Aldershot, Avebury, 1989, pp. 182.

Chapters include: 'Kent State: How the War in Vietnam became a War at Home'; 'Congress and the Anti-War Movement'; 'US Presidential Campaigns in the Vietnamese Era'; 'Opposing the War in Vietnam – the Australian Experience'; 'Vietnam War Resisters in Quebec'; 'Anger and After – Britain's CND and the Vietnam War'.

498. Feinberg, Abraham, L.. *Hanoi Diary*, Ontario, Longmans, 1968, pp. 258.

Rabbi Feinberg's account of his participation in a mission to North Vietnam in 1966-67 to investigate and publicize the effects of the US bombing. The other participants in the mission were the veteran US pacifist and socialist, A.J. Muste, Rev. Martin Niemoller, the Protestant pastor incarcerated in Dachau during part of World War II for opposing Hitler, and Rt Rev Ambrose Reeves, former Bishop of Johannesburg exiled for speaking out against apartheid.

499. Havens, Thomas, *Fire Across the Sea: The Vietnam War and Japan, 1965-1975*, Princeton NJ, Princeton University Press, 1987, pp. 330.

Covers growth of a major anti-war movement of rallies and marches against Japanese government support for the US in the war and the use of US bases in Japan.

500. Weiss, Peter and Ken Coates, eds., *Prevent the Crime of Silence: Reports from the Sessions of the International War Crimes Tribunal founded by Bertrand Russell*, London, Allen Lane, 1971, pp. 384. Online at: http://raetowest.org/ vietnam-war-crimes/russell-vietnam-war-crimes-tribunal-1967.html.

501. Young, Nigel, *An Infantile Disorder? The Crisis and Decline of the New Left*, London, Routledge and Kegan Paul, 1977, pp. 490.

The New Left became closely associated with opposition to the Vietnam War, and there are frequent references to this opposition in the US and UK, including a critique in chapter 9 'Vietnam and Alignment', of New Left support for North Vietnam, pp. 163-88.

See also: Prasad, *War is a Crime Against Humanity: The Story of War Resisters' International* (391 D.1.), pp. 371-85, which also includes in full the eloquent WRI Statement on Wars of Liberation.

b. Australia

502. 'Australia's Draft Resistance and the Vietnam War – Statement by Michael Matteson and Geoff Mullen', *Peacemaker*, vol. 33 nos. 9-12, Sept-Dec 1971. Online at Takver's Initiatives, Radical Tradition http://www. takver.com/history/matteson.html

Statements by two anarchists in the draft resistance movement, who went underground and then to jail, commenting critically upon it. An introduction by Takver notes the important role played by individual anarchists and anarchist g roups in the anti-war movement.

503. Forward, R. and B. Reece, Chapter 4 'Conscription, 1964-1968' in *Conscription in Australia*, Brisbane QLD, University of Queensland Press, 1968, pp. 79-142.

504. Hammell-Greene, Michael E., 'The Resisters: A History of the Anti-Conscription Movement 1964-1972' in Peter King, ed., *Australia's Vietnam: Australia in the Second Indo-China War*, Sydney, Allen and Unwin, 1983.

505. Noone, Val, *Disturbing the War: Melbourne Catholics and Vietnam*, Richmond VIC, Australia Spectrum, 1993, pp. 333.

506. Summy Ralph V., 'Militancy and the Australian Peace Movement 1960-67', *Politics* (Journal of the Australasian Studies Association), vol. 5 no. 2 (Nov. 1970), pp. 148-62. Downloadable from: http://www.tandfonline.com His MA thesis 'Militancy and the Australian Peace Movement: A Study of Dissent, pp. 273, is available at: http://espace.library.uq.edu.au

507. York, Barry, 'Power to the Young' in Verity Burgmann and Jenny Lee, eds., *Staining the Wattle: A People's History of Australia*, Ringwood VIC, McPhee Gribble/Penguin Books, 1988, pp. 228-42.

c. South Vietnam – Buddhists

Opposition to the war within South Vietnam was demonstrated most dramatically by Buddhist monks, but students and academics also protested.

508. Halberstam, David, *The Making of a Quagmire*, London, Bodley Head, 1965, pp. 323. Revised edn. Rowman and Littlefield , 2007, pp. 248, pb.

Includes helpful information on the Buddhist resistance in 1963, see especially pp. 194-243 in original edition.

509. Roberts, Adam, ' Buddhism and Politics in South Vietnam', *World Today*, vol. 21 no. 6 (June 1965), pp. 240-50.

Account of the 1963 Buddhist revolt, its origins and aftermath. See also later article by Roberts assessing thje political potential of the Buddhists. 'The Buddhists, the War and the Vietcong', *World Today*, vol. 22 no. 5 (May 1966), pp. 214-22. Both articles now available online: http://www.j.stor.org (but only via contributing libraries).

510. Thich Nhat Hahn, *Lotus in a Sea of Fire*, New York, Hill and Wang , 1967, pp. 128.

Well known theorist of nonviolence puts the Buddhist case.

d. USA

511. Bannan, John F. and Rosemary Bannan, *Law, Morality and Vietnam: The Peace Militants and the Courts*, Bloomington IN, Indiana University Press, 1974, pp. 241.

Explores the conflict between law and morality, and case for civil disobedience, with reference mainly to six well known prosecutions, including: the Fort Hood Three (GIs who refused to be posted to Vietnam); Dr Spock and others in 1967-68 charged with conspiracy to violate draft laws; and Daniel and Philip Berrigan and five other who burnt draft files at Catonsville in 1968.

512. De Benedetti, Charles and Charles Chatfield (assistant editor), *The Antiwar Movement of the Vietnam Era*, Syracuse NY, Syracuse University Press, 1990, pp. 495.

Detailed and well researched account. Final chapter by Charles Chatfield analyses the strengths and weaknesses of the movement and influence on US policy. Concludes that anti-war activists contributed to the growth of public disaffection with the war, but could not harness it, but that both Johnson and Nixon Administrations adapted their policies in response to pressure from dissenters.

513. Boardman, Elizabeth Jellinek, *The Phoenix Trip: Notes on a Quaker Mission to Haiphong*, Bournsville, Celo Press, 1985, pp. 174.

Diary of a participant in this defiance of the US prohibition on taking supplies to the Democratic Republic of Vietnam.

514. Boyle, Richard, *The Flower of the Dragon: The Breakdown of the US Army in Vietnam*, San Francisco CA, Ramparts Press, 1972, pp. 283.

Traces the growth of disillusionment with the war amongst American GIs and the increasingly militant opposition within the US forces. Extracts published as pamphlet 'GI Revolts: The Breakdown of the US Army in Vietnam', available online: http://theanarchistlibrary.org/library/

515. Chatfield, Charles, 'Ironies of Protest: Interpreting the American Anti-Vietnam War Movement' in Guido Grunewald and Peter Van den Dungen, eds., *Twentieth Century Peace Movements*, Lewiston NY, Edwin Mellen Press, 1995, pp. 198-208.

Argues radical left never had a cohesive centre and that when movement most confrontational, its liberal wing was working most effectively with the political system. Suggests the movement became associated with social and cultural iconoclasm, which appeal to sections of middle classes, but that the broader public eventually opposed both the war and the antiwar protest, because 'both seemed to threaten the established social order'.

516. Cortright, David, *Soldiers in Revolt: The American Military Today*, Garden City NY, Anchor Press, 1975; reissued as *Soldiers in Revolt: GI Resistance During the Vietnam War*, Haymarket, 2005, pp. 364, pb.

517. Foner, Philip S., *American Labor and the Indochina War: The Growth of Union Opposition*, New York, International Publishers, 1971, pp. 126. Re-issued as *US Labor and the Vietnam War*, 1989.

Traces the emergence of (belated) trade union opposition from a November 1967 conference in Chicago, attended by 523 trade unionists from 38 states and 63 international unions, which established the trade union division of the peace organization SANE. Includes a chapter on labour-student alliances.

518. Hall, Simon, *Peace and Freedom: The Civil Rights and the Antiwar Movements in the 1960s*, Philadelphia PA, University of Pennsylvania Press, 2004 (hb) and 2006 (pb), pp. 280.

Using archival research, explores both how the Civil Rights Movement reacted to the Vietnam War, and also examines relations between black groups opposed to the War and the wider peace movement, and difficulties that arose.

519. Hall, Simon, *Rethinking the American Anti-war Movement*, London and New York, Routledge, 2011, pp. 208.

Structured in sections covering key events and key individuals in movement against Vietnam War, and includes a chapter assessing strength and weaknesses of movement. Extensive footnotes and bibliography.

520. Halstead, Fred, *Out Now! A Participant's Account of the American Movement Against the Vietnam War*, New York, Monad Press, 1978, pp. 759; reissued by Pathfinder, 2001, pp. 886, pb.

Traces the rise of the anti-Vietnam War movement, including accounts of the ideological and institutional rivalries between organizations, and covers all the major demonstrations and civil disobedience actions from the Students for a Democratic Society March on Washington in 1965 to US withdrawal from Vietnam in 1973.

521. Hunt, Andrew E., *The Turning: A History of Vietnam Veterans Against the War*, New York, New York University Press, 1999; 2nd edn.. 2001, pp. 296, pb.

Covers origins and development of Vietnam Veterans Against the War and key events, as well as attempts to recruit Afro-American veterans and the role of women in the organization.

522. Lynd, Alice, *We Won't Go: Personal Accounts of War Objectors*, Boston, Beacon Press, 1998, pp. 332.

Deals with conscientious objection in US during the Vietnam War, 1961-1975.

523. Menasche, Louis and Ronald Radosh, *Teach -ins USA: Reports, Opinions, Documents*, New York, Praeger, 1967, pp. 349.

Records how the Teach-In movement began modestly in a mid-West campus in 1965 but spread across the country, engaging many students and professors, and released a vast quantity of material about the Vietnam War. For first teach-in see: 'History of Education: Selected Moments of the 20th Century: 1965 First 'Teach-in' held at University of Michigan: New Tool for Further Education is Born':
http://schuguren sky.faculty.asu.edu./moments/1965.teachin.html

524. Moser, Richard R., *The New Winter Soldiers: GI and Veteran Dissent During the Vietnam Era*, New Brunswick NJ, Rutgers University Press, 1996, pp. 232, pb.

Draws on interviews and personal stories to examine how the ideal of the 'citizen soldier' encouraged thousands to move towards opposition to the Vietnam war.

525. Powers, Thomas, *The War at Home: Vietnam and the American People, 1964-1968*, Boston MA, G.K. Hall, 1984, pp. 348.

Argues that, although all forms of opposition had some effect, those that involved the greatest self-sacrifice tended to work best. However, these sacrifices had most impact first time or two, before the public came to accept and then ignore them. Concludes that opposition to the war did not cause US failure, but forced the government to recognize this failure.

526. Sale, Kirkpatrick, *SDS*, New York, Random House, 1973, pp. 752. Online: http://archive.org

Traces emergence of Students for a Democratic Society from 1960-1970, with a major focus on campaigns against the Vietnam War, including the 1965 March on Washington.

527. Simons, Donald L., *I Refuse: Memories of a Vietnam War Objector*, Trenton NJ, Broken Rifle Press, 1997, pp. 184.

A personal account which includes a brief summary of the course of the war and statistics on the scale of draft resistance and desertion.

528. Small, Melvin, *Covering Dissent: The Media and the Anti-Vietnam War Movement*, New Brunswick NJ, Rutgers University Press, 1994, pp. 228.

529. Small, Melvin, *Johnson, Nixon and the Doves*, New Brunswick NJ, Rutgers University Press, 1988, pp. 319.

Focus on the presidents and their relationship with the Vietnam Anti-War Movements between 1961 and 1975.

530. Taylor, Clyde, *Vietnam and Black America*, New York, Anchor Books, 1993, pp. 335.

Includes essays, articles and poems by black opponents of the war, including Martin Luther King, James Baldwin, and (in a section 'The Black Soldier') extracts from the diaries of black GIs and the Statement of Aims of 'GIs United Against the War in Vietnam'. Taylor notes how the advice to African Americans from some leaders to 'prove themselves worthy' by taking part in the war in Vietnam became increasingly discredited.

2. Opposing the Wars against Iraq – the Gulf War 1991 and US-led Invasion 2003

There were important differences in the origins and justification of these two wars. In 1991 Iraq had invaded Kuwait, and in the new atmosphere of detente the Soviet Union did not block a vote in the UN Security Council. So the western war had UN backing, and after defeating Saddam Hussein's army, the victorious forces limited themselves to liberating Kuwait. Views of the justification for the war in leftist and liberal circles varied, although there was quite significant opposition.

In 2003 the US-led invasion of Iraq was justified by the dictatorial and dangerous nature of the regime and, in Britain in particular, was presented as necessary to prevent Saddam Hussein potentially using his stockpile of weapons of mass destruction (although their presence was not proven at the time of going to war, and subsequent attempts by weapons inspectors to find them indicated the stockpiles did not exist). British troops participated in the invasion and subsequent occupation, along with other more symbolic contingents from the 'Coalition of the Willing' forged by the US Administration. Many governments opposed the invasion, it was not supported by the UN , and there were very large demonstrations reflecting unusually widespread opposition in Britain, Europe and elsewhere. There was also growing resistance inside the US. Individual soldiers conscientiously refused to fight in both Iraq wars, and bereaved families became prominent in protest in both the US and Britain. Although the movement against the war in 2003 and against the continuing occupation of Iraq was the more politically significant, so far the literature is fairly limited.

531. Brittain, Victoria, ed., *The Gulf Between Us: The Gulf War and Beyond*, London, Virago, 1991, pp. 186.

Published immediately after the war to discuss key issues raised. Gives background information and comments on the conduct of the war, in particular the killing from the air of large numbers of Iraqi troops flying white flags. On opposition to the war see: Grace Paley, 'Something about the Peace Movement: Something about the People's Right Not to Know', which comments on the US-based opposition, including references to soldiers refusing to support the war, pp. 64-5 and 70-71.

532. German, Lindsey and Andrew Murray, *Stop the War: The Story of Britain's Biggest Mass Movement*, London, Bookmarks, 2005, pp. 286.

Book by organizers of the Stop the War Coalition, created in 2001 after the September 11 attacks in the USA, which demonstrated against the Afghan War. It played a central role in mobilizing up to a million people to march in London in February 2003 and continued to demonstrate against the presence of western troops in both Iraq and Afghanistan. Although the role of the Socialist Workers Party in the Coalition was sometimes criticized, it succeeded in mobilizing large numbers of British Muslims in peaceful protest and in drawing in people from a broad political spectrum.

533.'The Iraq War Protests 10 Years Later', 2013.
Online: http://mobilizingideas.wordpress.com

Assessments of degree of success or failure, unintended consequences, and lessons to be learned about movements. Contributors include David Cortright, William A. Gamson, Kathy Kelly, Lisa Leitz and Eric Stoner.

534. Jiminez, Manuel, 'Mobilizing Against the Iraq War in Spain: Background, Participants and Electoral Implications', *South European Society and Politics*, vol. 12 no. 3 (2007), pp. 399-420.

535. Walgrave, Stefaan and Dieter Rucht, eds., *The World Says No to War: Demonstrations Against the War on Iraq*, Minneapolis MN, University of Minnesota Press, 2010, pp. 312, pb.

See also on opposition to 1991 Gulf War: Burrowes, 'The Persian Gulf War and the Gulf Peace Team' in Moser-Puangsuwan and Weber, eds. *Nonviolent Intervention Across Borders* (Introduction 1.c.), pp. 305-18; Meaden, *Protesting fort Peace*, and Peace, *A Just and Lasting Peace* (386 390 D.1).

3. Opposing Other Wars and Occupations

This section covers opposition and resistance to a variety of very different wars and military action: the 1968 Soviet-led invasion of Czechoslovakia; the 1971 Pakistani military repression of East Bengal's movement for independence and subsequent war between India and Pakistan which created Bangladesh. It also covers opposition to the US Administration's active support for the Contra war against the left-wing government of Nicaragua in the 1980s and to the wars in former Yugoslavia that led to its disintegration in the early 1990s. The East Timorese resistance to Indonesia occupation in the 1990s is referenced in Vol. 1 (E.II.2.c.), but a transnational solidarity protest against the occupation is cited below. All these examples of resistance, protest or solidarity are listed together here because the available references are limited.

536. Carter, April and Randle, Michael, *Support Czechoslovakia*, London, Housmans, 1968, pp. 64.

Account of four transnational teams going to Warsaw Pact capitals to protest against the 1968 Warsaw Pact invasion.

537. Coulson, Meg, 'Looking behind the Violent Break-up of Yugoslavia', *Feminist Review*, no. 45 (1993), pp. 86-101.

Examines post-1945 history of Yugoslavia and causes of its breakdown. Notes emerging feminist peace and ecological movement in the 1980s and the role of women in ongoing opposition to the war, including Serbian women demonstrating against the war with Croatia and demanding return of their husbands and sons.

538. Gorbanevskaya, Natalia, *Red Square at Noon*, London, Andre Deutsch, 1972, pp. 285.

On the demonstration in Red Square, Moscow, against the Soviet invasion of Czechoslovakia in August 1968, and subsequent trial and sentences.

539. Kronlid, Lotta, Andrea Needham, Joanna Wilson and Angie Zelter, *Seeds of Hope: East Timor Ploughshares: Women Disarming for Life and Justice*, London, Seeds of Hope, 1996, pp. 59.

Account by four women who 'disarmed' a Hawk fighter-bomber bound for Indonesia at the time of the war against East Timorese resisters. In July 1997 Liverpool Crown Court acquitted the four, accepting that under international law their action aimed to prevent a crime.

540. McMillan, Andrew, 'The Voyage of the Lusitania Espresso' in Moser-Puamgsuwan and Weber, *Nonviolent Intervention across Borders* (Introduction.1.c), pp. 73-100.

Critical account by Australian participant of Portuguese initiated act of solidarity with East Timorese victims of Indonesian occupation and repression: to sail a boat from Darwin to Dili in 1992 and lay a wreath in Santa Cruz cemetery in memory of 50 killed there attending a funeral in November 1991.

541. Mladjenovic, Lepa and Vera Litricin, 'Belgrade Feminists 1992: Separation, Guilt and Identity Crisis', *Feminist Review* no. 45 (1993), pp. 113-19.

Reviews development of Yugoslav feminism from 1978 and notes strains created by vig ils against the war in Croatia and later in Bosnia. See also: Women in Black, *Compilation of Information on Crimes of War against Women in ex-Yugoslavia – and Actions and Initiatives in their Defence,* Belgrade, Women in Black, 1993.

542. 'Operation Omega' in Hare and Blumberg, eds., *Liberation Without Violence,* (Introduction 1.c.), pp. 196-206.

After Pakistani repression of the 1971 East Bengali independence movement and outbreak of the India-Pakistan war, a transnational team tried with some success to take relief supplies into East Bengal. Their aim was to provide practical aid to refugees and protest against Pakistani army repression. At the same time US activists blocked arms supplies to Pakistan (see Taylor below).

543. Peace, Roger, *A Call to Conscience: The Anti-Contra War Campaign,* Manchester University of Manchester Press, 2012, pp. 328, pb.

History of the 8 year anti-Contra campaign, its links in Nicaragua and its impact on deterring the US President from sending troops to oust the left-wing Sandanista government. See also on border monitoring: Griffin-Nolan, *Witness for Peace* [in Vol. 1, A.5.] and shorter version in Moser Puangsuwan and Weber, eds., *Nonviolent Intervention across Borders* (Introduction 1.c.), pp. 279-304.

544. Schweitzer, Christine, 'Mir Sada: The Story of a Nonviolent Intervention that Failed' in Moser-Puangsuwan and Weber, eds., *Nonviolent Action Across Borders* (Introduction 1.c.), pp. 269-76.

Attempt in 1993 to set up a transnational peace caravan in Sarajevo during the war in Bosnia.

545. Taylor, Richard K., *Blockade: A Guide to Nonviolent Intervention,* Maryknoll NY, Orbis Books, 1977, pp. 175.

Account of how a nonviolent fleet of canoes and kayaks blocked Pakistani shipping at East Coast ports of the USA to oppose US support for Pakistan's repression in East Bengal. Part 2 is a manual for direct action.

See also for women's resistance to wars in ex-Yugoslavia: Korac, *Linking Arms* (635 F.5.).

F. Feminist Movements and Protests

The first wave of feminism in the 19th and early 20th centuries was predominantly western, with US and British women starting to campaign for legal and political rights from the 1840s, and New Zealand and Australian women achieving the first successes in gaining votes for women in national and state elections. Feminism spread during the 19th century to other parts of the world: there were campaigning groups in Turkey, India and especially Japan before 1900. Feminist internationals created around the beginning of the 20th century (one specifically focused on the right to vote) had members in many parts of the world, although the organizations were western dominated. Many women in colonized countries focused their energies on the national liberation struggle, although political involvement could encourage activism on the rights of women. Huda Sharawi, who led a women's demonstration in support of the nationalist struggle in Cairo in 1919 and became Egypt's first prominent feminist and suffragist, epitomized this dual commitment. Radical and working class women often supported socialist movements, which endorsed in principle women's rights, but gave priority to socialist goals; although prominent women could influence party agendas, as Alexandra Kollontai did in Russia in the early years after the Bolshevik Revolution. The first wave of feminist protest in the west helped create better education opportunities for girls and young women, and exerted pressure for legislative change. Feminist activism also included mass demonstrations and (by some in Britain and the US) forms of civil disobedience and direct action. Tactics such as chaining oneself to railings have been taken up by more recent movements.

The experiences of the first wave of feminism had parallels in the second wave which began at the end of the 1960s in English-speaking countries and parts of Europe. These protests occurred in a context where women had already won basic legal and political rights, but where they still faced many forms of legal or de facto discrimination at work, in the family and in their personal lives. The early protests were primarily by young middle class women and included brief symbolic actions to highlight particular issues:

against beauty contests and products, and forms of direct action were later sometimes used in a number of countries to challenge restrictions on abortion, tolerance of rape, and promotion of pornography But the political strand of the movement focused primarily on political lobbying, sometimes supplemented by marches and rallies, or using the courts to achieve new rulings in favour of equality.

Although second wave feminism in the west was primarily a middle class movement, there were (as in the first wave) also significant expressions of militancy among working class women, notably in Britain. Many feminist pressure groups sprang up in the 1970s, and pre-existing ones were revitalized. But women's liberation was also a social movement which grew partly out of the New Left, but criticized male chauvinism on the left. Although, as in its first manifestation, key demands were those of 'liberal feminism', e.g. equal pay, equality in the professions, the right to contraception and abortion, Marxists and/or radical feminists were also influential in the movements in many countries.

Second wave feminism's roots in the 1960s were reflected in its emphasis on consciousness raising, sexual freedom and challenging dominant cultural and theoretical constructions of femininity. A new feminist literature arose, heralded by polemical and widely read books by authors such as Andrea Dworkin, Eva Figes, Shulamith Firestone, Betty Friedan, Germaine Greer, Kate Millet and Juliet Mitchell, and developed into a sustained critique of many academic disciplines.

Indeed one of the lasting impacts of the movement was the rise in feminist publishing and the creation of women's studies or gender courses in many universities. There were also important feminist experiments in communal organization to complement protest: for example rape counseling centres and refuges for women subject to domestic violence, which often lasted well after protests had subsided and in some countries gained government funding.

Radical feminism was also associated with a strong commitment to an anti-hierarchical mode of organisation. These feminist views influenced many major environmentalist direct action campaigns in the west in the 1970s and campaigns against nuclear weapons in the 1980s (see Barbara Epstein, *Political Protest and Cultural Revolution* (Introduction, 1.c.).

During the 1980s in Britain and the USA the momentum of feminist campaigning subsided, although some significant new groups representing women in racial minorities emerged. The divisions between different ideological strands of the movements also became more marked. Committed radical feminism emerged in part of the nuclear disarmament movement, symbolized by the Greenham Common camp at the cruise missile base in England and by the Seneca Falls peace camp in the USA Since the rise of feminism in the 19th century, there has been a close (though complex and contested) link between feminist activists and peace movements (a number of feminists in all the combatant countries opposed the First World War), and feminist activism has also emerged in recent decades in protests against a number of wars (see F.5). Since the rise of the Green movement some feminists have also argued that women have a particular role in preserving the environment. This 'ecofeminism' has been expressed through theoretical analysis, for example by Vandana Shiva, (298 C.1.a.) as well as by protests, and by promoting constructive roles for women in their local contexts – for example Wangari Maathai's campaign to plant trees (321 C 1.c.).

Although second wave feminism was waning in some western countries during the 1980s, in many other parts of the world feminism was gaining momentum, though often with different agendas reflecting varied political and cultural contexts. In some countries women have been struggling for the most basic rights. Women have also been active in many movements against repressive political rule, but have not been able to focus specifically on women's rights until greater political freedom had been achieved. In Spain, for example, a campaign for legislative reform emerged after the death of Franco, whilst in South Africa, it has only been since the end of apartheid in 1994 that major feminist issues, such as violence against women, have come to the fore. The collapse of apartheid gave women an opportunity to influence the new constitution, and an alliance of women's groups achieved a constitution embodying women's rights.

In much of the Global South feminist activism was growing in the 1980s and 1990s, encouraged by the UN Decade for Women and its non-governmental conferences, which culminated in the 1985 Nairobi Forum. Established women's organizations played an important part, but many new groups sprang up and had a prominent role. Feminism internationally was then given a substantial boost by the 1995 UN Conference on Women in Beijing. At an international level tensions had emerged between some western feminists and activists in Africa, Asia, the Middle East and Latin America, sensitive to neo-imperialist attitudes and assumptions by western spokeswomen and aware of the complexity of their own history and contexts. But one key theme, on which all women were able to unite at Beijing, was that of violence against women, and other issues such as the importance of education and political representation were also unifying.

When feminist campaigning re-emerged in Britain and other western countries in the 21st century, it was part of a wider global movement and awareness of the struggles of women and girls in other parts of the world. This revived feminism has been reflected in the annual Billion Women Rising demonstrations, initiated in 1998; by 2013 protests by dancing women were held in 207 countries, and the protests have strengthened local activists and legislators in the UK and US as well as in countries as diverse as Guatemala and Somalia. Feminist activism in the 21st century is strongly influenced by the new social media: in the UK a number of campaigns have been coordinated by and expressed through the internet or Twitter. Whilst proving a powerful tool for mobilizing protest, the new media also provided widespread opportunities for targeting feminists with hate messages and threats, and revealed the strength of hostility towards women in the most apparently liberal, as well as the more obviously patriarchal, societies.

There is a large literature focusing on women's general position in society, rather than on movements and protests. This wider literature is not covered here, although some books and chapters of course discuss both. Since this Guide focuses on post-1945 campaigning it does not cover the earlier history of feminism in any detail. But a few books providing a historical perspective on both western and non-western feminism are listed below:

546. Bouchier, David, *The Feminist Challenge: The Movement for Women's Liberation in Britain and the USA*, London, Macmillan, 1983, pp. 252.

Traces the course of the feminist movement from its beginnings at a meeting in Seneca Falls, USA, in 1848, through the campaign for voting rights in the early 20th century to the emergence of radical feminism in the 1960s and 1970s.

547. Cliff, Tony, *Class Struggle and Women's Liberation: 1640 to the Present Day*, London, Bookmarks, 1984, pp. 271.

Sweeping historical and transnational survey from a socialist standpoint, noting industrial action by working women and criticizing class base and focus of second wave American and British feminism.

548. Costain, Anne N., 'Women's Movements and Nonviolence', *PS: Political Science and Politics*, vol. 33 no. 2 (June 2000), p. 175-80.

Discusses nonviolent direct action by US feminists in both early suffrage movement and the 1970s.

549. Jaywardina, Kumari, *Feminism and Nationalism in the Third World*, London, Zed Press (Third World Books), 1986, pp. 288, pb.

Study of women's rights movements in Middle East and Asia from 19th century to 1980s, covering Egypt and Turkey, China, India, Indonesia,

Korea and the Philippines. Argues feminism was not an alien ideology but indigenous to these countries.

550. Offen, Karen, ed., *Globalizing Feminisms, 1789-1945*, London and New York, Routledge, 2010, pp. 472, pb.

Collection of essays providing a comparative history of women's activism round the world.

1. The 'Second Wave' of Feminism: Pressure and Protests in the West

1.a. Organizing, Lobbying and Protesting

551. Breines, Winifred, *The Trouble Between Us: An Uneasy History of White and Black Women in the Feminist Movement*, New York, Oxford University Press, 2007, pp. 280, pb.

552. Coote, Anna and Beatrix Campbell, *Sweet Freedom: The Struggle for Women's Liberation in Britain*, London, Pan Books, 1982, pp. 258.

Study of British movement since 1960s, legislative changes and political developments affecting women in work, the family, sex and culture. Chapter 1, pp. 9-47, charts the evolution of the movement in terms of key protests, campaigns and organization, including some examples of nonviolent action.

553. Duchen, Claire, *Feminism in France from May 1968 to Mitterand*, London, Routledge, 1986, pp. 165.

Chapter 1, 'Beginnings' examines role of women in May 1968 and the emergence of the Mouvement de Liberation des Femmes in 1970, laying of a wreath on the tomb of the unknown soldier to commemorate his wife (leading to arrests), support for women strikers (e.g. in a hat factory in Troyes) and the 5th April 1971 Manifesto by 343 prominent women who had resorted to illegal abortions. Later chapters explore ideological divisions within the movement, theoretical issues and the relationship of feminists to socialist government in France.

554. Evans, Sara, *Personal Politics: The Roots of Women's Liberation in the Civil Rights Movement and the New Left*, New York, Vintage, 1980, pp. 288, pb.

Using her personal experience the author examines how women were dismayed by their treatment in radical movements, and how they turned their activist skills to feminist campaigning.

555. Freeman, Jo, *The Politics of Women's Liberation*, New York, Longman, 1975, pp. 268.

Examines the evolution of second wave feminism in the USA from the early protests.

556. Gelb, Joyce, 'Feminism and Political Action' in R.J. Dalton and M. Kuechler, eds., *Challenging the Political Order: New Social and Political Movements in Western Democracies*, Cambridge, Polity, 1990, pp. 137-56.

Comparing the US, British and Swedish movements.

557. Haug, Frigga, 'The Women's Movement in West Germany', *New Left Review*, no. 155 (Jan/Feb. 1986).

Discusses paradox of decline of women's movement in 1980s, despite significant public gains and state support for feminist causes.

558. Malagreca, Miguel, 'Lottiamo Ancora: Reviewing One Hundred and Fifty Years of Italian Feminism', *Journal of International Women's Studies*, vol. 7 no. 4 (May 2006), pp. 69-89.

Includes material on the second wave of Italian feminism in 1960s and 1970s and developments on divorce, family law and employment law in the 1970s and 1980s, Ends with some discussion of lesbian and queer struggles for recognition.

559. Ryan, Barbara, *Feminism and the Women's Movement: Dynamics of Change in Social Movement Ideology and Activism*, New York, Routledge, 1992, pp. 272.

After looking at earlier history of US feminism, examines 2nd wave and in particular the mobilization around the Equal Rights Act passed in 1975; also explores ideological divisions within the movement.

560. Threlfall, Monica, 'The Women's Movement in Spain', *New Left Review*, no. 151 (May/Jun 1985), pp. 44-73.

Discusses post-Franco development of feminist movement and legislative results.

561. Wilson, Elizabeth, *What Is to be Done about Violence Against Women?* Harmondsworth, Penguin, 1983, pp. 256.

Chapter 6, 'Feminists fight back' (pp.169-224) covers the protests in Britain against male violence, and also constructive organizational responses and the campaign for legal change and challenges to prevailing attitudes.

I.b. Women's Strikes and Engagement in Industrial Action in UK

This sub-section covers a number of significant strikes by women in Britain. The best known is the 1968 strike at Ford Dagenham by women machinists demanding equal pay with men doing jobs of equivalent skill, which helped to achieve the Labour government's Equal Pay Act of 1970. The Grunwick strike by Asian immigrant women in 1976-77 against very low pay and enforced overtime was (although ultimately unsuccessful) a landmark in mobilizing white male workers in support of immigrants and gaining widespread sup port, for examples from MPs. There were other strikes by women in very badly paid work, such as cleaners. In addition, wives and mothers of miners engaged in the major 1984 strike became actively involved on the picket lines and in providing practical support, and in the process gained a new sense of empowerment.

562. Alexander Sally, 'The Nightcleaners' Campaign' in Sandra Allen, Lee Sanders and Jan Wallis, eds., *Conditions of Illusion*, London Feminist Books, 1974, pp. 309-25. See also: 'Striking Progress' a list of strikes involving women 1973-74, pp. 332-48.

563. Bohanna, John, 'Finally Making the Grade', *Red Pepper* (Dec/Jan 2011), pp. 54-55.

Recalls that the 1968 Ford Dagenham strike for equal pay, although it achieved a substantial pay rise and eventual parity with men on the same grade, did not recognise the skilled nature of the sewing-machinists work by upgrading them. Provides brief account of later 1984 strike by women machinists demanding upgrading, which led to an independent inquiry, which recognised their claim. A film *Making the Grade* by the Open Eye Film, Video and Animation Workshop documents this second struggle.

564. Dromey, Jack, *Grunwick: The Workers' Story*, London, Lawrence and Wishart, 1978, pp. 207.

The author was secretary of Brent Trades Council in London when the non-unionised women strikers at the mail-order plant contacted him for help in 1976, and became a member of the strike committee. He also wrote an obituary of the inspirational leader of the strike, Jayaben Desia, when she died 23 December 2010 (*Guardian*, 29 Dec 2010, p.30). (For a celebration of Desia's role and life see also Yasmin Alibhai-Brown, 'Remembering an unsung heroine of our modern history', *Independent*, 3 Jan 2011, p.5.)

565. Friedman, Henry and Sander Meredeen, *The Dynamics of Industrial Conflict: Lessons from Ford*, London, Croom Helm, 1980, pp. 386.

This is an account and analysis of the 1968 Ford Dagenham women sewing machinists' strike by two men on opposing sides (trade union convener of plant and Ford negotiating team) involved in the dispute. A lively semi-fictionalized account of the dispute from the women's viewpoint is the 2010 film 'Made in Dagenham'.

566. Miller, Jill, *You Can't Kill the Spirit: Women in a Welsh Mining Village*, London, Women's Press, 1987, pp. 177.

567. Rogaly, Joe, *Grunwick*, Harmondsworth, Penguin, 1977, pp. 199.

Account by journalist who gave prominent coverage to the women's struggle during the strike.

568. Stead, Jean, *Never the Same Again: Women and the Miners' Strike*, London, Women's Press, 1987, pp. 177.

See also: Gillian, Audrey talking to 1984 activist Betty Cook, 'I was always told I was thick. The strike taught me I wasn't', *Guardian* (10 May 2004), pp. 10-11, looking back after 20 years; and Loach, Loretta, 'We'll be Here Right to the End...and After: Women in the Miners' Strike' in Hugh Beynon, ed., *Digging Deeper: Issues in the Miners' Strike*, (34 A.1.a.ii) chapter 9. See also for list of articles and books relating to Grunwick: http://www.leeds.ac.uk/strikingwomen/resources

2. Women under Communism and under Post-Communism

Under Soviet-style Socialism women appeared to enjoy rights that women in the west were demanding: for example in higher education and at work, access to affordable child care and the right to maternity leave, and abortion. However they were noticeably under-represented in politics, on average paid less well than men (tending to have less skilled jobs), and patriarchal attitudes meant that women had to undertake all the burdens of shopping, housework and child-rearing in addition to employment outside the home. There was also concern that abortion was used in lieu of contraception, and women were expected to return to work after paid maternity leave, although in the 1960s and 1970s some countries introduced unpaid maternity leave for up to a year and/or child allowances. The possibility of expressing feminist criticisms was limited by the stringent controls on any autonomous protest – a very small feminist group in the USSR in the 1980s immediately came under KGB surveillance. Moreover when in the post-Stalinist era dissent began to emerge, active women were likely to focus on basic human rights rather than women's issues, although in the ferment of the late 1980s feminist issues began to be voiced. A stronger feminism existed in the GDR in the 1980s, where it tended to be linked to peace issues.

Since 1989 the economic, political and cultural situation has changed radically, and also varies between countries, for example in the political power of the Orthodox or Catholic Churches. In Russia in particular women's position rapidly worsened: as a result of the new market economy (and ensuing economic chaos, poverty and rise in criminality), many more women than men became unemployed and women's average wages had by 1995 dropped to 40% of men's (compared with 70% in the Soviet era). Businesses openly advertised for secretaries who were 'young, blonde, long-legged and without inhibitions'; and rates for the rape and murder of women soared between 1991 and the mid-1990s.

Feminist organizations emerged in the 1990s in Russia and in other parts of the former Communist bloc, for example to provide aid to raped and battered women, and to promote women's representation in politics. In the second decade of the 21st century small but well-publicized radical groups like Pussy Riot have challenged the authorities.

569. Bull, Anna, Hanna Diamond and Rosalind Marsh, eds., *Feminisms and Women's Contemporary Movements*, London, Macmillan, 2000, pp. 286.

Covers Europe in the 1990s, including essays on 'Theorizing Feminism in Postcommunism', 'Something Unnatural: Attitudes to Feminism in Russia', 'New Mothers' Campaigning Organization in Russia', '"Its about Helping women to Believe in Themselves": Grassroots Women's Organizations in Contemporary Russian Society' and 'Women's Discordant Voices in the Context of the 1998 Elections in the Ukraine'.

570. Einhorn, Barbara, 'Socialist Emancipation: The Women's Movement in the GDR', in Sonia Kruks, Rayna Rapp and Marilyn B. Young, eds., *Promissory Notes: Women in the Transition to Socialism*, New York, Monthly Review Press, 1989, pb.

571. Einhorn, Barbara, 'Feminism in Crisis: The East German Women's Movement in the "New Europe"', *Australian Journal of Politics and History*, vol. 41 no 1 (April 1999), pp. 14-28.

572. Femen and Galia Ackerman, *Femen*, Cambridge, Polity Press, 2014, pp. 240, pb.

Femen was founded in the Ukraine in 2008 by four women to protest against patriarchy embodied in dictatorship, religion and the sex industry. Their well publicised bare-breasted protests have included a dangerous demonstration in Belarus and opposition to President Putin. They have moved to France and this book was first published in French. A film 'Ukraine is not a Brothel' claimed that Femen's protests were orchestrated and the women controlled by a male svengali. This claim is addressed in an addendum to the English version of the book.

573. *Feminist Review*, Issue on 'Post-Communism,' no. 76 (2004).

The editorial comments on key changes for women in the transition from Communism: political representation had dropped; more women were overrepresented among the unemployed; socialist reproductive rights were being challenged; women's domesticity promoted as a virtue; and pornography and marketing of women's bodies seen as 'freedom'. Women were also more vulnerable to various sorts of violence, including sexual harassment at work, domestic violence and sex trafficking.

574. Funk, Nanette, 'Feminism in Former East Germany', *Dissent* (Spring 1992), pp. 152-56.

575. Gessen, Masha, *Words Will Break Cement: The Passion of Pussy Riot*, Riverhead Books, 2014, pp. 308, pb.

Discusses roots of the group founded in 2011 and their international support, especially among musical celebrities, after their 2012 demonstration in Moscow Cathedral, leading to imprisonment of the three involved. See also: *Pussy Riot: A Punk Prayer for Freedom*, London, Feminist Press, 2013, pp. 152, including letters from prison, court statements, poems and tributes by international admirers.

576. Graff, Agnieszka, 'A Different Chronology: Reflections on Feminism in Contemporary Poland', in Gillis, Howie and Munford, eds., *Third Wave Feminism* (616 F. 4.), pp. 142-55.

Argues 'wave' chronology does not apply to Poland.

577. Guenther, Katja, *Making Their Place: Feminism after Socialism in Eastern Germany*, Palo Alto CA, Stanford University Press, 2010, pp. 262, pb.

Examines feminist activism in two East German cities, Erfurt and Rostock, in context of economic and political upheaval in former socialist bloc, and the trends undermining the rights and status of women.

578. Haug, Friga, 'The End of Socialism in Europe: A New Challenge for Socialist Feminism', *Feminist Review*. no. 39 (1991).

579. Holland, Barbara, ed., *Soviet Sisterhood: British Feminists on Women in the USSR*, Bloomington IN, Indiana University Press and Fourth Estate, 1986, pp. 272

Includes chapter by Alix Holt, 'The First Soviet Feminists' on Leningrad group associated with The Almanach: 'Women and Russia' and their club 'Maria'.

580. Jancar, Barbara, 'The New Feminism in Yugoslavia' in Pedro Ramet, ed., *Yugoslavia in the 1980s*, Boulder CO, Westview Press, 1985.

581. Mamonova, Tatyana, *Women and Russia: Feminist Writings from the Soviet Union*, Boston MA, Beacon press, 1984, pp. 272.

Mamonova and three others in the group were forced into exile by the KGB.

582. Marsh, Rosalind, 'Polish Feminism', Opus, 2009. Online at: http://opus.bath.ac.uk

583. Martens, Lorna, ed., *The Promised Land: Feminist Writing in the German Democratic Republic*, New York, State University of New York Press, 2001, pp. 273.

Writings by prominent intellectuals, including Christa Wolf, exploring how far the GDR gave women the equality it proclaimed.

584. Molyneux, Maxine, 'The "Woman Question" in the Age of Perestroika', *New Left Review*, no. 183 (1990), pp. 23-49.

Useful overall summary analysis of changing position of women in communist (and post-communist) countries (including China), with detailed references.

585. Posadskaya, Anastasia, *Women in Russia: A New Era of Russian Feminism*, London, Verso, 1994, pp. 256.

Study spanning women's position in Tsarist Russia, th e Communist period and immediate aftermath of dissolution of USSR.

586. Racioppi, Linda and Katherine O'Sullivan Lee, *Women's Activism in Contemporary Russia*, Philadelphia PA, Temple University Press, 1997, pp. 277, pb.

The opening chapters provide historical context, but the focus of the book is on interviews with leading activists, representing the great variety of ideological standpoints and concerns, to develop an analysis of feminism since the later 1980s.

587. Renne, Tanya, ed., *Ana's Land: Sisterhood in Eastern Europe*, Boulder CO, Westview Press, 1997, pp. 256.

Includes over 30 contributions from nine countries indicating women's activism on issues such as reproduction, health and abortion, political and legal change and violence against women.

3. The Global Women's Movement: 1970s–2000s

Western feminism had some impact on women in other parts of the world, even though the western feminist agendas (and the style of protest and rhetoric) often had little relevance to the most pressing problems of women in very different social circumstances.

Western feminist scholars could also be criticized for misunderstanding feminist struggle in other continents and cultures: see for example: Oyeronke, Oyewimi *African Women and Feminism: Reflecting on the Politics of Sisterhood*, 2003.

The strength of feminist groups around the world has varied considerably, depending on the political context, the social, cultural and religious obstacles they had to overcome, and how far there was an earlier history of women's political activism, although feminism could emerge in very repressive contexts, as in Afghanistan in the 1950s and 1970s. In Latin America there were lively women's movements in the 1970s and Latin American and Caribbean feminists began to meet regularly at a regional level in 1981. In China feminist protest is constrained by lack of political freedom; in India women do have democratic freedoms and have been campaigning on women's issues for decades, but as the brutal gang rape and murder of a woman student in Delhi in December 2012, and also the 'dowry deaths' of young brides, have illustrated, women in India are threatened by alarming levels of public and sometimes family violence. The position of women in the Middle East has been mixed; women were often prominent in the 2011 Arab uprisings, but also vulnerable to public violence, as in Egypt. In conservative monarchical Saudi Arabia women taking part in a campaign of driving cars on 22 May 2012 were committing an act of civil disobedience; but (after several women challenged their lack of a vote) the King decided in September 2011 to allow women to vote and to stand in municipal elections.

Local and national campaigns have often gained publicity and support from transnational feminist organizations and networks created since the 1980s. These bodies often lobby at the level of the UN and issue policy documents, but many also offer solidarity through transnational conferences, training institutes, research resources, spreading news, issuing action alerts, supporting demonstrations or offering practical help. They also often cooperate with other transnational feminist organizations. For more information and details of current action by a few of these organizations with varied agendas, see:

DAWN (Development Alternatives with Women for a New Era) founded in 1984 to assess crises faced by women and impact of neoliberalism: http://www.dawnnet.org

SIGI (Sisterhood Is Global Institute) created in 1984 as 'the first international feminist think tank': http://sigi.org

WEDO (Women's Environment and Development Organization} campaigning for 'a just world, human rights, gender equality and the integrity of the environment', which supported People's Climate Change March September 2014 in New York: http://www.wedo.org

WLUML (Women Living Under Muslims Laws) is 'an international solidarity network with groups in about 40 countries and reaching over 110 countries that provides information, support and a collective space' for women seeking their rights and challenging repressive interpretations of Islam. Their website, available in Arabic, French and English, is: http://www.wlumi.org

3.a. General, Regional and National Studies

588. Ahmed, Leila, 'Feminism and Feminist Movements in the Middle East: a Preliminary Exploration', *Women' Studies International Forum*, vol. 5 (1982), pp. 153-68.

589. Ahmed, Leila, *A Quiet Revolution*. Newhaven CT, Yale University Press, 2012, pp.360, pb.
Discusses reasons for the resurgence of veil-wearing among Muslim women, and the social and political implications. Argues (contrary to author's own earlier position) that Islamists rather than secularists often prominent in struggle for social justice and women's rights.

590. Alpizar, Lydia, Anahi Duran and Anali Russo Garrido, eds., *Building Feminist Movements: Global Perspectives*, London, Zed Books, 2006, pp. 288, pb.
The chapters cover a wide range of countries and issues, including: The Korean Women's Trade Union, the feminist movement in Indonesia, the

Algerian 'Twenty Years is Enough' campaign, widening the base of the feminist movement in Pakistan, advocacy of women's rights in Nigeria, re-politicizing feminist activity in Argentina, new modes of organizing in Mexico, and two chapters on Israel, one on an Arab women's organization.

591. Al-Sharmani, Mulki, ed., *Feminist Activism, Women's Rights and Legal Reform*, London, Zed Books, 2013, pp. 200.

Explores both attempts at legal reform and those reforms achieved in Islamic countries (Palestine, Yemen, Iran and Egypt) and problems of implementing reform, for example the domestic violence law in Ghana.

592. Alvarez, Sonia, 'Advocating Feminism: The Latin American Feminist NGO "Boom"', *International Feminist Journal of Politics*, vol. 2 no. 1 (1999), pp. 181-209.

593. Basu, Amrita, ed., *The Challenge of Local Feminisms: Women's Movements in Global Perspective*, Boulder CO, Westview Press, 1995, pp. 510.

Worldwide overview, but with especial focus on postcolonial states in Africa, Asia and Latin America.

594. Chang, Doris, *Women's Movements in Twentieth Century Taiwan*, University of Illinois Press, 2009, pp. 248.

Discusses mixed fortunes of women's movement in changing political contexts, and how Taiwanese women made selective use of western feminist theory.

595. Chaudhuri, Maitrayee, ed., *Feminism in India*, London, Zed Books, 2005, pp. 416.

Collection of essays by academics and activists on condition of women in colonial and independent India, and the challenges to Indian feminism from globalization and the Hindu Right. Indicates a vigorous if uneven women's movement over several decades.

596. Fiedler, Rachel Nyagondwe and Johannes Wynand Hofmeyr, 'The Conception of Concerned African Women Theologians: Is it African or Western?', *Acta Theological*, vol. 31 no. 1 (2011), pp. 39-57. Online at: http://www.uovs.ac.za/ActaTheologica

Discusses origins in 1988 of an Africa-wide group that promotes theological debates between Christians, Muslims, Jews and adherents of African religions, gives African women a voice through numerous publications and has focused on social issues such as the stigma attached to HIV/AIDS. For background and current information: http://www.thecirclecawt.org

597. Loonba, Ania and Ritty A. Lukose, eds., *South Asian Feminisms*, Durham NC, Duke University Press, 2012, pp. 432.

Building on 40 years of activism and scholarship, contributors assess recent feminist issues and campaigns in India, Pakistan, Sri Lanka and Bangladesh.

598. McFadden, Patricia, 'The State of Feminism in Africa Today', Nordic Affairs Institute, 2002. Online at: http://www.nai.uu.se/publications/news/archives/002mcfadden

599. Moghadam, Valentine, *Globalizing Women: Transnational Feminist Networks*, Baltimore MD, John Hopkins University Press, pp. 272, pb.

Explores pressures of globalization on women and reactions against it and rise of transnational networks, such as DAWN (Development Alternatives with Women for a New Era), WEDO (Women's Economic and Development Organization), SIGI (Sisterhood is Global Institute) and WLUML (Women Living Under Muslim Laws).

600. Molyneux, Maxine, 'Mobilization without Emancipation? Women's Interests, the State and Revolution in Nicaragua', *Feminist Studies*, vol. 11 no. 2 (1985), pp. 227-52.

601. Morgan, Robin, *Sisterhood is Global: The International Women's Movement Anthology*, New York, City University of New York Feminist Press, [1984] 1996, pp. 821.

Anthology of essays and documents from women in 70 countries round the world, especially the Global South. Authors are a mix of well known and less well known grass roots activists, politicians and scholars. A global strategy meeting organized to mark publication in 1984 led to the creation of the Sisterhood Is Global Institute (SIGI).

602. Naples, Nancy A. and Manisha Desai, eds., *Women's Activism and Globalization: Linking Local Struggles and Transnational Politics*, New York and London, Routledge, 2002, pp. 352.

Focuses on women's inequalities in rural and urban areas, and considers forms of organization and solidarity across borders. Includes a study of women activists in Mali.

603. Pietila, Hikka and Jeanne Vickers, *Making Women Matter: The Role of the United Nations*, London, Zed Books, 1996 (3rd edn), pp. 224.

Assesses critically UN attempts to improve the position of women over half a century.

604. Salime, Zakia, *Between Feminism and Islam: Human Rights and Sharia Law in Morocco*, Minneapolis MN, University of Minnesota Press, 2011, pp. 248.

Study of both feminist and Islamist organizations in Morocco showing how two have influenced each other's agendas through decades of activism.

605. *Signs: Journal of Women in Culture and Society*, vol. 17 no. 2 (1992) section on 'Feminisms in Latin America: From Bogota to San Bernado'', pp. 393-434.

606. Stephen, Lynn, *Women and Social Movements in Latin America: Power from Below*, University of Texas Press, 1997, pp. 352.

Covers six cases of grassroots activism in Mexico, El Salvador, Brazil and Chile, which use interviews with activists and provide histories of organizations and movements involved. The activists are concerned with economic and health issues, but also stress problems relating to contraception and abortion, rape and domestic violence.

607. Stienstra, Deborah, 'Making Global Connections Among Women' in Cohen and Rai, eds., *Global Social Movements* (see Introduction 1.c.), pp. 62-82.

Discusses the significance of UN Conferences on Women and the role of both established and newly created women's organizations in relation to them and the wider movement.

608. Tripp, Aili Mari, *African Women's Movements: Transforming Political Landscapes, Changing Political Landscapes*, Cambridge, Cambridge University Press, 2009, pp. 280, pb.

Focuses on Cameroon, Uganda and Mozambique within wider African context.

609. Woodward, Alison E., Jean-Michel Bonvin and Merce Renom, eds., *Transforming Gendered Well-Being in Europe*, Aldershot, Hants, Ashgate, 2011, pp.308.

Primarily examines role of women activists. Part I includes some historical studies from 18th and 19th centuries. But Part II covers period from 1970s -2000s in Netherlands and Poland and examines claims and projects of European movement. Part III examines how women's movements have embraced global issues and role of minority groups within Europe.

3.b. Individual Campaigns and Activists

Some brave individuals and movements challenging profound inequalities have caught the attention of mainstream or leftist media and feminists, and therefore have been written about in English. Some accounts are very brief. *New Internationalist* has published several short accounts of women activists: for example: 'Making Waves: Interview with The Rescue Foundation: Liberating Sex Slaves in India' (June 2006 p. 33); 'Making Waves: Nepal's Trailblazing Dalit Feminist Durga Sob' (May 2010, p. 33); 'Making Waves: Interview with Rosi Orozco.on the Fight against Human Trafficking and Sexual Exploitation in Mexico' by President of the Special Commission in the Combat of Sexual Trafficking (November 2011, p. 56); 'Interview with Khanim Latif', Iraqi feminist campaigner and director of Kurdistan-based women's rights organization Asuda (December 2012, p. 42) A few book length studies are listed below.

610. Brodsky, Anne E., *With All Our Strength: The Revolutionary Association of the Women of Afghanistan*, London, Routledge, 2004, pp 336.

Account of feminist organization founded in 1977, which uses literacy classes, underground papers and pamphlets and demonstrations, based on more than 100 interviews with key activists by author, a US feminist scholar. The founder of the Association, who left university in Kabul to struggle for women's rights, was assassinated in 1987.

611. Fontanella-Khan, Amana, *Pink Sari Revolution: A Tale of Women and Power in India*, W.W. Norton, 2013, pp. 304, hb. In paperback Oxford, One World Publications.

Describes Sampat Pal and the now 20,000 strong Pink Gang she founded, which uses 'social power' to defend individual women treated unjustly and to challenge misogyny in general, The women carry sticks and sometimes attack corrupt politicians and policemen. See also: Sampan Pal as told to Anne Berthod, *Warrior in a Pink Sari*, Zubaan Books, 2012, pp. 220, pb.

612. Joya, Malalai, *Raising My Voice: Story of the Afghan Woman Who Spoke Out*, London, Rider, 2010, pp. 288, pb.

Explores life of young woman who secretly ran schools for girls in Herat during Taliban rule, was elected to the Afghan parliament in 2005 at the age of 23, but was thrown out of it for raising women's issues, and who had by 2009 already survived five assassination attempts. When she visited Britain in 2009, where she opposed NATO involvement in Afghanistan, the *Independent* ran a long interview with her by Johann Hari (Supplement *Independent Life* 28 July 2009, pp. 1-5).

613. Mam, Somaly, *The Road of Lost Innocence: The True Story of a Cambodian Heroine*, New York, Random House Circle, 2009, pp. 224.

Memoir by Cambodian activist against sexual slavery, who herself as a child was sent to brothels in Southeast Asia and as a campaigner has been threatened frequently by brothel keepers and traffickers. Her organizations try to rescue, shelter and teach children and women escaping from sexual exploitation, in Cambodia, Thailand, Laos and Vietnam, and more globally. See also: http:// www.somaly.org

614. Yousafzai, Malala with Christine Lamb, *I Am Malala: The Girl Who Stood Up for Education and was Shot by the Taliban*, London, Weidenfeld and Nicholson, 2013, pp. 288.

The schoolgirl Pakistani campaigner for girls' education who was awarded the Nobel Peace Prize in 2014 tells her story.

See also: Maathai, *Unbowed* (321 C.1.c.)

4. Feminism in the West with Global Connections: 'Third Wave' to 'Fourth Wave'

4.a. The Third Wave 1990s-2000s

In the 1990s and at the turn of the millenium many young women in countries where they enjoyed full access to education, formal equal rights at work and personal freedom seemed to turn against the feminism of the second wave. Some who still believed feminism was important reassessed its relevance to their times and articulated a set of ideas usually labelled 'third wave feminism'. This was primarily a theoretical tendency, influenced by postmodernism, arguing that 'women' could not be understood as a single category and stressing the diverse identities and experiences of women. The third wave also rejected what it saw as the sexual puritanism of the 'second wave', engaged with popular culture, including its projections of 'strong' women, and tended to prioritise narratives of personal experience. This theoretical strand did reflect a real trend for diverse groups to organize under the banner of feminism – for example African American women in the USA, and some writings explored the position of lesbians and transgenders. But third wave feminism was not primarily a call to action, unlike the 'fourth' wave of activism, embracing a new generation of young women, that came to the fore by the second decade of the 21st century.

615. Findlen, Barbara, *Listen Up: Voices from the Next Feminist Generation*, Seattle, Seal [1995] 2001 (expanded edition), pp. 300, pb.

Collection featuring writers and activists – including Rebecca Walker, Nomy Lama and Inga Musci – and editors of several women's periodicals – discussing range of issues.

616. Gillis, Stacy, Gillian Howie and Rebecca Munford, *Third Wave Feminism: A Critical Exploration*, New York, Palgrave Macmillan, 2007 (expanded 2nd edition), pp. 344.

Wide range of theoretical perspectives organized in 3 parts: Generations and Genealogies; Locales and Locations; Politics and Popular Culture. Part II includes essays on 'Imagining Feminist Futures: The Third Wave, Postfeminism and Eco/feminism' by N. Moore, and 'Global Feminism, Transnational Political Economies, Third World Cultural Production' by W. Woodhull.

617. Heywood, Leslie and Jennifer Drake, *Third Wave Agenda: Being Feminist, Doing Feminism*, Minneapolis MN, Minnesota University Press, 1997, pp. 232.

Discusses submerged histories of black women and working class women and also stresses experience of multiple identity – multicultural, biracial, bisexual and transgender.

618. Snyder, R. Claire, 'What is Third Wave Feminism? A New Directions Essay', *Signs*, University of Chicago Press, pp. 23. http://jstor.org/stable/10/1086/588436

Clear critical analysis of third wave feminism, which also provides a list of relevant texts

4.b. The Fourth Wave since 2010 and Impact in UK

By 2010 there was evidence of a feminist revival in many parts of the west. In the USA Jennifer Siebel Newsom made the documentary film 'Miss Representation' challenging the representation of women in the mainstream media, where very few women hold positions of power, and US students joined Campus Rising, protesting against the high levels of violence experienced by women on university campuses and demanding greater safety. In Italy women began to demonstrate in large numbers against the sexism epitomized by Silvio Berlusconi's government and promoted by his mass media. Whilst in Spain, where women have been prominent in challenging the worst effects of the recession (see A.8.b on Indignados), they were faced in 2014 with an Abortion Bill, passed by the right wing Partido Populare close to the Catholic Church, which rescinded the right to an abortion that they had gained 30 years earlier. Women protested vigorously against the Bill, including queues to register symbolically their own bodies as their own property, and gained support from some regional and municipal authorities, but to no avail. The issue did however reignite awareness of feminism.

One manifestation of this feminist consciousness is the SlutWalk Movement, which began in North America but rapidly spread to much of Europe and Australia, but also to Latin America, Asia (e.g. India and South Korea) and to Northern Africa and South Africa. The movement was sparked by a Canadian police officer telling university students that to avoid rape they should not dress like 'sluts'. The first 'Slut Walk' in Toronto April 2011 attracted several thousand protesters, and was followed by Walks in many other cities in 2011 and continued into2012 and 2013. The movement developed into a wider challenge not only to sexual violence and harassment but patriarchal attitudes and culture, and it has been supported by members of the LGBT community. But it has been criticized, for example by Black Women's Blueprint in the US and by some feminists doubtful about the message conveyed.

Alongside this revival of feminism, groups representing minorities within western countries, who began to assert their special interests and perspectives in the 1980s, are campaigning on a range of national and global issues, For example, London's first young poet laureate, Warsan Shire, wrote a poem in February 2014 supporting the campaign against female genital mutilation.

This section focuses in particular on the UK, where a surprisingly vigorous array of campaigning groups has sprung up. This rebirth of feminist campaigning is beginning to promote a new literature which has a global dimension but refers primarily to the UK.

619. Aune, Kristin and Catherine Redfern, *Reclaiming the F Word: Feminism Today*, London Zed Press, 2013. A reprint with a new Preface of their 2010 book: *Reclaiming the F Word: The New Feminist Movement*, Zed Books, 2010, pp. 244.

Based on a survey of over 1000 feminists discusses revitalized movement, the areas in which change is necessary, and how to struggle for change. International perspective but especial focus on UK.

620. Barnard, Kat, *The Equality Illusion: The Truth about Women and Men Today*, London, Faber and Faber, 2011, pp. 320, pb.

In 2012 Barnard founded UK Feminista, which gives support and training to local activists, and together with Object began the campaign in 2013 Lose the Lads' Mags. Her book argues that feminism is still very necessary in the light of continuing inequality at work, prevalence of sexual harassment, rape and domestic violence, and treatment of women's bodies in magazines, lap dancing clubs and on the internet. UK Feminista offers workshops for schools: http://ukfeminista.org.uk

621. Carr, Joetta, L. 'The Slutwalk Movement: A Study in Transnational Activism', *Journal of Feminist Scholarship*, no. 4 (Spring 2013), pp. 24-37.

North American initiative, but taken up in Britain and transnationally.

622. Cochrane, Kira, *All the Rebel Women: The Rise of the Fourth Wave of Feminism*, London, Guardian Shorts Originals ebook, 2013, pp. 71: guardianshorts.com
See also her article 'The Fourth Wave of Feminism: Meet the Rebel Women', *Guardian*, 10 Dec. 2013: http://www.theguardian.com/world/2013/dec/10fourth-wave-feminism-rebel-women

Describes wide range of feminist activities and groups (both established like the Fawcett Society, and new) and wider attitudes to feminism in mainstream organizations such as Girl Guides and Mumsnet.

623. *Feminist Review*, issue 108, 2015. Special issue on 'Black British Feminism'.

Looks back at pioneering issue 30 years earlier on black feminism (no. 17, 1984) and examines role of black feminists today and the mobilizing impact of cyber feminism.

624. Gupta, Rahila, *From Homebreakers to Jailbreakers: Southall Black Sisters*, London, Zed Press, 2003, pp. 301.

Southall Black Sisters was founded by Asian women in 1982 to campaign about issues specific to women in racial minorities in Britain. Over the years it has become the focus for racial and ethnic minorities in Britain and gained an international profile. Issues tackled include: 'honour' killings, domestic violence, forced marriages and resistance to deportations. See also: *Against the Grain*, Southall Black Sisters, 1990,: a collection of essays covering the first ten years, and available from SBS. For current activities: http://www.southallblacksisters.org.uk

625. Okolosie, Lola, 'Feminism for All', *Red Pepper* (Apr./May 2012), p. 66.
Account of first Go Feminist conference designed to link up and inspire activists.

Feminist campaigns in Britain in 2014 included the following:

Daughters of Eve works against female genital mutilation and supports victims: http://www.dofeve.org

Eaves focuses on trafficking, helping women leave prostitution and on domestic violence, offering practical support as well as engaging in research and campaigning: http://www.eavesforwomen.org.uk

The End Violence Against Women Coalition, created in 2005, brings together both organizations and individuals to campaign against violence against women in all its forms, lobbies local, regional and national government bodies in the UK and challenges cultural attitudes: http://www. endviolenceagainst women.org.uk

The Everyday Sexism Project runs a website encouraging women to add their experiences of sexism ; it aims to show that sexism exists and that it is important to discuss and expose it. http://everydaysexism.com

A new feminist magazine, *Feminist Times*, was launched online in October 2013, with the aim of becoming available in print, but had to close down in July 2014, when it ran its last weekly issue.

5. War and Women's Resistance

Introduction

The relationship between women and war is of course complex; sometimes, as in liberation wars, they have actively supported armed resistance; but in many wars they become victims and survivors; sometimes they actively try to promote peace and cross 'enemy' lines. The emphasis in this section is on resistance to war. Opposing wars has in recent decades quite often been linked to broader feminist commitments and campaigns, although sometimes women are prompted to act simply by the urgency of ending brutal and devastating wars. In both cases wider theoretical issues arise about whether women are particularly disposed to resist war and about links between militarism and patriarchy. The theoretical debates are not central to this Guide, which focuses primarily on examples of resistance, but a few relevant theoretical references are included below.

626. Bethke Elshtain, Jean and Sheila Tobias, eds., *Women, Militarism and War: Essays in History, Politics and Social Theory*, Latham MD, Rowman and Littlefield, 1990; 2nd edn. (with new Epilogue) University of Chicago Press, 1995, pp. 318, pb.

627. Cockburn, Cynthia, *From Where We Stand: War, Women's Activism and Feminist Analysis*, London and New York, Zed Books, 2007, pp. 288.

Examines women's resistance to war in many parts of the world, including Sierra Leone, Colombia and Gujerat, India. It also covers women's cooperation across enemy lines in the former Yugoslavia and in Israel/ Palestine, and resistance in the west to imperialist war, and develops theoretical questions about gender and militarism. See also: Cynthia Cockburn, 'Women in Black: The Stony Path to "Solidarity"', in Clark, ed., *People Power*, pp. 156-63 (Introduction, 1.c.).

628. Cockburn, Cynthia, 'The Women's Movement: Boundary Crossing on Terrains of Conflict' in Cohen and Rai, eds. *Global Social Movements* (Introduction 1.c.), pp. 46-61.

Focuses on action-research project Women Building Bridges in Northern Ireland, Israel/Palestine and Bosnia Hercegovina, and comments on role of transnational women's networks, including Women in Black.

629. Cook, Alice and Gwyn Kirk, *Greenham Women Everywhere*, London, Pluto Press, 1983, pp. 127.

630. Eglin, Josephine, 'Women and Peace: from the Suffragists to the Greenham Women', in Taylor and Young, eds., *Campaigns for Peace* (392 D.1.), pp. 221-59.

631. Evans, Jodie and Medea Benjamin, *Stop the Next War Now: Effective Responses to Violence and Terror*, Novat CA, New World Library, 2005, pp, 256, pb.

The editors were among the women who launched the campaign Code Pink: Women for Peace in November 2002, which has since undertaken a wide range of nonviolent direct action protests in the United States and forged links with women in many other countries. (For details see: http:// www.codepink4peace.org). The book is a collection of essays by peace activists and scholars exploring a range of issues but including an emphasis on dissent and movement building.

632. Giles, Wenona, Malathi de Alwis, Edith Klein and Neluka Silva, eds., *Feminists Under Fire: Exchanges Across War Zones*, Toronto, Between the Lines, 2003, pp. 238.

Examines role of women's organizations in civil wars in former Yugoslavia and Sri Lanka.

633. Harford, Barbara and Sarah Hopkins, eds., *Greenham Common: Women at the Wire*, London, The Women's Press, 1984, pp. 171.

634. Jones, Lynne, ed., *Keeping the Peace*, London, The Women's Press, 1983, pp. 162.

Gives transnational examples of women's peace activism.

635. Korac, Maja, *Linking Arms: Women and War in Post-Yugoslav States*, Uppsala, Life and Peace Institute, 1998, pp. 91.

636. Krasniewicz, Louise, *Nuclear Summer: The Clash of Communities at the Seneca Women's Peace Encampment*, Ithaca NY, Cornell University Press, 1992, pp. 276.

637. Kwon, Insook, 'Gender, Feminism and Masculinity in Anti-Militarism', *International Feminist Journal of Politics*, vol. 15 no. 2 (June 2013), pp. 213-33.

Feminist analysis of the conscientious objection movement in South Korea in which women activists challenge dominant militarized conception of masculinity.

638. Liddington, Jill, *The Long Road to Greenham: Feminism and Militarism in Britain since 1820*, London, Virago, Syracuse NY, Syracuse Press, 1991, pp. 341.

639. Mama, Amina and Margo Okazawa-Reis, 'Militarism, Conflict and Women's Activism in the Global Environment: Challenges and Prospects for Women in three West African Countries', *Feminist Review*, no. 101 (July 2012), pp. 97-123.

Focus on examples from Nigerian, Sierra Leone and Liberian civil wars over several decades.

640. Natanel, Katherine, 'Resistance and the Limits: Feminist Actions and Conscientious Objection in Israel', *Feminist Review*, no. 101 (July 2012), pp. 78-96.

Assesses effectiveness of feminist resistance on movement to refuse the draft, looking primarily at experience of individual feminist COs, rather than organized women's groups.

641. Roseneil, Sasha, *Disarming Patriarchy: Feminism and Political Action at Greenham*, Buckingham, Open University Press, 1995, pp. 225.

This PhD thesis is a detailed account of the history and everyday life at Greenham, based on participation in the peace camp and interviews with other women. See also Roseneil, *Common Women, Uncommon Practices: The Queer Feminism of Greenham*, London, Cassell, 2000, which explores life-style and lesbian issues connected with the camp.

642. Ruddick, Sara, *Maternal Thinking: Towards a Politics of Peace*, London, Women's Press, 1989, pp. 297.

Influential, but also much criticized, argument linking women's inclination towards peace with their role as mothers.

643. Sjoberg, Laura, 'Viewing Peace through Gender Lenses", *Ethics and International Affairs*, vol. 27 no. 2 (Summer 2013), pp. 175-87.

See also: Epstein, *Political Protest and Cultural Revolution*, esp. pp. 160-68, which briefly describe the Women's Pentagon Action and Seneca Falls Peace Camp in USA (Introduction, 1.c.).; Elster and Sorensen, *Women Conscientious Objectors* (412 D.2.b.); and Coulson, "Looking Behind the Violent Break-up of Yugoslavia', and Mladjenovic and Litricin' Belgrade Feminists 1992' – for further material on women in ex-Yugoslavia opposing the war, and the Belgrade 'Women in Black' campaign (537 & 541 E.3.).

G. LGBT: Movements for Lesbian, Gay and Transgender Rights

The position of lesbians, gays and transgender people has varied considerably over time and in different cultures, and still varies strikingly between different countries despite the 2001 UN Declaration for global decriminalization of homosexuality. In 2014, whilst lesbian and gay couples in Britain and an increasing number of states of the USA were celebrating their new right to get married, in some countries gays and lesbians still face the death penalty, and ILGA (International Lesbian Gay Bisexual Trans and Intersex Association) noted in their 2014 world survey of laws that in 2013 there were worrying developments in India, Uganda, Nigeria and Russia. In all countries lesbians, gays and trans can be subjected to bullying and hate crimes, and police violence has often been an issue. The major gains in rights in the west since the 1950s have generally been the result of sustained campaigning for legal change and through the assertion of LGBT identity and community (for example through gay pride marches) and direct action. LGBT activism has become a transnational movement challenging repression and pressing for greater rights and has its own international organizations.

Gay Liberation arose in the context of the Civil Rights Movement in the USA, the student protests of 1968, resistance to the Vietnam War (see section E.1) and in parallel with the Second Wave of feminism (see section F.1). It reflected the new willingness to challenge long-held beliefs, aspiration for a fundamental change in society, and the adoption of a more confrontational style of campaigning and assertion of identity. The ferment of ideas and protests led to ideological and organizational splits , but this did not undermine the momentum towards cultural and social change in the west (although deep seated attitudes and discrimination are not easily altered, as the Fourth Wave of feminism also testifies). The Gay Liberation movement created bookshops, newspapers and journals, encouraged a new literature and prompted new academic courses.

LGBT activists have often had links with others social movements, most obviously in the overlap between lesbian activists and feminism. There have also been demonstrations of solidarity between movements – for example ACT UP and the Health GAP challenging policies on HIV/AIDS joined a Global Justice Movement protest in Washington DC in April 2000, and earlier the London-based Lesbians and Gays Support the Miners (LGSM) was active during the strike of 1984-45 (for references see A.1.a.ii.). There have also been connections with the peace movement, notably at the Greenham Common Women's peace camp in the 1980s (see Roseneil, *Common Women, Uncommon Practices* 641 F.5.)

There is, however, a long history of often more discreet attempts to assert lesbian and gay identity and to achieve legal reforms, partly covered in the next section. We list below a few books providing an introductory overview of historical change and campaigns:

644. Adam, Barry D., *The Rise of a Gay and Lesbian Movement*, Boston Twayne [1987] 1994 revised edn., pp. 240, pb.

Scholarly study of world wide campaigning for gay and lesbian rights, looking at earlier history as well as the militant protests and organizations of the 1960s-1970s.

645. Bullough, Vern L., ed., *Before Stonewall: Activists for Gay and Lesbian Rights in Historical Context*, New York, Routledge, Haworth Gay and Lesbian Studies, 2002, pp. 464, pb.

Survey of gay and lesbian rights issues in USA. Part 1 covers period before 1950, Parts 2 and 3 organizational activists and national figures , and Part 4 'Other Voices'.

646. David, Hugh, *On Queer Street: Social History of British Homosexuality, 1895-1995*, London, Harper Collins, 1997, pp. 305.

647. Hekma, Gert, Harry Oosterhuis and James Steakley, eds., *Gay Men and the Sexual History of the Political Left*, New York, Harrington Press, 1995, pp. 408.

Includes chapters on the often difficult relationship between socialist, anarchist or social democratic movements and homosexuality in countries such as pre-First World War Netherlands, Civil-War Spain, the German Weimar Republic and post-1945 East Germany.

648. Jivani, Alkarim *Its Not Unusual: History of Lesbian and Gay Britain in the 20th Century*, Bloomington IN, Indiana University Press, 1997, pp. 224, pb.

Looks briefly at early 20th century, focusing on celebrities. But based primarily on interviews with 36 lesbians and gay men and covers changing social and legal contexts of World War Two, 1950s, 1960s-70s and emergence of gay liberation, and setbacks of HIV/AIDS and Section 28 in the 1980s.

649. Robinson, Lucy, *Gay Men and the Left in Post-War Britain: How the Personal got Political*, Manchester, Manchester University Press, 2011, pp. 232, pb.

650. Stryker, Susan, *Transgender History*, Berkeley CA, Seal Press, 2008, pp. 208, pb.

Survey of US Transgender movement from mid 20th century to early 2000s in chronological order.

651. Willett, Graham, *Living Out Loud: A History of Gay and Lesbian Activism in Australia*, St Leonards NSW, Allen and Unwin, 2000, pp. 320, pb.

Account of gay and lesbian activism in Australia, from 1950s to 1990s, its successes and contribution to Australian society.

1. The 'Homophile' Movement and Rise of Gay Liberation Protest and Organization in the West: 1950s -1970s

Groups directly challenging legal repression and social discrimination against lesbians and male homosexuals arose in a number of countries in the years between 1919 and 1939, but the rise of fascism and Nazism and the outbreak of war brought an end to such campaigning. In countries like Spain and Portugal calling for gay rights was virtually impossible until their dictatorial regimes came to an end in the 1970s. In Spain legalizing of gay and lesbian sexual relations was seen as part of the necessary post-Franco liberalization, and occurred in 1979, when the first Gay Pride march was held in the country. The Nazis had destroyed the Institute for Sexual Research set up by a pioneer of homosexual (and women's) rights, the German Jew Magnus Hirschfeld, passed a more draconian law against male homosexuals in their amendment of paragraph 175 of the Criminal Code in 1936, and sentenced as estimated 50,000 to imprisonment. Lesbians were less specifically targeted, although some were arrested for 'prostitution' or 'asocial' behaviour. Of the men arrested it is estimated that between 5,000 and 15,000 were sent to concentration camps where they forced to wear a pink triangle, and up to 60 per cent may have died. (A reference for this period provided by the American Library Association is: http://www.ala.org/glbtrt/popularresources/holocaust) However, after the War homosexual victims of the camps were not acknowledged and a memoir by one survivor, Heinz Heger, *The Men with the Pink Triangle,* was not published until 1980. (It has since been re-issued in English and translated into several languages.) In West Germany the Nazi version of paragraph 175, which made it criminal to look at another man 'in a lewd manner', was not repealed until 1969. Although East Germany under Communist Party rule was less open to public protest, the regime amended the Nazi version of paragraph 175 in 1950, but the paragraph was not formally repealed until 1968 (though it was not enforced after 1957).

Even after the Second World War, homosexuals were not only stigmatized by widespread social and institutional discrimination, but also in many cases faced legislation prohibiting sexual activity and possible imprisonment or chemical castration. As a result they were subject to police harassment and entrapment, vulnerable to blackmail and vilification in the media and liable to arrest. Some were driven to suicide – as was the celebrated British mathematician, Enigma Code breaker during World War Two and pioneer of computer science, Alan Turing . (He received a retrospective 'pardon' for 'gross indecency' from the Queen in December 2013, but others persecuted in Britain received no official recognition.) During the 1950s campaign organizations focused on seeking legal and social reform, many of these groups (some revivals from the inter-war years) were linked to the transnational 'homophile' network. One of the best known organizations was Arcadie in France, founded in 1954, with its own club and publication; it attracted prominent intellectuals like Jean Cocteau and Michel Foucault. In Britain pressure for law reform began in the 1950s, and liberal minded parliamentarians succeeded in passing a Private Members Bill in 1967, which meant that sex in private between men over 21 was no longer illegal in England and Wales – though this only became law in Scotland in 1980 and in Northern Ireland in 1982 (lesbianism had not been previously banned).

Legislation decriminalizing sex between consenting male homosexuals was also passed in Canada in 1967 and came into effect in 1969. In the United States the McCarthyist purges and paranoia of the earlier 1950s tended to repress all nonconformists. Many gay men and lesbians lost government jobs, and although groups were formed to change the law in the later 1960s, at the end of the decade homosexual sex was still illegal in all states except Illinois.

A trigger for change was the June 1969 confrontation at the Stonewall Inn in New York between police and gays (including drag queens who were at the forefront of resisting police). The rapid rise of the Gay Liberation movement afterwards resulted in a much more openly challenging and radical style of protest and organizing, including the spread of Gay Pride marches from 1970, and various forms of direct action, such as occupations of police stations and interrupting church services in Britain. The movement was also diverse, stressing the rights of women as well as men and embracing transgender people and drag queens, although divisions and controversies also arose. Gay Liberation spread rapidly to the UK and Australia and rather more slowly to New Zealand. It also had a strong impact on campaigning for gay and lesbian rights in much of Western Europe. But one difference between the United States movement and Gay Liberation in many other western countries was that the latter were often concerned about their relationships with the socialist left, as some titles below indicate.

Alongside decriminalization of homosexuality there was pressure for demedicalization. Labeling homosexuality as a mental illness meant that lesbians, gays and transgender people could be given psychiatric treatment to change their sexual orientation. At the 1971 American Psychiatric Association convention, gay activist Dr Franklin E. Kameny seized the microphone as part of a long-standing opposition to the diagnosis of homosexuality, and initiated wider gay rights protest. One outcome was a session at the 1972 conference on homosexuality and mental illness entitled 'Psychiatry: Friend or Foe to Homosexuals: A Dialogue'. Kameny was on the panel. Here John E. Fryer made his famous 'I am a homosexual, I am a psychiatrist' speech, disguised by a mask and wig and calling himself Dr H. His speech (the first time a psychiatrist publicly admitted to being homosexual) has been cited as a key factor in achieving the removal of homosexuality from the Diagnostic and Statistical Manual of Mental Disorders a year later. Some orthodox psychiatrists fought a rearguard action against what they saw as capitulation to gay activism, and demanded a referendum of all the members, who ratified the decision in 1974. The American Psychological Association followed suit in 1975. However, it took until 1990 for the World Health Organization to remove homosexuality from its tenth international classification of diseases and health problems (ICD 10).

652. Altman, Dennis, *Homosexual: Oppression and Liberation*, New York, New York University Press, [1971 and 1974] 1993, pp. 304, with new Introduction by Jeffrey Weeks and Afterword by author commenting on his book in light of developments since 1970s.

Key work on early period of Gay Liberation in 1960s/70s in the USA, examining different strands of movement and arguing need for struggle for common goals.

653. Bayer, Ronald, *Homosexuality and American Psychiatry: The Politics of Diagnosis*, Princeton NJ, Princeton University press, 1987, pp. 244, pb.

Account of 1973 decision by American Psychiatric Association to stop listing homosexuality as a mental disorder and attempts by some psychiatrists to overturn this decision.

654. Carter, David, *Stonewall: The Riots that Sparked the Gay Revolution*, New York, St Martins Press, [2004] 2010, pp. 352, pb.

Detailed account of protests that erupted on 28 June 1969 when New York police raided the Stonewall Inn in Greenwich Village (popular among gays), when many others joined in, and demonstrations spread across the city for several days. The 'riots' led to the founding of the Gay Liberation Front and the first Gay Pride marches in New York, Chicago, Los Angeles and San Francisco a year later.

655. D'Emilio, John, *Sexual Politics, Sexual Communities: The Making of a Homosexual Minority in the United States 1940-1970*, Chicago IL, Chicago University Press, [1983] 2nd edn. 1998, with new preface and afterword, pp. 282, pb.

Highly regarded book on the American Homophile movement by historian and gay activist, including biographical sketches of prominent lesbian and gay figures.

656. Gallo, Marcia M., *Different Daughters: A History of the Daughters of Bilitis and the Birth of the Lesbian Rights Movement*, Seattle WA, Seal Press (Avalon Publishing), [2006] 2007, pp. 274, pb.

'DOB' was founded in 1955 as a social group in San Francisco, but developed over two decades into a national organization. See also 'Del' Martin and Phyllis Lyon below.

657. Jackson, Julian, *Living in Arcadia: Homosexuality, Politics and Morality in France from the Liberation to AIDS*, Chicago IL, University of Chicago Press, 2009, pp. 336.

Account of the French 'homophile' organization Arcadie.

658. McLeod, Donald, *Lesbian and Gay Liberation in Canada: A Selected Annotated Chronology 1964-1975*, Toronto, ECW Press/Homewood Books, 1996, pp. 302.

Covers 12 years of the 'homophile' movement, represented by ASK (Association for Social Knowledge) in Vancouver, and early Gay Liberation activity to founding of the National Gay Rights Coalition in 1975. Emphasis on demonstrations, lobbying and other political activities and legal reform, but also covers expressions of lesbian and gay concerns in culture and arts.

659. Marotta, Toby, *The Politics of Homosexuality*, Boston MA, Houghton Mifflin Harcourt, 1981, pp. 361.

Examines struggle for gay rights in USA from 1950s to early 1970s, charting the different political and cultural issues and types of campaigning and the contradictions between political reformism and radical hippy culture. Part III covers the Lesbian Feminist Movement.

660. Martin, 'Del' (Dorothy L. Taliaferro) and Phyllis Lyon, *Lesbian/ Woman*, Volcano CA, Volcano Press, [1972 and 1980, Bantam Press] 1993, pp. 384.

By two women journalists at forefront of US gay and lesbian rights struggle from the 1950s, founders of Daughters of Bilitis and active in the feminist campaign NOW (National Organization for Women) where they argued that lesbian issues were feminist issues. A couple since the 1950s, they married in San Francisco in February 2004.

661. Milligan, Don, *The Politics of Homosexuality*, London, Pluto Press, 1975, pp. 19.

Studies in Anti-Capitalism series. Available as pdf at: http:// www. donmilligan.net

Brief survey, which raises issue of how homosexuality should be addressed in the socialist movement.

662. Nancy, Gregory, 'The Gay and Lesbian Movement in the United States' in Moyer, *Doing Democracy: The MAP Model for Organizing Social Movements*, (833 J.1.), pp.152-64.

Analyses the US LGBT movement from 1945-2000 using the model of the Movement Action Plan developed by Moyer.

663. Ross, Liz, *Revolution is for Us: The Left and Gay Liberation in Australia*, Melbourne, Interventions, 2013, pb.

The author, an active socialist, argues contrary to widely held views that the left and working class supported earlier gay rights campaigns and that the left is central to Gay Liberation.

664. Rupp, Leila, 'The Persistence of Transnational Organizing: The Case of the Homophile Movement', *American Historical Review*, vol. 116 no. 4 (Oct. 2011), pp. 1014-1039.

Study of the reformist groups which were active in Scandinavia, West Germany, France, the UK, Canada and USA, primarily in the 1950s and 1960s, which joined in the International Committee for Sexual Equality (1951-1963) founded by the Dutch COC (the first 'homophile' group).

665. Scasta, D .I. 'John E. Fryer, MD and the Dr. H. Anonymous Episode', *Journal of Gay and Lesbian Psychotherapy*, vol. 6 no. 4 (2002), pp. 73-84.

Recounts Fryer's anonymous appearance on stage, at the 1972 American Psychiatric Association session on psychiatry and mental illness, to announce his homosexuality. (He spoke anonymously – as he explained later – through fear of being refused tenure at his university.)

666. Schilts, Randy, *The Mayor of Castro Street: The Life and Times of Harvey Milk*, New York, St Martins Press, 1998; Atlantic Books, 2009, pp. 480.

The career of Milk, the first openly gay man to be elected to political office in the USA – as a councilor in San Francisco – reflects the rise of the gay community in the 1970s. He was assassinated in November 1978. His life is also the subject of a 1984 documentary film, 'The Times of Harvey Milk', 1984, directed by Rob Epstein, and a feature film 'Milk' 2008, directed by Gus Van Sant.

667. Sibalis, Michael, 'The Spirit of May '68 and the Origins of the Gay Liberation Movement in France' in Lessie Jo Frazier and Deborah Cohen, eds., *Gender and Sexuality in 1968: Transformative Politics in the Cultural Imagination*, Basingstoke, Palgrave Macmillan, 2009, pp. 235-53. See also: Sibalis, *Gay Liberation Comes to France: The Front Homosexuel d'Action Revolutionnaire*, Paper for George Rude Seminar, 2005, pp. 12. Online: http://www.h-france.net/rude/2005conference/Sibalis2.pdf

668. Taylor, Verta and Nancy E. Whitaker, 'Collective Identity in Social Movement Communities: Lesbian Feminist Mobilization', in Aldon D. Morris and Carol McClure Mueller, eds., *Frontiers in Social Movement Theory*, New Haven C T, Yale University Press, 1992, pp. 104-29.

Examines development of lesbian feminism in the US from the early 1970s and explores its collective identity and engagement in range of actions challenging status quo.

669. Walter, Aubrey, ed. *Come Together: The Years of Gay Liberation 1970-73*, London, Heretic Books, 1981, pp. 218, pb.

Based on articles from the newspaper *Come Together*. Walter was one of the founders of the British Gay Liberation Front.

670. Whisnant, Clayton J. *Male Homosexuality in West Germany: Between Persecution and Freedom 1945-69*, New York, Macmillan Palgrave, 2012, pp. 280.

Looks at prejudice and role of police, the homophile movement, the gay scene and the rejection of Paragraph 175 of the Constitutional Code.

G.2. Gay Liberation: Protest and Organization in the West: 1980s-2010s

The impact of HIV/AIDS in the 1980s created common problems for gays, but we focus here primarily (though not exclusively) on the response in the USA (see G.2.a.). Since the 1980s gays, lesbians and trans have also sought equal civil rights and the right to express their identity. Some common themes have emerged and common forms of protest and celebration of identity – notably in Pride marches. An important common experience has been violent attacks on members of LGBT community which have often not been taken seriously enough by the police, and also examples of brutality by police forces themselves. For US studies see:

671. Amnesty International, USA, *Stonewalled: Police Abuse and Misconduct against LGBT People in the US*. 2005, pp. 149, pb. Available at: http://.www.amnesty.org/en/library/info/AMR51/122/2005 and as a pdf.

672. Bernstein, Mary, 'Lavender and Blue: Attitudes About Homosexuality and Behavior Toward Lesbians and Gay Men Among Police Officers', *Journal of Contemporary Criminal Justice*, vol. 18 no. 3 (Aug. 2002), pp. 302-28.

673. Berrill, Kevin T., 'Anti-Gay Violence and Victimization in the United States: An Overview', *Journal of Interpersonal Violence*, vol. 5 no. 3 (1990), pp. 274-94. Online: http://jiv.sagepub.com

There have been significant campaigns to protect and promote LGBT rights in the USA, including a series of National Marches on Washington in 1979, 1987, 1993 and 2000, but also in many other western countries, which are not so well covered in English publications. The political, legal , religious and cultural contexts vary, however, between countries, so LGBT communities can face somewhat different problems. (For the UK see G.2.b.)

674. Brandao, Ana Maria, 'Not Quite Women: Lesbian Activism in Portugal', in Woodward, Bonvin and Renom, *Transforming Gendered Well-Being in Europe* (609 F. 3.a.).

675. D'Emilio, John, *The World Turned: Essays on Gay History and Politics and Culture*. Durham NC, Duke University Press, 2002, pp.264 pb.

A collection of diverse essays, not a comprehensive survey of LGBT history in the US, but explores the movement's growth and activities from the 1970s to 1990s, the impact of AIDS in increasing resources and organization in the LGBT community, and the role of several organizations, including the influential National Gay and Lesbian Task Force (NGLTF) founded in 1973 to promote grass roots power and its role in resisting hostile referenda and promoting positive legislation. NB. NGLTF records from 1973-2008 are based in the Cornell University library: http://www.thetaskforce.org

676. Flam, Helena, ed., *Pink, Purple, Green: Women's Religious, Environmental, and Gay/Lesbian Movements in Central Europe Today*, New York, Columbia University Press, 2001, pp. 175.

Covers variety of movements, but three chapters on problems of gay/lesbian groups in Hungary, Poland and the eastern part of Germany.

677. Jay, Karla and Allen Young, eds., *Out of the Closet: Voices of Gay Liberation*, New York, New York University Press, 1997, pp. 367, pb.

Views and experiences of US activists and their assessment of how much or little had changed since Stonewall.

678. Martel, Frederic, *The Pink and the Black: Homosexuals in France Since 1968*, Palo Alto CA, Stanford University Press, 1999, pp. 464, pb. (transl. Jean Marie Todd).

Examines activist lesbian and gay organizations in relation to post-1968 feminism, gay 'ghettoes' and the gay press, and explores the impact of AIDS and revival of militancy in the 1990s. Notes influence of American movement, but also stresses differences.

679. Stone, Amy, "Dominant Tactics in Social Movement Tactical Repertoires: Anti-Gay Ballot Measures, 1974-2008', in Patrick G. Coy, ed., *Research in Social Movements, Conflicts and Change*, vol. 31 of series, Bingley, Emerald, 2010, pp.141-74.

Examines how LGBT movement responded to over 200 attempts by religious right in US to promote discrimination through anti-gay referenda.

See also, Willett, *Living Out Loud*, Part 3 on Australia from 1980s (651 G. Introduction).

a. The Impact of HIV/AIDS

The emergence of AIDS in the 1980s precipitated a shift in global gay activism and the perception of the LGBT community – although outside the west it was not experienced or seen as almost exclusively a problem for gays, it was a focus for gay activism (for example in South Africa). Within this shift there was a re-emergence of direct action groups and a move towards support volunteerism. The impact of the AIDS crisis and the rise of fear affected all and mobilized those who had not previously identified with gay activism. The most notable of the support volunteerism groups was Gay Men's Health Crisis (GMHC) formed in 1981 in the USA in response to the impact on the gay community, which provided a model for support groups elsewhere. GMHC created an AIDS hotline in 1982, as did the People with AIDS foundation (PWA) in 1983. Moreover in the process of providing this support network and opening up a dialogue, the gay community initiated a process of education and self-identity , which had a lasting impact on the gay community and culture.

However, a significant proportion of the US gay community believed that support volunteerism promoted by GMHC and PWA could not enact genuine change. Consequently in 1987 the AIDS Coalition to Unleash Power (ACT UP) was formed in New York, and led to other ACT UP groups in the US and other countries (for example in the UK, Australia and France). Comprising a variety of different protest and pressure groups ACT UP sought to affect public opinion and government policy directly through both political protests and civil disobedience. Perhaps their most famous campaign was Silence=Death, which responded to the media blackout of HIV/AIDS in the gay community. This campaign combined political protest and civil disobedience to place AIDS more centrally in the minds of Americans. Civil disobedience was, for example, directed against the pharmaceutical companies, attempting to get them to invest in alternatives to the drug AZT .

These two distinct approaches – support volunteerism promoting awareness and self help within the community, and direct pressure on the political system through protest and direct action – are still reflected in gay culture today.

680. ACT UP, *Accomplishments and Chronology in Brief: 1987-2012.* Available at: http://actupny.com

Lists range of nonviolent direct action protests by ACT UP since 1987, involving marches, sit-ins, blockades, political funerals, die-ins, disrupting political occasions and speeches, etc. Main targets have been pharmaceutical companies (for profiteering and failure to produce new drugs or provide adequate access to them in Africa), the medical establishment in the US, health insurance companies, the Catholic Church and President Bush Snr and President Clinton and Vice-President Gore.

681. Altman, Dennis, *AIDS in the Mind of America*, New York, Anchor Press, 1986, pp. 240, pb.

682. Altman, Dennis, *Power and Community Organizational and Cultural Responses to AIDS*, London and Bristol PA, Taylor and Francis, 1994, pp. 179.
Assessment of role of community-based organizations world-wide in responding to AIDS.

683. Edwards, Jeff, 'AIDS, Race and the Rise and Decline of a Militant Oppositional Lesbian and Gay Politics in the US', *New Political Science*, vol. 22 no 4 (2000), pp. 485-506.

684. Gamson, Josh, 'Silence, Death and the Invisible Enemy: AIDS Activism and Social Movement "Newness"', *Social Problems*, vol. 36 no. 4 (1989), pp. 358-67.

685. Gilbert, Elbaz, 'Beyond Anger: The Activist Construction of the AIDS Crisis', *Social Justice*, vol. 22 no. 4 (1995), pp.43-76.
Discusses ACT-UP in relation to two contrasting approaches in social movement theory: 'resource mobilization' and the 'identity' paradigm.

686. Gould, Deborah B. *Moving Politics: Emotion and ACT UP's Fight Against AIDS*, Chicago IL, University of Chicago Press, 2009, pp. 524.
Analysis of emergence, development and decline of ACT UP, highlighting emotional dimension in movement politics.

687. Holt, Martin, 'Gay Men and Ambivalence about 'Gay Community': from Gay Community Attachment to Personal Communities', *Culture, Health and Sexuality*, vol. 13 no. 8 (2011), pp. 657-71.

688. Power, Jennifer, *Movement, Knowledge, Emotion: Gay Activism and HIV/AIDS in Australia*, Canberra, Australian National University E-Press, 2011, pp. 204. Available at: http://epress.anu.edu.au/ Also available in print on a print-on-demand basis.
In three Parts: 1. 'Fear and Morality', 2. '(Mis)trust of Medicine, 3. 'Grief and Activism'.

Provides historical background and uses interviews with members of early AIDS Councils and covers role of ACT UP.

689. Ramirez-Valles, Jesus, *Companeros, Latino Activists in the Face of AIDS*, Chicago, University of Illinois Press, pp. 192.

A professor of community health tells the stories of 80 gay, bisexual and transgender activists and volunteers in Chicago and San Francisco.

690. Rand, Erin J., 'Gay Pride and its Queer Discontents: ACT UP and the Political Deployment of Affect', *Quarterly Journal of Speech*, vol. 98 no. 1 (2012), pp. 75-80.

691. Roth, Benita, 'Feminist Boundaries in the Feminist-Friendly Organization. The Women''s Caucus of ACT UP/LA', *Gender and Society*, vol. 12 no. 2 (April 1998), pp. 129-45.

692. Stoller, Nancy, *Lessons from the Damned: Queers, Whores and Junkies Respond to AIDS*, New York and London, Routledge, 1998, pp. 175.

See also: Martel, *The Pink and the Black*, Part III on 1980s and Part IV 1989-96 (678 G.2. Introduction); Willett, *Living Out Loud*, Part 3 (1980s and 1990s) on Australia (651 G. Introduction).

2.b. Campaigning for Equal Rights: UK

AIDS not only had a disastrous impact on the health and lives of gay men, but influenced public attitudes. In Britain a move towards greater acceptance of the gay community from the 1970s to the early 1980s was undermined by fear and prejudice about what was often projected as a gay plague. This was also a period of harassment by the authorities, symbolized by the 1984 raid by Customs and Excise on the Gay's The Word bookshop in London.

In the context of a more hostile public opinion the Conservative government enacted in 1988 Section 28, banning the 'promotion' of homosexuality by local authorities through publications or education (on the assumption that sex education was 'promoting' homosexual lifestyles). This was seen by the LGBT community as discriminatory and an encouragement to prejudice and bullying. In response the LGB lobby group Stonewall was formed in 1989 to overturn Section 28, finally achieved, after numerous attempts, under a Labour government in 2003. Stonewall has gone on to lobby for change on other issues, including repealing the ban on gays serving in the military, protection from discrimination in the provision of goods and services and in the workplace, protection from hate speech and hate crime, and same-sex adoption.

A more radical and controversial campaigning body was OutRage! formed in 1990 at a meeting to commemorate the murder of a gay actor a year earlier. Peter Tatchell, who was vilified for being gay whilst contesting Bermondsey in London for Labour in a 1983 bye-election, and has been a prominent gay activist nationally and internationally, was a founding member and wrote the first draft of its statement of aims. Early actions in 1990 were protests at Hyde Park against Metropolitan Police entrapment of gay men in public toilets, and a 'kiss-in' in Piccadilly Circus to challenge police arrests of gay men kissing in public. OutRage! went on to diversify its campaigning and were active in pressing for the age of consent for gay sex (then 21) to be the same as for heterosexual sex – i.e. 16. When the House of Commons debated the issue in 1994, OutRage held a prominent demonstration outside parliament, and when news cam through that equality had been rejected there was – despite the organizers call for a peaceful presence – a near riot. After the vote OutRage! invaded the Labour Party National Executive Committee meeting to protest about the 35 Labour MPs who had voted against equality. The age of consent was not equalized until the Sexual Offences (Amendment) Act 2000.

Police attitudes to and treatment of members of the LGBT community was a major issue in the 1980s and 1990s. The Gay London Policing Group (GALOP) created in 1984 provided moral and legal support to individuals in their dealings with the police, and also liaised with the police to promote more tolerant attitudes among new recruits. In 1991 GALOP was part of a coalition of groups – the London Lesbian and Gay Policing Initiative – who met with Scotland Yard to discuss policing in London. By 2007 police officers in uniform were joining Pride marches.

Stonewall, alongside the 'Equal Love' campaign (formed by Peter Tatchell) campaigned in 2010 for the right to same sex marriage, and were strongly opposed by organizations upholding traditional marriage and by newly formed groups contesting same-sex marriage, such as Scotland for Marriage and the Coalition for Marriage. In response LGBT groups Out4Marriage and the Coalition for Equal Marriage were created. The Marriage (Same Sex Couples) Act was passed in 2013, and same sex couples in England were able to marry from March 2014.

Despite high levels of success by LGBT activists in the UK in the last few decades, transgender rights have lagged behind. The legal right to change gender was introduced in 2005, but the Same Sex Couples Act included a 'spousal veto', requiring that the partner's consent is required for the marriage to continue if a Gender Recognition Certificate is issued to a transgender person. The Coalition for Equal Marriage continued to lobby the government to amend this clause.

For websites covering the history of LGBT campaigning in the UK and the role of various groups, see: http://lgbthistory.uk.org and http://www.gayinthe80s.com

The Stonewall website also provides historical information, as well as news of current issues and campaigns: http://www.stonewall.org.uk

693. Jeffrey-Poulter, Stephen, *Peers, Queers and Commons: The Struggle for Gay Law Reform from 1950 to the Present*, London, Routledge, 1991, pp.320, pb.
Detailed account of post-war gay movement using contemporary newspaper reports, articles and letters.

694. Komhiya, A., 'Britain: Section 28' in James Thomas Sears, ed. *Youth Education and Sexualities: An International Encyclopedia*, vol. 1 (A-J), Westport CT, Greenwood Press, 2005.

695. Lucas, Ian, *OutRage! An Oral History*, London, Continuum, 1998, pp. 256, pb.

696. Terence Higgins Trust, *Rewriting History: Key Moments and Issues of the Last 50 Years of British LGBT History* http://www.tht.org.uk//media/Files/Publications/Resources/rewriting-history-resources,ashx

Divided into sections on 1. Campaigns against homo/transphobia; 2.Law and change; 3. Health and wellbeing; and 4. Community and diversity (covering Pride, representation in the media and LGBT communities and spaces). Includes coverage of policing, Section 28, civil partnerships and HIV/AIDS and mental health issues.

See also: Jivani, *Its Not Unusual* on the 1980s (648 G. Introduction).

3. LGBT Globally and Transnational Campaigning

Pride marches and festivals were held in many parts of the world on 29 June 2014 to celebrate the 45th anniversary of the Stonewall riots. But whilst there has been progress towards recognition of LGBT rights and acceptance of gays, lesbians and trans, in some parts of the world – for example Latin America, other regions such as the Caribbean, Africa and the Middle East remain generally hostile. (Exceptions are Cuba and South Africa – though in the latter liberal laws conflict with many examples of deep social prejudice and violence.) In some countries the position has got worse. In

2013 the Indian Supreme Court overturned the liberal ruling of the Delhi High Court on section 377 (originally introduced under the British) – effectively re-criminalizing gay sex, and Putin's Russia passed a law banning homosexual propaganda to minors, providing a basis for clamping down on LGBT organization and activism. The Russian police had for years been breaking up pride demonstrations and assaulting protesters, and the BBC reported on 17 August 2012 that Moscow's leading court had upheld a ban on gay pride marches in the Russian capital for 100 years.

Widespread international concern was expressed over Uganda's plans for draconian legislation against lesbians and gays – first proposed in 2009 and widely seen as a response to strong pressure from American Evangelicals. Although the final law, signed by President Museveni in February 2014, did not incorporate the death sentence (as had been indicated earlier) it did propose life sentences for same sex activity, enabled the government to extradite Ugandan gays and lesbians living abroad and made it a criminal offence not to report on those suspected of being lesbian or gay. Archbishop Tutu eloquently attacked the proposed legislation, comparing it with the former apartheid rules on sexual relationships in South Africa (*Guardian*, 24 February 2014). Rights groups and some MPs took legal action to get the law declared invalid, and judges struck down the law in August 2014, on the grounds that Parliament was not quorate when it passed the bill. However, homosexuality remains illegal under colonial-era law. By the end of 2014 the government was proposing new draconian legislation.

Detailed information on the state of LGBT rights globally is available from ILGA (at: http://www.ilga.org) and from ILGA Regional bodies such as ILGA-Europe. The International Gay and Lesbian Human Rights Commission (IGLHRC), also publishes reports on individual countries and annual reports on its activities, available at: http:// iglhrc.org The UK lobbying group Stonewall includes reports on international developments on its website: http://www.stonewall.org.uk

Transnational organizations also engage in various forms of campaigning. IGLHRC engages in advocacy and reporting and gained consultative status at the UN in 2010; ILGA attend conferences of international organizations such as the UN and its agencies, provide speakers and policy papers and issue press releases. In 2013-14 ILGA-Europe also campaigned in the context of EU parliamentary elections, submitted third party interventions to the European Court of Human Rights, ran the 'No hate Campaign' jointly with the European Network against Racism, and supported the first Cyprus Pride march and the Belgrade Pride march.

697. Altman, Dennis, 'Global Gaze/Global Gays', *GLQ: A Journal of Gay and Lesbian Studies* (Toronto, Duke University Press) vol. 3 no. 4 (1997), pp. 417-36.

698. Altman, Dennis, 'Globalization, Political Economy and HIV/AIDS', *Theory and Society*, vol. 28 (1999), pp.559-84.

Notes threat to developing countries but also potential of new forms of global cooperation through UN AIDS programmes, and discusses how best to analyze the spread and impact of AIDS. See also: Altman, 'Aids and the Globalization of Sexuality', *World Politics Review* (Aug. 10 2010) at: http://www.worldpoliticsreview.com/artices/print/6233

699. Ekine, Sokari and Hakima Abbas, *The Queer African Reader*, Cape Town, Pambazuka Press, 2013, pp. 220.

Wide ranging reader including poetry and analysis, personal testimonies, and activist accounts and discussions of strategy. Testament to resistance of LGBT communities across the continent.

700. Epprecht, Marc, *Sexuality and Social Justice in Africa: Rethinking Homophobia and Forging Resistance*, London, Zed Books, 2013, pp. 220, pb.

Covers activism for rights and over HIV. Notes external influences exacerbating position of lesbians, gays and trans, as well as role of some African leaders and cultural influences.

701. Hochberg, Gil Z., 'Introduction: Israelis, Palestinians and Queers: Points of Departure', *GLQ*, vol. 16 no 4 (2010), pp. 493-516.

702. ILGA: International Lesbian Gay Bisexual Trans and Intersex Association, *State-Sponsored Homophobia: A World Survey of Laws: Criminalization, Protection and Recognition of Same Sex Love*, by Lucas, Paoli Itaborahi and Jingshu Zhui, May 2014, pp. 95. Available at: http://www.ilga.org

Provides global overview of LGB legislation and country-by-country summary of states that still criminalize same-sex acts between consenting adults in private.

703. Manalaslan IV, Martin F., 'In the Shadows of Stonewall: Examining Gay Transnational Politics and the Diasporic Dilemmas', *GLQ*, vol. 2 no. 4 (1995), pp. 425-38.

704. Samba, Chesterfield, 'Solidarity Based on Sexual Orientation: Regional Organising in Africa' in Clark, ed., *Unarmed Resistance and Global Solidarity* (Introduction, 1.c.), pp.171-76.

Discusses attempts to develop African regional organization and activism and difficulties encountered up to 2006.

705. Whitaker, Brian, *Unspeakable Love: Gay and Lesbian Life in the Middle East*, Palo Alto CA, University of California Press, 2006, pp. 264, pb.

Argues Middle East moving away from sexual diversity, which is demonized by clerics and persecuted by governments – but notes 'pockets' of change and tolerance.

4. Minorities within LGBT

4.a. Transgender Issues and Activism Globally

Trans people often experience extreme dangers and difficulties, and their particular problems tend to be peripheral to campaigns for gays and lesbians, although transnational organizations like IGLHRC and ILGA do take up trans cases and support initiatives like the Transgender Day of Remembrance on 1st December for those murdered (the 16th annual remembrance was held in 2014).

But there are now groups and projects which focus on trans people. Transgender Europe monitors and lobbies organizations like the EU and the Council of Europe and national governments and launched the Trans Murder Monitoring project, see: http:www.tgeu.org

The Trans Awareness Project (a poster and digital media campaign challenging stereotypes and promoting respect for people of all genders) is sponsored by the University of Minnesota, see: http://www.transawareness. org A new dedicated journal on trans issues is *Transgender Studies Quarterly*: http://tsq.dukejournals.org

706. Arkles, Gabriel, Pooja Gehi and Elana Redfield, 'The Role of Lawyers in Trans Liberation: Building a Transformative Movement for Social Change'. *Seattle Journal for Social Justice*, vol. 8 no. 2 (summer 2010). http://digitalcommons.law.seattleu.edu/sjsj/vol8/iss2/7

707. Broad , K.L., 'GLB +T?: Gender/Sexuality Movements and Transgender Collective Identity (De)Constructions', *International Journal of Sexuality and Gender Studies*, vol. 7 no. 4 (Oct. 2002), pp. 341-64.

708. Brossi, Lionel, Naria Ines Landa and Amalia Ortiz de Zarate, 'The Intersex Movement: Empowering Through New Technologies', *International Journal of Humanities and Social Science*, vol. 2 no 22 (Special Issue – Nov. 2012), pp. 64-75. http://www.ijhanet.com/journal/index/1422

709. Feinberg, Leslie, *Trans Liberation: Beyond Pink or Blue*, Boston, Beacon Press, 1998, pp. 147 (pb. 1999).
Collection of speeches by Feinberg (poet and grassroots activist in US) covering range of issues including health care reform and infant genital mutilation.

710. Hines, Sally, *TransForming Gender: Transgender Practices of Identity, Intimacy and Care*, University of Chicago Press, Policy Press (distributed by University of Bristol), 2007, pp. 232.
Drawing on interviews with transgender people charts impact of changing legislation in UK. Primarily about individual experience and social context, but there is a chapter on: 'Transgender Care Networks, Social Movements and Citizenship'.

711. *Liminalis*, no. 3 (2009), Issue on 'Intersex and Transgender in Movement'. http://www.liminalis.de/articles.html
Includes article on 'Intersex and Transgender Activism in South Africa' and interviews with activists from Africa, Latin America and Europe discussing situation of trans people, forms of organization and role transnational organizations in these regions.

712. Moreno, Alumine, 'The Politics of Visibility and the GLTTBI Movement in Argentina', *Feminist Review*, issue 89 (June 2008), pp. 138-43.

713. Motmans, Joz, 'We Can't Have Men Giving Birth! (But We Do). The Impact of the Belgian Transgender Movement on the Well-Being of Transgender Persons in Belgium', in Woodward, Bonvin and Renom (609 F.3.a.).

714. Silva de Assis, C., *Transgendering the Media: Trans Media Watch and the Struggle over Representations o f Transgender in the British Media*, Utrecht, Utrecht University, Faculty of Humanities Theses, 2014. Online at: http// dspace.library.uu.nl/hand le/1874/298700

715. Stone, Amy, 'Transgender Movement' in Snow et al. eds., *Wiley Blackwell Encyclopedia of Social and Political Movements* (8 Introduction 1.a.). Online: http://onlinelibrary.wiley.com/book/10.1002/9780470674871

Examines evolution of US transgender movement from 1960s as it challenged violence, demanded legal recognition and resisted employment discrimination, poverty and media misrepresentation.

4.b. Queer Movements

From the late 1980s, in response to the growing acceptance of lesbian and gay identity in mainstream society, the 'mainstreaming' of LGBT organizations and at the same time a (perceived) increase in homophobic violence, new queer movements arose, initially in the USA. Queer Nation emerged as an activist group out of ACT-UP, and anonymously distributed a pamphlet at the 1990 New York Pride entitled 'Queers Read This' (online at: http://zinelibrary.info/queers-read). The movement spread later to Europe and to some other parts of the world, notably Latin America and some countries in Asia, as well as to South Africa.

The term 'queer', originally a derogatory term, was reclaimed by queer activists with a new meaning, based on the rejection of fixed identities (the hetero/homo or male/female dichotomies), and opposition to 'normalization' and respectability and an assimilationist approach to LGBT liberation. Queer politics and queer theory developed along side each other endorsing similar values, though often with an uneasy relationship. Queer activism links queer politics with social justice, anti-racism, feminism and global justice issues, refusing absorption into mainstream society. In addition to Queer Nation groups such as the Lesbian Avengers, Bash Back!, Queeruption, Queer Mutiny and many more evolved to promote radical queer activism. Today queer activism partially overlaps with tran and feminist activism, and is closely linked to some other radical movements (for example queer anarchism).

716. Gray, Mary L., '"Queer Nation is Dead/Long Live Queer Nation": The Politics and Poetics of Social Movement and Media Representation', *Critical Studies in Media Communication,* vol. 26 no. 3 (2009). http://www.tandfonline.com/doi/abs/10.1080/1529503015062

717. Highleyman, Liz, 'Radicals Queers or Queer Radicals? Queer Activism and the Global Justice Movement', in Benjamin Shepard and Ronald Hayduk, eds., *From ACT-UP to the WTO: Urban Protest and Community-Building in the Era of Globalization,* London, Verso, 2002, Part II. Online at: http://www.black-rose.com/articles-liz/actupwto.html.

718. Lopez Penedo, Suzana, 'Queer Politics in Spain: There is Life after Same -Sex Marriage Legislation', *Jindal Global Law Review,* vol. 4 no. 1 (2012), pp. 238-63.

719. Rand, Erin J., *Reclaiming Queer Activist and Academic Rhetorics of Resistance*, Tuscaloosa, University of Alabama Press, 2014, pp. 224. See also: Rand, E.J. 'A Disunited Nation and a Legacy of Contradiction: Queer Nation Construction of Identity', *Journal of Communication Inquiry* , vol. 28 no. 4 (Oct 2004), pp. 288-306.

720. Sears, Alan, 'Queer Anti-Capitalism: What's Left of Lesbian and Gay Liberation?', *Science and Society,* vol. 69 no. 1 (2005), pp. 92-117. At: http:/ philpapers.org/rec/SEAQAV

721. Wickman, Jan, 'Queer Activism: What Might That Be?', *Trikster,* no. 4, 2010, online: http://trikster.net/4/wickman/singlepage.html

722. Zimmerman, Bonnie, 'A Lesbian-Feminist Journey Through Queer Nation's Construction of Identity', *Journal of Lesbian Studies,* vol. 11 nos. 1-2 (2007). http://www.tandfonline/doi/abs/10.1300/Jl55vlln01_03

Websites recommended:

Against Equality: http://www.againstequality.org. An anti-capitalist collection of radical queer and trans writers, thinkers and artists

Queer Zine Archive Project (QZAP): http://archive.gzap.org. A lot of the early debates (pre-internet) related to queer activism (as opposed to queer theory) took place in zines. The QZAP is aiming to make many of them available online.

H. Campaigns Against Government

This section covers a range of protests against government policies (e.g. neoliberalism leading to greater inequality) and styles of government (e.g. corruption and misspending). It begins with the Chilean student-led challenge to the Pinochet legacy in 2011-12 and three mass movements that erupted in 2013 (and sometimes compared to each other) in Bulgaria, Turkey and Brazil. Secondly it focuses more specifically on campaigns for greater transparency and against corruption, using a number of examples from India, including the well publicized anti-corruption movement that arose in 2011. Thirdly, this section illustrates campaigns for just taxation and against overtaxing the poor.

1. Challenging Authoritarianism, Neoliberalism, Corruption and Misspending: 2013-2014

The student-led protests in Chile in 2011-12 were hailed as the most significant movement in Chile since the resistance to General Pinochet in the 1980s, and were a direct challenge to Pinochet's legacy of neoliberalism, involving privatization (including of higher education) and profound inequalities, enshrined in the 1981 Pinochet Constitution.

There were in 2013-2014 significant protests in terms of both duration and scale in three countries which are formally democratic (regular multiparty elections in which the conduct and outcome is not seriously challenged), but are in varying degrees corrupt, authoritarian, or both. In Bulgaria the protesters demanded the resignation of governments, and in Turkey targeted the role of the prime minister; in both protesters also challenged the nature of the political regime. But in Brazil protests were directed against aspects of the regime and socio-economic system, rather than the Socialist government in power.

Opposition to corruption was one of the important issues behind the Bulgarian protests and became a major focus in Turkey by 2014, and was also one target of the Brazilian demonstrations.

Poverty, deep social and economic inequalities and the power of big business, have been other motives for mass agitation. In Bulgaria the spark was the doubling of electricity bills in the city of Blagoevgrad; and anger at the impact of neoliberal economic policies and government support for corporations motivated demonstrators in Turkey and Brazil. In both these countries a related issue was government commitment to major urban or sporting projects, at the expense of the local inhabitants.

The protests in Turkey and, especially, Bulgaria, where students became central in the final stage, had similarities with the earlier Chilean resistance to neoliberalism.

1.a. Chile: 2011-12

An impressive student movement erupted in Chile in 2011 and maintained its activism for months, employing a wide range of tactics (including not only mass marches and temporary occupations of educational and political buildings, but also hunger strikes, 'kiss-ins' in public squares, bicycle rides and performances of pop songs). They also organized an informal referendum again the profit motive in which many thousands took part to show their opposition to higher education policy. The students challenged the neoliberal nature of higher education, where total privatization had linked high quality to high fees and state investment was very low. But they also criticized the impact of this ideology on society and the economy as a whole. So – after police violently attacked a student march through the centre of Santiago – the wider public began to join the protests. Students began to receive major support from trade unionists and workers, who went on strike, built barricades and took part in 'carcerolazos' (organized banging of pots and pans). A public opinion poll suggested three quarters of the population supported the students, and their demands received major media coverage for months. This challenge to the regime had been preceded in 2006 by the 'penguin revolution' of secondary school pupils (named for the colours of their school uniforms), which did manage to get the Pinochet law on education repealed, but the new law failed to promote real educational reform. The demonstrations of 2006 also failed to ignite wider social unrest.

The students in 2011 did manage to wring a series of concessions from the government, and leaders of the Student Federation negotiated with President Pinera; but the students rejected several attempts by the government between June and August 2011 to find solutions as superficial. Student protesters in April 2012 were still rejecting the government concessions. When elections took place in December 2013, against a background of widespread public activism, student leader Camila Vallejo stood for Congress and the socialist

Michelle Bachelet became President, promising educational, constitutional and tax changes to promote greater equality. But the coalition government was then divided on reforms in 2014, and the debate took place primarily at the parliamentary level.

The developments in Chile were quite widely reported, but much of the literature is in Spanish. We list below a number of commentaries and analyses, mostly available online.

723. Cabalin, Cristian, 'Neoliberal Education and Student Movements in Chile: Inequalities and Malaise', 10pp. Available as pdf at: http:// www. academia.edu.

Looks at 2006 and 2011 protests.

724. Contreras, Dan, 'Chile's Educational and Social Movement: Quality Education for Everyone...Now!', *Broken Rifle*, London, War Resisters' International, no. 90 (Dec. 2011): http://www.wri-irg/node/14359

Briefly explains problem in higher education and how privatization promotes gap between rich and poor. Describes wide range of nonviolent direct action used by the students, but notes wider support and activism.

725. Figueroa-Clark, Victor, 'The Meaning behind Protests in Chile', *International Affairs at LSE*, Aug. 2011, pp. 3. http://blogs.lse.ac.uk/ ideas/2011/08

Discusses context of protest, the school and university education system, extent of inequality in Chilean society, and implications if movement successful.

726. McIntyre, Jody, 'How to Grow a Student Movement, Chilean Style', *New Internationalist* (October 2012), pp. 26-7.

Stresses challenge to Pinochet legacy and links with workers' unions. Includes timeline of protests from May 2011 – August 2012.

727. Munoz-Lamartine, Ernesto, 'Chile: Student Leaders Reinvent the Movement', *Berkeley Review of Latin American Studies* (Fall, 2011), pp. 4. Online: http://clas.berkeley.edu/research

Account of talk by Giorgio Jackson, President of the Catholic University's Student Association in Chile.

728. Salinas, Daniel and Pablo Fraser, 'Educational Opportunities and Contentious Politics: The 2011 Chilean Student Movement', *Berkeley Review of Education*, vol. 3 no. 1 (2012), pp. 17-47. Online: http://escholarship.org/ ucbgse_bre

Considers the reasons for emergence of movement and its challenge to free market provision of education. Argues experience of this education provides both mobilizing grievances and resources for political mobilization.

729. Somma, Nicolas M., 'The Chilean Student Movement of 2011-2012: Challenging the Marketization of Education', *Interface: a journal about social movements*, vol. 4 no. 2 (Nov. 2012), pp. 296-309.

The author is assistant professor of sociology at the Catholic University of Chile. Examines causes of protests and educational system, 'horizontalism' of student organization, tactics, use of media and maintenance of internal unity.

1.b. Bulgaria: 2013

Major protests took place in Bulgaria in three stages. The first stage, which began in February with the burning of electricity bills that had doubled in a month, involved resistance to unemployment and government austerity policies (similar to the protests in Greece, Spain and elsewhere in Europe in response to the economic downturn), but included anger about corruption. These protests, which involved a mass demonstration outside parliament and seven people setting fire to themselves, and mobilized the poor and many from the countryside, demanded the resignation of the centre-right government led by Boiko Borisov. This demand was successful and resulted in a general election. A new government led by the Bulgarian Socialist Party in coalition with the (largely Turkish) Movement for Rights and Freedom was formed in May reliant on parliamentary support from the far-right Ataka MPs. The new government, headed by Plamen Oresharski, aroused popular anger in June when the government was seen to be reverting to collusion with corporate oligarchs in nominating a 'media mogul with shady connections' to a key national security post. Demonstrators immediately and successfully demanded his resignation, but continued throughout the summer to demand the resignation of the government as a whole. These protests, primarily by the urban middle class, did not succeed in their stated aim and began to reflect divergent political ideologies. They did, however, gain some support from European governments and the EU. (See: Ivan Krastev, 'Why Bulgaria's Protests Stand Out in Europe', *Guardian*, 30 July 2013}.

The third phase was initiated by students at Sofia occupying the main lecture hall in late October, prompting other student occupations round the country (with some support from their lecturers) and promoting an 'Occupy Bulgaria' movement against corruption and calling for electoral reforms, easier removal of MPs and greater transparency. The students also backed the demand for the resignation of the government and highlighted the gap between rich and poor. In November they joined with trade unions to demonstrate outside parliament. Despite apparent widespread popular support, the student protests began to lose momentum by December. However, observers noted that the protests in 2013 had been almost entirely nonviolent, and had involved a range of imaginative and artistic actions – for example the recreation on July 14 of the Delacroix painting 'Liberty Leading the People', but substituting the Bulgarian for the French flag – which might provide a hopeful precedent for future mobilization.

730. Drezov, Kyril, 'A Neighbour in Turmoil: Two Waves of Popular Protest in 2013 Bulgaria', in Gokay and Xypolia, eds., *Reflections on Taksim – Gezi Park Protests in Turkey* (see 744 1.c. below), pp. 52-57.

731. Gurov, Boris and Emilia Zankina, 'Populism and the Construction of Political Charisma: Post-Transition Politics in Bulgaria', *Problems of Post-Communism*, vol. 60 no. 1 (Jan/Feb 2013), pp. 3-17.

Article published just before protests erupted in February.

732. Junes, Tom, 'Students Take Bulgaria's Protests to the Next Level. Can They Break the Political Stalemate?', *Transit: Europaische Revue*, no. 44 (2013), pp. 13. Available from Institut for die Wissenschaften Menschen online at: http:// www.iwm

Useful and well referenced analysis of student phase of protests, in context of earlier student protests in 1997 and wider national demonstrations in 2013.

733. Lipkis, Sarah, '2013: The Year of Bulgarian Protest', *World Policy Journal Blog*, (17 Dec., 2013), pp. 3. At: http://www.worldpolicy.org/blog/2013/12/17/2013-year-bulgarian-protest

734. Nikolov, Nikolay et al., 'Bulgaria: Lost in Transition', *openDemocracy* (10 Dec. 2013), pp. 4: http://www.opendemocracy.net

Stresses that Bulgaria's corrupt and incompetent governments are result of the nature of the 1989 transition, the opportunities created then for members of the security services to seize economic, social and political power, and lack of public debate about the past.

I.c. Turkey: 2013 and 2014

Authoritarianism was a major focus of the Turkish 2013 protests, which gathered momentum after brutal police reaction to a small peaceful sit-in from May 28-31 in Gezi Park, Taksim Square, Istanbul. Although the prime minister Recep Tayyip Erdogan, who had won three successive elections since 2002, could claim significant political achievements – curbing the army and (despite repression of Kurdish militants) promoting a peace process with the Kurds – his style was increasingly autocratic. Under his government artistic and media freedom were suppressed – Reporters Without Borders placed Turkey no. 154 out of 180 countries in its 2014 Press Freedom Index. Secondly, although the Turkish economy had prospered under neo-liberal policies, anger about the gap between rich and poor was a second element in the Turkish protests (as it has been in many popular uprisings). The government has fostered close links with big business, including construction and mining companies, at the expense of workers, as the deaths of 282 miners in May 2014 (against a backdrop of government refusal to impose stronger safety rules in mines, which according to the ILO are the third most dangerous in the world) dramatically illustrated. A third factor in the Turkish protests was the government's policy of rapid urban development overriding local concerns – resistance to the destruction of Gezi Park in central Istanbul began the May-June 2013 movement. The government planned to replace the park with a rebuilt Ottoman barracks and a shopping mall, and it was one of the last public parks in the city. Another concern for many demonstrators was the government's attack on secular lifestyles, for example tighter rules on sales of alcohol.

The rapidly growing demonstrations from 1 June 2013 included a much larger occupation of Gezi Park and protests across the country, mobilizing over 3 million people in 50 towns and cities. Erdogan ordered a crackdown in mid -June: in the violent police operation eight died, 104 had serious head injuries and about 8,000 were hurt; many who showed sympathy (even by tweets) lost their jobs, and a year later hundreds were still on trial. The repressive response was met initially by individuals mounting solitary 'standing' protests in public places. Although after June there was not a sustained movement, there have been frequent protests since on varied issues, including corruption, in late 2013 and in 2014. The funeral processions in March 2014 for a 14 year old boy who died after nearly months in a coma (induced by being hit by a gas canister fired by police during the Gezi Park protests) was attacked by the police, triggering new demonstrations across the country. Corruption allegations had surfaced in December 2013, there were leaks on social media, and Erdogan was being accused of removing police and prosecutors in order to delay investigations which might incriminate his family and business and political allies. The mine disaster in May 2014 (noted above) prompted angry street protests in major cities.

Although a majority of Turkey's 80 million population has continued to support Erdogan and his Justice and Development Party (AKP) – for example in voting in the municipal elections in 2014 – the Gezi protests and their aftermath brought about a more critical attitude by many to government and the subservient mainstream media. In the view of some activists the protests also promoted greater tolerance among those with diverse attitudes to Islam and differing lifestyles, and brought together very diverse groups: Turks and Kurds, Kemalists and conservative Muslims, Greens, Marxists, anarchists, feminists and LGBT activists. The protesters were predominantly young – those who flocked to Gezi Park to protest against police violence included young liberals and members of the activist pro-democracy Young Civilians – but included older men and women and gained support from many white collar and professional groups, including doctors who tended the wounded. Businesses in Istanbul also offered some support.

Erdogan did receive a setback in the June 2015 parliamentary elections – despite being elected president in 2014 – when his AKP party failed for the first time in 13 years to win a majority in parliament. He had campaigned for a constitutional change to strengthen presidential powers, and some voters apparently wished to curb his authoritarian ambitions.

I.c.i. Reports and Immediate Analyses of May-June 2013

The Gezi Park protests gained international media coverage, as did their brutal suppression in mid-June. The reports below are all from Turkish commentators.

735. Bechev, Dimitar, 'Turkey, a People-Power Tide', *openDemocracy*, (2 June 2003), pp. 2: http://www.opendemocracy.net)

736. Gokpinar, Ali, 'Neither Turkish Spring nor Velvet Revolution', *openDemocracy*, (5 June 2013), pp. 4: http://www.opendemocracy.net

737. Shafak, Elif, 'The View from Taksim Square', *Guardian*, (4th June 2013), pp. 2. Online: http://www.theguardian.com

738. Tocci, Nathalie, 'A U-Turn in Turkish Politics? Gezi Park in Perspective', *openDemocracy* (3 June, 2013), pp.4: http://www.opendemocracy.net

I.c.ii. Journal Articles and Substantial Assessments

739. Abbas, Tahir, 'Political Culture and National Identity in Conceptualising the Gezi Park Movement', *Insight Turkey*, vol.15 no. 4 (Fall 2013), pp. 19-28. Online: http:// www.insightturkey.com/ and: http://www.academia.edu

740. Arat, Yesim, 'Violence, Resistance and Gezi Park', *International Journal of Middle East Studies*, vol. 45 no. 4. (Nov 2013), pp. 807-9.

Examination of violence from a gender perspective by academic specializing in women's political participation in Turkey.

741. Cansun, Sebnem, 'The Gezi Park Protests and Youth in Turkey: Perceptions of Hurriyet Columnists', *International Journal of Social Sciences and Humanity Studies*, vol. 6 no. 1 (2014), pp. 92-105. Online: http:// www. academia.edu

Article discusses why, despite major role of young people using social media in the first three weeks of protests, columnists in the major Turkish daily *Hurriyet (Liberty)* often failed to mention, or underplayed, the significance of the young demonstrators.

742. Cook, Steven A., 'Turkey's Democratic Mirage: The Powerbrokers Ankara Back', *Foreign Affairs, SNAPSHOT* (Jan 8 2014). Online: http:// www.foreignaffairs.com

Assessment of Turkey's progress towards being a consolidated democracy since the Justice and Development Party came to power in 2002, arguing that despite some significant gains there are still 'profound' problems as the corruption allegations against Erodgan illustrate.

743. Gokay, Bulent and Ilia Xypolia, eds., *Reflections on Taksim-Gezi Park Protests in Turkey*, Keele European Research Centre, Southeast Europe Series, Keele University, 2013, pp. 70. Online: http://www.keele.ac.uk

Includes a range of brief essays on the Taksim protests, but also includes Immanuel Wallerstein on 'Turkey: Dilemma of the Kurds', and chapters making comparisons with Mexico 1968 and with Brazil, plus an analysis of 'Two Waves of Popular Protest in 2013 Bulgaria'.

744. Gul, M. Dee J. and Cunuk, C.N., 'Istanbul's Taksim Square and Gezi Park: The Place of Protest and the Ideology of Place', *Journal of Architecture and Urbanism*, vol. 38 no. 1 (March 2014), pp. 63-72.

Discusses the protests and their symbolism and the ideological conflicts evoked.

745. Letsch, Constanze, 'A Year after the Protests, Gezi Park Nurtures the Seeds of a New Turkey', *The Guardian* (29 May, 2014). Online: http://www.theguardian.com/

746. Tugal, Cihan, 'Democratic Janissaries? Turkey's Role in the Arab Spring', *New Left Review*, no. 76 (Jul-Aug 2012), pp.5-24.

Criticizes the western view of Turkey as model for the Islamic world and analyses the Erdogan government's domestic and foreign policy. Written the year before Gezi Park , but provides relevant background.

747. Yayla, Atilla, 'Gezi Park Revolts: For or Against Democracy?', *Insight Turkey*, vol. 15. no.4 (Fall 2013), pp. 7-18. Also available at: Liberal Dusunce Toplulugu (Association for Liberal Thinking): http:// www.liberl.org.tr/ldt

Critical examination of the multiplicity of the Gezi movement, the underlying factors and its repercussions . The author stresses the degree of violence and claims 'the broader Gezi Park agenda represented a fundamentally Kemalist reaction against democracy', citing the role of the Republican People's Party as supporting evidence.

d. Brazil 2013 and 2014

The mass demonstrations that broke out in Brazil on 6 June 2014 began as a protest against a rise in bus and metro fares in Sao Paolo (organized by the leftist and anarchistic Movement for Free Passes), but a brutal police response prompted the demonstrations to swell rapidly in numbers and spread across the country. As a movement erupted the demands also grew, including improvement in social services such as transport, health and education, calls for electoral and constitutional reform and opposition to corruption. Another central focus for protests was the lavish government expenditure on preparations for holding the World Cup in the summer of 2014 and the Olympics in 2016. This expenditure should, demonstrators asserted, have been directed instead to improving the welfare of ordinary Brazilians.

The protests drew on students and young people alienated by the link between government and corporations and the role of money in politics, the poor from the slums, but also many from the middle classes. This diverse constituency and the largely spontaneous nature of the protests meant that the demonstrations lacked a clear sense of political priorities and had no organizational focus. The movement arose outside the party political system and although some protesters indicated support for small leftist parties and support for the ruling Workers' Party waned during June

2014, there was no concerted call for President Dilma Roussef, who made a number of promises in response to the protests, to resign.

Demonstrations continued periodically in 2013 and into 2014 against the World Cup, and slum clearance and demolitions in preparation for the Olympics aroused anger in the favelas. But a movement on the scale of June 2013 did not reappear.

748. Branford, Sue and Hilary Wainwright, 'Ructions in Rio', *Red Pepper* (Aug/Sep 2013), pp. 40-41.

749. Campos, Nauro F., 'What Drives Protests in Brazil? Corruption, Ineptitude and Elections', VOX (23 July 2013), pp. 4. Online: http:// www. voxeu.org
Economics professor suggests three main causes of the protests.

750. Gatehouse, Tom, 'Copa de Cash' *Red Pepper* (Jun/Jul 2014), pp. 38-39.
On the negative impact of preparations for the World Cup and increasingly repressive police tactics.

751. Pinheiro-Machad, Rosana and Alexander S. Dent, eds. 'Protesting Democracy in Brazil', Fieldsights-Hot Spots, *Cultural Anthropology Online* (20 Dec 2013): http://www.culanth.org
Series of 22 posts covering numerous aspects of protests, their cause, and issues of policing.

752. Saad-Filho, Alfredo, 'Mass Protests under "Left Neoliberalism": Brazil, June-July 2013,' *Critical Sociology*, vol. 39 no. 5 (Sep. 2013), pp. 657-69.
Examines causes, range of demands, social base and 'contradictory frustrations' of the mass protests. Discusses political dilemmas and proposes 'constructive alternatives for the left'.

753. Singer, Andre, 'Rebellion in Brazil', *New Left Review*, no. 85 (Jan /Feb 2014), pp.19-38.
Analyzes varied class, age and political beliefs of the protesters (sometimes resulting in conflict between them).

754. Winters, Matthew S. and Rebecca Weitz-Shapiro, 'Partisan and Nonpartisan Protests in Brazil', *Journal of Politics in Latin America*, vol. 6 no. 1 (2014), pp. 137-50. Online: http:// www.jpla.org
Uses evidence of two surveys to examine effects of protests on party-alignment and suggests a drop in support for the ruling Workers' Party, but that no other party gained in support.

2. Campaigns for Transparency and against Corruption: India since 1990

Anger about government and business corruption is frequently one theme in popular movements, as the studies of Bulgaria, Turkey and Brazil illustrate, and has prompted protests in many parts of the world: for example the 'Million People March' in Manila in 26 August 2013. A valuable recent study of how popular organization and nonviolent action (taking many forms) has challenged corruption in many countries, from Italy to Korea, India, Indonesia, Afghanistan, Brazil and Uganda, is:

755. Beyerle, Shaazka, *Curtailing Corruption: People Power for Accountability and Justice*, Boulder CO, Lynne Rienner, 2014, pp.261, pb.

It is impossible in this Guide to cover all anti-corruption protests. The focus here is on India, where an internationally well-publicized Anti-Corruption Movement arose in 2011 and had repercussions on Indian politics. However, this significant but controversial movement should be seen in the wider context of many earlier and varied forms of struggle in India to promote greater government transparency and to prevent corruption.

2.a. Analyzing Corruption in Indian Politics and Civil Society Responses

This sub-section gives references for the role of civil society bodies, and in particular the work of the radical Mazdoor Kisan Shakti Sangathan (Association for the Empowerment of Workers and Farmers), which waged a campaign including direct action in the state of Rajasthan in the 1990s for a Right to Information Act. This Act became law in Rajasthan in January 2001. The MKSS encouraged campaigns in other parts of India, and a national Right to Information Act was passed in 2005. The Act now provides a basis for campaigners to seek out examples of corruption.

756. Jenkins, Rob, 'Civil Society versus Corruption in India', in Sumil Ganguly, Larry Diamond and Marc F. Plattner, eds., *The State of Indian Democracy*, Baltimore MD, John Hopkins University Press, 2007, pp. 161-67.

757. Jenkins, Rob, 'Democracy, Development and India's Struggle Against Corruption', *Public Policy Research*, vol. 3 no 3 (Sep-Dec 2006), pp. 155-63.

758. Jenkins, Rob and Anne Marie Goetz, 'Accounts and Accountability: Theoretical Implications of the Right-to-Information Movement in India', *Third World Quarterly*, vol. 20 no. 3 (1999), pp. 603-22.

Examination of the grass roots work of the MKSS in developing campaign for right to information as part of their wider campaigning and their use of jan sunwals (public hearings) in communities where official documents regarding public works, anti-poverty programmes etc. are read out and people are encouraged to add their own testimony about diversion of funds and fraud. The article also covers the MKSS use of public protest, such as a 52 day sit-in in the capital of Rajasthan, Jaipur, in 1997. See also: Commonwealth Human Rights Initiative, 'Right to Information. State Level: Rajasthan': http://www.humanrightsinitative.org Brief elaboration and update on work of MKSS and Right to Information Acts up to 2005.

759. Kumar, C. Raj, *Corruption and Human Rights in India: Comparative Perspectives on Transparency and Good Governance*, Delhi, Oxford University Press, 2011, pp. 234.

Analyzes corruption as a violation of human rights and proposes a multi-pronged approach to tackling corruption, including a greater role for civil society. A postscript takes account of the 2011 Anna Hazare movement against corruption.

760. Webb, Martin, 'Disciplining the Everyday State and Society? Anti-Corruption and Right to Information Activism in Delhi', *Contributions to Indian Sociology*, vol. 47 no 5 (Oct 2013), pp. 363-93.

On use of legal mechanisms under the 2005 Right to Information Act by anti-corruption and right to information groups.

2.b. Anna Hazare and the 2011-13 Anti-Corruption Movement

A significant popular movement against corporate and government corruption was ignited on 5 April 2011, when Anna Hazare, a 73 year-old former soldier, and campaigner against corruption in Maraastha state since 1991, embarked on a 'fast to death' to secure a national ombudsman to fight corruption. His action mobilized many thousands of supporters in different cities, who flocked to the streets, undertook candlelit processions or fasted in sympathy. The Congress-led government, which was embroiled in a 24 billion pound telecoms fraud and allegations about bribery over the 2010 Commonwealth Games, hastened to respond. After the Prime Minister promised to bring a bill into the Lower House of Parliament, Harare called off his fast on 9 April, but set a deadline for 15 August for bringing the bill into parliament. The government brought in an anti-corruption ombudsman bill which Hazare and his supporters argued was wholly inadequate; Hazare demanded that the draft drawn up by his advisers should be put before parliament instead. In order to prevent a further public hunger strike, the government on 16 August 2011 imprisoned Harare in Delhi's Tihar jail and arrested hundreds of his supporters. Hazare began his fast in jail, whilst supporters protested across India. The government rapidly ordered his release, but Harare refused bail until allowed to fast in public, which he did until 28th August, when parliament passed a 'sense of the house' resolution endorsing his demands, and thousands celebrated a 'people's victory'.

The government brought in a bill which passed in the lower house in late December 2011, but in the view of Hazare and his supporters it did not give the ombudsman sufficient powers, such as the right to prosecute offenders, and he embarked on another fast on 27 December, but on doctors' advice ended it three days later. The proposed ombudsman was not finally voted into law until two years later, when the lower house approved amendments to the original bill endorsed by the upper house. Anna Hazare, who had been undertaking another fast, ended it and announced the setting up of 'watchdog bodies' to monitor how the new law was enforced. The creation of the national ombudsman was the culmination of eight previous unsuccessful attempts to set up such a body since the 1960s. However, some leftists critics of Hazare's campaign argued a national body would be unwieldy and was contrary to the Gandhian approach he claimed to adopt.

Harare began his national campaign by a statue of Gandhi and used the tactics of fasts and disobedience, and comparisons with Gandhi were promoted by his supporters and the media. One strand in negative comments on his campaign has queried the validity of this comparison. But the major criticisms on the left have been that the campaign was predominantly middle class and not focused on issues facing the poor, and that Hazare leaned towards the Hindu right, who were represented among his campaign team. Coverage of his movement did tend to be more favourable in Hindu language media, and the rightwing Hindu party the BJP supported his anti-corruption demands, in part to embarrass the Congress-led government. However, others have argued that the significance of the movement Hazare helped to mobilize should not be ignored. Indeed, a newly-created anti-corruption party the Aam Aadmi (Common Man) Party (AAP), formed by a former Gandhian activist and key associate of Hazare, Arvind Kejriwal, received spectacular support in elections to the Delhi assembly in December 2013. Kejriwal resigned as Delhi's chief minister 49 days later with his colleagues because, he claimed, the two major parties (Congress and the BJP) had blocked his anti-corruption measures. Hazare has, however, refused to support the AAM, citing his distrust of party politics.

The 2011-13 movement has been quite well covered in the international media, especially during the fasts and protests in April, August and December 2011, and some reports in Indian newspapers, such as the *Times of India,* are available online. Substantial journal articles and commentaries are so far more sparse.

761. Baisakh, Pradeep, 'We Will Give People a Political Alternative: An Interview with Arvind Kejriwal', *openDemocracy* (8 Mar. 2013), pp. 5: http:// www.opendemocracy.net

762. Jayaram, N. 'Frenzied Argument in India', *openDemocracy* (29 Aug. 2011), pp. 3: http:// www.opendemocracy.net

Article written at peak of Hazare movement, noting the divided views on the movement and criticisms of it, including the dangers of 'messianic campaigns' for parliamentary democracy.

763. Mishra, K.P., 'Gandhian Views on Democracy', *Gandhi Marg*, vol 34 nos 2-3 (Jul-Dec 2012), pp. 205-16.

Primarily an exposition of Gandhi's theory of democracy, but commenting on Hazare's anti-corruption movement as a starting point.

764. Nigam, Aditya and Nivedita Menon, 'Anti-Corruption Movement and the Left: Commentary', *Economic and Political Weekly*, vol. 46 no 37 (10 Sep. 2011), pp. 5. At: http://www.epw.in

Comments on the potential of a large and nonviolent movement and criticizes hard line leftist criticisms.

765. Patnaik, Prabhai, 'Anna Hazare and Gandhi -Whatever devalues Parliament strikes at the root of democracy', *The Telegraph* Calcutta (21 June 2011): http://www.telegraphindia.com

Criticizes coercive nature of a 'fast to the death' and dangers of civil society activism that bypasses parliament.

766. Sengupta, Mitu, 'Anna Hazare and the Idea of Gandhi', *Journal of Asian Studies,* vol. 71 no. 3 (Aug 2012), pp. 595-601. Originally published in *Dissent.* Online: http://www.internationalpolicydigest.org

Raises caveats about comparisons with Gandhi, discusses Hazare's diagnosis and prescriptions for corruption and comments on the nature of the Hazare movement. Argues against claims that it is a pawn of the extreme right RSS and/or CIA, noting the extent of mass protests and the depth of anger about corruption.

767. Shabnoor, Sultana, 'Dig Deep into Corruption in India', *openDemocracy* (24 Aug. 2011), pp. 2.: http:// www.opendemocracynet

Brief summary of key disagreements between government and Hazare camp on role and powers of proposed ombudsman.

See also: Kumar, *Corruption and Human Rights in India*, postscript (759 H..2.a.).

3. Campaigning for Just Taxes

Opposition to taxes seen as unjust or illegitimate has long been a spur to popular resistance, as in the English Peasants' Revolt and in the preludes to the English Civil War and the American Revolution. Taxes may also be withheld to demonstrate opposition to particular policies, for example military budgets and preparations (see D.2.b.), or as part of a wider revolt against state policies, as in the Poujadist movement among small farmers in France in the 1950s. An important example of widespread resistance to a tax on the grounds it was unjust was the British poll tax movement of 1989-90, sparked by Mrs. Thatcher's introduction of a 'poll tax' – a new flat rate local government tax on all individuals, regardless of their income. This movement, which led to the tax being revoked and helped to undermine Mrs. Thatcher's tenure in office, has inspired a significant literature.

Unfair targeting of the poor is one form of tax injustice. The other side of the coin, which has come increasingly into focus in recent years, is the failure of the very rich (individuals and in particular corporations) to pay their fair share of tax. Sit-in campaigns on this issue were promoted by UK Uncut, which targeted companies making large profits in Britain, but used accounting mechanisms to avoid paying any (or sufficient) tax to the UK exchequer (see A.8.d.). UK Uncut tactics and demands spread to some other countries, and were part of wider public, media and parliamentary criticism of the social irresponsibility of banks and large corporations. Tax avoidance and evasion is a global issue – particular important for poorer countries – and a range of civil society bodies in different countries have combined since 2011 to demand an end to secrecy on tax havens. The Tax Justice Network published a report in 2012 suggesting that 13 trillion pounds in financial wealth (excluding property) was hidden in secret tax havens. A whistleblower in the UK Revenue and Customs department in 2011 drew the attention of two parliamentary committees to another potential source of unfairness – tax authorities failing to enforce taxes of millions of pounds on major companies. Although there is potential for forms of direct action such as sit-ins and boycotts targeting companies (as Uncut demonstrated) much of the campaigning involves 'tracing the tax' and symbolic protests of the kind promoted by Christian Aid.

3.a. Poll Tax Protests, Britain, 1989-90

768. Bagguley, Paul, 'Protest, Poverty and Power: A Case Study of the Anti-Poll Tax Movement', *Sociological Review*, vol. 43 (1995), pp. 693-719. First published online 28 June 2008 at: http://onlinelibrary.wiley.com

Examines social base, organization and tactics of the anti-poll tax movement and relates it to theoretical debates about new social movements and poor people's movements. See also: Bagguley, 'Anti-Poll Tax Protest' in C. Barker and P. Kennedy, eds., *To Make Another World: Studies in Protest and Collective Action*, Aldershot, Avebury Press, 1996, pp. 7-24.

769. Hoggett, Paul and Danny Burns, 'The Revenge of the Poor: The Anti-Poll Tax Campaign in Britain', *Critical Social Policy*, vol. 11 (Dec 1991), pp. 95-110, See also reply by Lavalette, Michael and Gerry Moony, 'The Poll Tax Struggle in Britain: A Reply to Hoggett and Burns', vol. 12 (Jan. 1993), pp. 96-108.

770. Lavalette, Michael and Gerry Mooney, '"No Poll Tax Here!": The Tories, Social Policy and the Great Poll Tax Rebellion, 1987-1991' in M. Lavelette and G. Mooney, eds. *Class Struggle and Social Welfare*, Abingdon, Routledge, 2000, pp.199-227.

771. Murgatroyd, Richard, *The Popular Politics of the Poll Tax: An Active Citizenship of the Left*, London, Brunel University, 2000 (published PhD thesis).

Detailed case study of poll tax protest in the London Borough of Ealing.

772. Ramsey, Kanaan (interviewed by David Solnit), 'How One Small Anarchist Group Toppled the Thatcher Government', in David Solnit, ed., *Globalize Liberation*, San Francisco CA, City Lights, 2004, pp. 397-410.

Discusses how the poll tax campaign spread beyond its origins in Edinburgh to the rest of Britain and describes its main tactics.

I. Regional Campaigns for Civil, Cultural or National Rights

Regional demands for cultural rights, for full civic rights which are being suppressed by central government, or for partial or total autonomy from the central government, are often voiced even in well-established 'nation states', and may take the form of regional political parties, calls for referendums, demonstrations and civil resistance or violent resistance. The movements in the Basque region of Spain – where despite success for moderate nationalists ETA has waged a prolonged armed struggle, and the rise since 2010 of a nonviolent Catalan nationalism, illustrate these tendencies. There are regional movements with varying degrees of public support in Italy (Sardinian activists proposed in 2014 that Sardinia should secede and become a canton of Switzerland), and in France (for example in Brittany). Where there are divisions within a region based on ethnicity, language or religion political solutions may be undermined by bitterness and tension, as in Kosovo's moves towards independence (see Vol. 1. *Guide to Civil Resistance*, D.I.).

In this section we are not attempting a comprehensive coverage of regional movements, but focus on those within the UK, which illustrate a variety of different political approaches and issues. Nationalists in Scotland have made major gains primarily through the political process: in September 2014 the nationalists won 44.7 per cent of the votes in a turnout of over 84 per cent of the electorate in an independence referendum, and the Scots were promised further significant measures of devolution. Radical nationalists engaged in a few spectacular exploits – for example four Scottish students removed then symbolic Stone of Scone from Westminster Abbey on Christmas Day 1951 – and a few symbolic targets such as letter boxes in Scotland with the Queen's name were bombed or dynamited. But these were a temporary and minority part of a predominantly constitutional campaign, which is not directly relevant to this Guide.

Movements which are relevant are the nonviolent action campaign for the use of the Welsh language in Wales, and the examples of civil resistance

– in particular the Civil Rights Movement of 1967-73 – in Northern Ireland. Welsh nationalists have otherwise primarily pursued a political path towards greater autonomy through Plaid Cymru contesting elections. The position in Northern Ireland is however complicated by its broader history within the movement for Irish independence, the divisions between the Protestant and Catholic communities with their distinct political allegiances, and the legacy of armed struggle embodied by the IRA (and in the late 1960s the Provisional IRA). Northern Ireland illustrates how nonviolent resistance can be overtaken by violent resistance and how this can lead in turn to inter-communal violence. But on the positive side Northern Ireland illustrates too the scope for creative initiatives towards reconciliation and peacemaking from below, which is another reason for including it here. Moreover, the long political peace process in Northern Ireland, involving both the British and Irish governments as well as parties on the ground and US mediators, has – despite continuing evidence of tensions – become a model for resolving bitter political conflicts in other parts of the world.

1.Welsh Nationalism and Nonviolent Action

The long campaign for the public use of the Welsh language – including Welsh language radio and TV stations, and for Welsh political autonomy or independence – has used a mix of constitutional tactics and more dramatic protest. Plaid Cymru has contested local, British and European elections in Wales, but Welsh language campaigners have also refused to pay BBC radio licences and prominent activist Gwynfor Evans engaged in public fasts. The movement has included some acts of sabotage, such as burning down English second homes in Wales, and a guerrilla style attack on a reservoir built in a Welsh valley to provide water for Liverpool, but the Welsh campaign has made varied use of nonviolent direct action tactics.

773. Dafis, Cynog, 'Cymdeithas yr Iaith – the Manifesto', translated by Harri Webb, *Planet Magazine: The Welsh Internationalist*, nos. 26/27, (Winter 1974/75).

774. Earnshaw, Helena and Angharad Penrhyn Jones, eds., *Here we Stand*, Aberystwyth, Honno, 2014, pp.450. pb.

Anthology of accounts by 17 British women campaigners, engaged in a range of militant direct action, including one by Welsh Language Society (Cymdeithas yr Iaith) activist, Angharad Thomas.

775. Evans, Gwynfor, *For the Sake of Wales: The Memoirs of Gwynfor Evans*, Caernarfon, Welsh Academic Press, [1986], Updated edition, 2001, with Foreword by Dafydd Elis Thomas, and epilogue by Steve Dubè, pp.281.

Memoirs of this key figure in the nationalist movement and committed advocate of nonviolence.

776. Evans, Gwynfor, *The Fight for Welsh Freedom*, Talybont, Y Lolfa, 2000, pp. 176, pb.

Covers Plaid Cymru, history and Welsh politics and government. An earlier book by Evans from the same publisher is: *Fighting for Wales*, 1992, pp. 221.

777. Howys, Sian, 'Breaking the law to make change', in John Brierley et al (eds.), *Gathering Visions, Gathering Strength*, co-published by GVGS organizing group and London, Peace News, 1998, pp. 13-15.

778. McAllister, Laura, *Plaid Cymru – The Emergence of a Political Party*, With a foreword by Gwynfor Evans, Bridgend, Seren, 2001, pp.224. pb.

Covers the period 1945-99 when Plaid was developing from a pressure group to established party with MPS and MEPs.

779. Madgwick, P.J., 'Linguistic conflict in Wales: A problem in the design of government', in Glyn Williams, ed., *Social and Cultural Change in Contemporary Wales*, London, Routledge and Kegan Paul, 1978, pp. 227-41, pb.

780. Morgan, Gerald, *The Dragon's Tongue: The Fortunes of the Welsh Language*, Cardiff, The Triskel Press, 1966, pp. 144.

781.Osmond, John, *Creative Conflict: The Politics of Welsh Devolution*, Llandysul, Gome Press; London, Routledge and Kegan Paul, 1978, pp. 314pp.

States the case for devolution, criticizes British regional policy, and traces the emergence and development of a distinctive Welsh politics.

782. Thomas, Ned, *The Welsh Extremist*, [Gollancz, 1971], Updated edition, Talybont,a, 1991, pp.144, pb.

Chronicles the Welsh cultural and national revival in the 20th century, including the nonviolent direct action campaign of the 1970s. Chapters on several of the leading figures in the movement. Critical assessment of the response of English socialists to the movement.

783. Tomos, Angharad, 'Realising a Dream', in Simon Blanchard and David Morley, eds., *What's This Channel Four? An Alternative Report*, Comedia Publishing Group, 1982, pp. 192, (pb edition Law Book Co of Australia, 1982).

2 Northern Ireland

The 1920 Government of Ireland Act created a Northern Ireland state within the UK with its own devolved parliament and government in the six North East counties of Ireland, which had constituted part of the nine counties of the province of Ulster. This constitutional arrangement was strengthened by the 1921 Anglo-Irish Treaty which created the Irish Free State, and also provided for Northern Ireland to choose to remain separate. The Treaty split the nationalist movement in the South and led to a bitter civil war between those for and against the Treaty.

Since Catholics/Nationalists formed a majority in two of the six counties of Northern Ireland and in the city of Derry/Londonderry, and since Irish republicans had fought for a united independent Ireland, the settlement created continuing sources of conflict. The demography of the new state and the political divide on Protestant/Unionist and Catholic/Nationalist lines ensured permanent Unionist control of the Provincial government at Stormont and the exclusion and political alienation of the Catholic minority. Unionist governments, fearful of this minority which mainly looked to the south and cherished the hope of a united Ireland, enshrined Protestant dominance through restricting voting rights in local elections, altering local electoral boundaries and controlling most aspects of government and society, including law and order. Thus judges and magistrates were almost all Protestants, many members of the Unionists Party. The police force, the Royal Ulster Constabulary (RUC) was 90 per cent Protestant and the Ulster Special Constabulary – the 'B-Specials' – entirely so. Many in the political, and religious establishment, and the security forces were also members of the Orange Order, founded in 1795 to defend the Protestant Ascendancy. Discrimination in jobs and housing, which pre-dated the creation of the new state, continued. This was the background to intermittent unrest, and to bombings and other military attacks by the Irish Republican Army (IRA).

Following the end of the IRA bombing campaign of 1956-62, a more effective challenge to the political status quo arose in the form of the Civil Rights movement which had its origins in various community initiatives dating back to the early 1960s. Thus in 1963 women in Dungannon, Co Tyrone, formed the Homeless Citizens League and supported homeless families who squatted in empty pre-fabs due for demolition. This was followed soon afterwards by the formation in the town of the Campaign for Social Justice in Northern Ireland which publicized the discrimination in housing operated by Dungannon and other councils. In 1968 the Nationalist MP in Stormont (the Northern Ireland Parliament) for East Tyrone, Austin Currie, squatted in a house which Dungannon Rural District Council had allocated to an unmarried Protestant woman ahead of a young Catholic family. His action proved a catalyst for the countrywide campaign for civil rights and an end to discriminatory practices.

In Derry/Londonderry, a city with high unemployment, acute housing shortage and a majority Catholic population ruled by a Protestant/Unionist City Council, a campaign in 1965 to have the second university for Northern Ireland sited there brought together a cross section of people, including Catholic, and some Protestant, business people. The suspicion was that the Council was reluctant to have a university in the city as that would alter the demographic and threaten Protestant/Unionist control. Although the group failed in its objective its experience enabled some of its members to provide useful organizational support for a more far-reaching campaign on discrimination in housing and employment launched by a small group of socialists, republicans and other radicals in 1968, the Derry Housing Action Committee (DHAC).

In January 1967 the Northern Ireland Civil Rights Association (NICRA) was launched in Belfast with support from trade unions, community and campaigning groups, republican bodies and representatives of all the Northern Ireland political parties. (The Unionist Party delegate walked out of the initial meeting but the Executive Committee subsequently co-opted two young Unionists.) NICRA called, not for the abolition of the border, but for an end to collective discrimination against Catholics on voting, housing and employment, the repeal of the Special Powers Act (which gave police sweeping powers of search and arrest and the right to ban meetings or publications), the disbandment of the B-Specials and the disarming of the RUC.

In August 1968 NICRA organized the first civil rights march from Coalisland to Dungannon in support of the campaign already under way there. Though prevented by police from entering the town centre, and facing provocation from a loyalist counter-demonstration led by Rev Ian Paisley, the majority of the march remained nonviolent.

However, the event which catapulted the campaign into the headlines, and can be seen in retrospect as marking the beginning of the mass movement for civil rights, took place in Derry on 5 October 1968 when police baton-charged a banned but relatively small march of around 400

208 A GUIDE TO CIVIL RESISTANCE – VOLUME 2

people organized by the DHAC, with the backing of NICRA. Two weeks later 4,000 to 5,000 took part in a peaceful sitdown in Guildhall Square, this time organized by the newly-formed, and generally more middle-class and 'respectable', Derry Citizens Action Committee (DCAC), drawn mainly from people who had been active in the campaign over the siting of the university. The demonstration concluded with people singing 'We Shall Overcome'. On 16 November the DCAC engaged in civil disobedience for the first time, defying a ban to march to the city centre. Around 15,000 people took part and the police had no option but to allow them through and leave the maintenance of order in the hands of a well-trained body of marshals.

On November 22 the Stormont government, announced its intention to introduce a package of reforms and on December 9 Prime Minister Terence O'Neil made a passionate appeal for people to give him their support and allow time for the promised reforms to succeed. NICRA and DCAC announced a temporary suspension of marches, but others argued that what the government promised fell far short of what was needed and that it was vital to keep up the momentum. In January 1969 a civil rights march from Belfast to Derry, the 'Long March', organized by the Peoples Democracy (PD) campaign, based at Queen's University Belfast, was attacked by Protestant loyalists at Burntollet Bridge a few miles from Derry.

A subsequent PD march in Newry, Co. Down,was followed by rioting and damage to property. In March, the Northern Ireland government set up a Commission of Enquiry under Lord Cameron to inquire into the causes of the disturbances which concluded there had indeed been partisan law enforcement, the gerrymandering of local government boundaries, and discrimination in the areas of housing allocation, and local government employment. The report also criticized the police for failing to protect the PD marchers at Burntollet.

The point of no return came in Derry on 12 August 1969 following clashes between the Protestant Apprentice Boys March and residents of the Catholic Bogside area of the city. The Bogside came under siege from loyalists, largely backed by the RUC and B-Specials, an event which came to be known as The Battle of the Bogside. The rioting escalated and spread to Belfast on 14 August, where 150 Catholic homes were burned, eight people killed and hundreds injured. The British government sent troops into the province, who were initially welcomed by Catholics. But increasingly the troops were seen as serving the interests of the Unionist government. In this period too, 1969-70, there was a split in the Republican movement between the 'Officials' who had been pursuing a political, Marxist, strategy, and the breakaway 'Provisionals' who favoured a continuation and stepping up of a military campaign to defend Catholic areas and ultimately to end partition.

In August 1971 in face of armed attacks and bombings by the Provisional IRA and loyalist paramilitaries, the British government introduced internment. Over 2,400 people were arrested in the first six months, the majority of them in the initial phase from the Catholic/Nationalist community. Although most were soon released, internment further antagonized the community, and the newly formed (mainly Catholic) Social Democratic and Labour Party (SDLP) announced a campaign of civil disobedience, including a rent and rates strike. Many Catholics also withdrew from public bodies.

The last civil rights march took place in Derry in January 1972 when the British Army Parachute Regiment opened fire on unarmed demonstrators, killing 14 people and wounding many more. Bitterness in the Catholic/ Nationalist community at the 'Bloody Sunday' massacre was intensified when later that year an official Commission of Inquiry, under Lord Widgery, largely exonerated the army – though commenting that its firing on the demonstrators 'bordered on the reckless' – and concluded that the organizers of the march bore the main responsibility for what happened by creating a situation where confrontation was inevitable. In March of that year the Northern Ireland government resigned, Stormont was suspended and direct rule from Westminster under a Secretary of State imposed. Thereafter violence escalated.

Despite the descent of Northern Ireland into violence, the Civil Rights movement did draw world attention to the injustices suffered by the minority community and forced the Northern Ireland and British governments to introduce reforms. These included one-person-one-vote in local council elections (1969), the creation of Parliamentary and local commissioners for complaints (1969), the replacement of the B-Specials with the Ulster Defence Regiment (1970), the establishment of a new housing executive (1971), proportional representation in local and European elections (1972), local government reorganization (1972), and the Fair Employment Act (1976). The movement also produced a new generation of political leaders and who continued to press for more far-reaching political and constitutional changes including, increasingly, the abolition of the border.

There were a number of initiatives at an official level to end the conflict in the course of the 1970s. In 1973 the British Government set up the Northern Ireland Assembly whose members were elected by proportional representation. The Sunningdale Agreement in December of that year provided for the establishment of a power-sharing Executive, a Council of

Ireland (with representatives from both parts of Ireland) and, as a reassurance to the Protestant/Unionist community, reaffirmed that the constitutional status of Northern Ireland could only be changed with the consent of the majority in the Province. The Executive took office in January 1974 with ministers drawn from the Ulster Unionist Party, the SDLP and the Alliance Party. But the Agreement proved divisive. Provisional Sinn Fein and IRA rejected it and the latter continued their attacks. The Unionist party split on the issue, its leader, Brian Faulkner, resigned, and all the Unionist MPs at Westminster opposed it. Anti-Sunningdale Unionist candidates won 11 out of 12 Westminster seats with 51 per cent of the votes in the UK February 1974 general election. Finally a strike by the Ulster Workers Council, in which gas and electricity workers played a critical role, brought the Province to a standstill, led to the downfall of the Executive and a decision by the British government to suspend the Assembly.

In a sense the UWC strike was an impressive demonstration of civil resistance, but it was far from nonviolent as there was widespread intimidation by Protestant paramilitary groups to enforce the strike. It also coincided with bombings of civilian targets in Dublin and Monaghan by the Ulster Volunteer Force (UVF) in which 33 people were killed. However, the downfall of the power-sharing Executive was perhaps an indication that the time was not yet ripe for a cross party alliance of this kind to succeed and that the 'extremes' on all sides, including paramilitary groups, had somehow to be included in the peacemaking process.

For discussion of the UWC strike see:

784. Fisk, Robert, *The Point of No Return: The Strike which Broke the British in Ulster*, London, Times Books: Deutsch, 1975, pp. 264.

Detailed account by journalist of the strike and its political repercussions.

See also:

McCann, Eamonn, *War and an Irish Town,* (815 I.2.c.), pp.142-145.

McCann cites reports that Prime Minister Harold Wilson was set to order the army to confront the UWC but was informed that the army would refuse to obey such an order (p.144).

McKittrick, David and David McVea, *Making Sense of The Troubles,* Chapter 5: 'Sunningdale, Strike and Stalemate' (791 I.2.a.), pp. 98-117.

Nairn, Tom, *The Break-up of Britain*, Chapter 5, 'Northern Ireland: Relic or Portent?' (795 I.2.a.)

The author comments: 'It [the strike] was without doubt the most successful *political* action carried out by any European working class since the World War' (p. 242).

After Sunningdale, there was slow and fitful progress at the official level. In 1975 a Constitutional Convention made recommendations as to how the government of Northern Ireland should be constituted. In 1983 representatives of the four main constitutionalist nationalist parties in Northern Ireland and the Republic set up the New Ireland Forum to discuss ways forward to ending the Troubles. Its report published in May 1984 indicated greater flexibility on the part of nationalists with respect to constitutional changes, and paved the way for the Anglo-Irish Agreement of the following year which gave the Republic an advisory role in the government of Northern Ireland. In 1993 the British and Irish governments signed the Downing Street Declaration which set out the broad principles of a settlement, and this was followed five years later by the Good Friday Agreement (GFA) – also known as the Belfast Agreement – which re-established a Northern Ireland Assembly and power sharing Executive. The Agreement was endorsed in referendums in both Northern Ireland and the Republic. There was also an additional referendum in the Republic, in accordance with the terms of GFA, to approve the amendment of Articles 2 and 3 of its constitution so that the claim that its jurisdiction extended to Northern Ireland was relinquished. This too received overwhelming endorsement.

Among significant events at the grassroots level post the civil rights years were the formation of the cross-community Peace People initiated by Mairead Corrigan and Betty Williams in 1976, the hunger strikes in 1980-81 by republican prisoners demanding the reinstatement of their former Special Category Status, the election of the hunger strike leader, Bobby Sands, as MP for Fermanagh and South Tyrone shortly before his death, and subsequently the death of nine other hunger strikers, and a gradual shift away from a military policy by Provisional Sinn Fein and IRA, which twice instituted cease-fires in the 1990s, and finally in 2005 declared an end to the military campaign. This shift was occasioned in part by the evidence that the campaign had reached a dead end, and perhaps also by the fact that civilian campaigns such as the Smash H-Block campaign in support of the hunger-strikers, and the Bloody Sunday Justice Campaign in Derry showed the potential of mobilizing mass civilian action. The election to the Westminster Parliament of Bobby Sands who had become such an iconic figure in the republican movement and the wider Catholic/nationalist

212   A GUIDE TO CIVIL RESISTANCE – VOLUME 2

community – his funeral in Belfast was attended by 100,000 people – strengthened the position of those within Provisional Sinn Fein and IRA who favoured some level of engagement in conventional politics.

On the loyalist side, the Ulster Defence Association and its armed wing, the Ulster Freedom Fighters (UFF) called a ceasefire in 2004 and announced an end to its military operations in 2007. The other main loyalist paramilitary group, the Ulster Volunteer Force (UVF), responsible for some of the worst sectarian killings, announced a ceasefire in 1994 and, in 2007, an end to its military campaign, but it has subsequently been deemed responsible for fomenting riots, and for attacks on the police and rival paramilitary groups.

The political breakthrough, which virtually no-one had anticipated, came when Provisional Sinn Fein on the Republican side and the Ian Paisley's Democratic Unionist Party, (DUP) won the majority of seats in Assembly elections and agreed to form a power-sharing Executive in 2007, with Ian Paisley as First Minister and his former arch-opponent, Martin McGuinness, as his deputy.

Communal tensions have, however, persisted related particularly to marches, the flying of the Union Flag at City Hall, sporadic attacks by breakaway republican and loyalist paramilitaries and the legacy of unsolved killings during the Troubles. By the autumn of 2014, these issues, plus wrangles over the administration budget and the implementation of welfare changes, threatened the collapse of the Assembly and Executive and a return to direct rule from Westminster. However, after 11 weeks of talks involving the five main parties in Northern Ireland, and British and Irish governments, a deal was reached on 23 December which averted the collapse, secured a £2 billion grant from the British government to cushion the effects of cuts and welfare changes, and established commissions to consider the unresolved issues of marches and flags.

2.a. Historical Background and Political Perspectives

785. Bew, Paul, Peter Gibbon and Henry Patterson, *1921-1994: Political Forces and Social Classes*, London, Serif 1995, pp.253. Updated edition, *Northern Ireland 1921-2001*, Serif, 2002, pp. 274.

An extended historical interpretation from a Marxist perspective, which makes use of the large volume of archive material released in the 1970s. Focuses on the interaction of class and other economic and political factors in the conflict in Northern Ireland. Maintains that the divisions in the country made some form of partition inevitable, the issue at stake being what form it would take.

786. Curtis, Liz, *The Cause of Ireland: From the United Irishmen to Partition,* Belfast, Beyond the Pale Publications, 1994, pp.436.

A history of the period from a nationalist perspective with the stated aim of putting in context the divisions and conflict in Northern Ireland. A postscript notes briefly some of the political developments in the 1920s and 1930s including the introduction of the Special Powers Act in 1933 and the emergence of the civil rights movement in the 1960s.

787. Elliott, Marianne, *The Catholics of Ulster: A History,* London, Allen Lane, The Penguin Press, 2000, pp. 642.

A major study looking at the history of Catholics in Ulster from the Anglo-Norman invasion of Ireland in 1169 to the signing of the Belfast agreement in 1998. The author, who defines herself an 'Ulster Catholic', takes a fresh look at the attitudes, assumption and convictions of the Catholic community, and at some of the causes of sectarian division. She notes that there has been a return of self-confidence among Ulster Catholics since the signing of the GFA and that the overwhelming majority of them support the constitutional arrangement based on majority consent.

788. English, Richard, *Armed Struggle: The History of the IRA,* [Macmillan, 2003], Pan Books 2012, pp.544, pb.

The chapters in this history of the IRA which deal with the gradual shift in the position of Provisional Sinn Fein and IRA, their engagement in the political process through discussions with both the rival nationalist SDLP and the British government, and their eventual decision to end the military campaign, provide valuable insights into the dynamics of the peace process in Northern Ireland. The final chapter subjects the republican case to critical – though not unsympathetic – scrutiny but rejects the contention that the struggle was in any straightforward sense an anti-colonial one or that its religious dimension can be ignored.

789. Farrell, Michael, *Northern Ireland: The Orange State,* London, Pluto Press, 1976 & 1980, pp.406.

A history of Northern Ireland, and socialist political analysis of the causes of the conflict there, by a leading civil rights campaigner and founding member of People's Democracy. He concludes that the choice in Ireland is 'between, on the one hand, a semi-fascist Orange statelet in the North, matched by a pro-imperialist police state in the South, and, on the other hand, an anti-imperialist and socialist revolution'.

790. McGarry, John & Brendan O'Leary, *Explaining Northern Ireland*, Oxford, Blackwell, [1995] 1996, pp. 533.

Critical examination of both Nationalist and Unionist accounts of the causes of the conflict. Authors distinguish broadly between explanations that focus on external factors – the policies of British and Irish governments – and those that identify the internal factors of religion, culture and ethnicity in Northern Irish society. They reject the proposition that the conflict is fundamentally a religious one, and are sceptical not only of the various Marxist accounts – Orange, Green and 'Red' – but of the essentially materialist accounts by many liberal commentators. While acknowledging the multiplicity of causal factors, they view the conflict as essentially one between groups which identify themselves along different national, ethnic and religious lines, though they hold out the hope of an accommodation between them to produce an 'agreed', though not necessarily a united, Ireland.

791. McKittrick, David and David McVea, *Making Sense of The Troubles*, Belfast, The Blackstaff Press, 2000. Revised edition, London, Viking, 2012, pp.404.

Coverage of major events during the Troubles. Includes a useful chronology and an account of the Ulster Workers Council strike in 1974. . The revised 2012 edition also covers political developments in Northern Ireland since the origonal publication including the historic power-sharing agreement between the DUP and Sinn Féin in 2007.

792. Miller, David ed,, *Rethinking Northern Ireland: Culture, Ideology and Colonialism*, London, Longman,1988; Abingdon, Routledge, 1998,pp.344, pb.

Aims, in words of editor, 'to give its readers a reasonably broad critical introduction to the Northern Ireland conflict'. Most of the 13 contributors to the book are academics working in the field of sociology, politics and media studies, plus writers and journalists. The thrust of the argument in the book is that the conflict needs to be understood as an anti-colonial struggle, not as a religious or ethnic one, and that tackling the inequalities brought about by colonialism is the key to securing a lasting peace.

793. Murphy, Dervla, *A Place Apart*, Harmondsworth, Penguin Books, [1978] 1980, pp 300, pb.

Records the experiences of this distinguished Irish travel writer during her cycling tour of Northern Ireland in 1976-77. Briefly recapitulates the historical background to the Troubles, and re-examines the rival myths and prejudices of the Protestant and Catholic communities, both of whom warmly welcomed her while remaining suspicious of each other. Informed by genuine affection for the people of Northern Ireland and an optimism about its future in the longer term though discounting the possibility of a united Ireland.

794, Murphy, Dervla, *Changing the Problem: Post Forum Reflections,* Lilliput Pamphlets No. 3, Gigglestown: Lilliput 1984.

Puts the case, following the publication of the report of the New Ireland Forum, for an independent Northern Ireland

795, Nairn, Tom, *The Break-up of Britain,* London, Verso, 1981, pp. 409. (First published New Left Books, 1977), pb.

Marxist analysis of the political and economic factors leading to a resurgence of national consciousness in the constituent parts of the UK. In a chapter on Ireland, he rejects what he sees as the oversimplified imperialist analysis of Ireland's situation by Irish nationalists and some fellow Marxists from Connolly to Farrell. Argues the case for an independent Northern Ireland.

796. O'Brien, Conor Cruise, *States of Ireland,* London, Hutchinson, 1972, pp. 336. Republished by Faber & Faber, 2015, pb.

Mixture of history, personal memoir and analysis by this Irish academic, writer and statesman. In chapter 8, 'Civil Rights: the Crossroads' (pp. 147-77) he argues that the campaign of civil disobedience begun by the civil rights movement in 1968 was bound in the context of Northern Ireland's deeply divided society to increase sectarianism and lead to violence. Defends Partition on the grounds that the alternative would have been a much bloodier civil war than the one that occurred in the South in 1922-23. Cites a loyalty survey conducted by Richard Rose in 1968 to dismiss as unrealistic the proposition that the Catholic and Protestant working class might unite in a struggle against a common class enemy and create a workers' republic in a united Ireland.

797. O Connor, Fionnuala, *In Search of a State: Catholics in Northern Ireland,* Belfast, The Blackstaff Press, 1993, pp. 393.

Investigation of the convictions and sense of identity of people in the Catholic Community in Northern Ireland based on recorded interviews with fifty-five individuals – not all of them necessarily practising Catholics – about their political allegiances, their relationship with Protestants, and their attitude to the IRA, Britain, Southern Ireland and the Church.

798. O'Dowd, Liam, Bill Rolston and Mike Tomlinson, *Northern Ireland: Between Civil Rights and Civil War*, London, CSE Books, 1980, pp.232

Examination from a socialist perspective of key issues by three Northern Ireland academics. Includes a chapter on the reform of the RUC in the 1970s.

799. Porter, Norman, *Rethinking Unionism: An Alternative Vision for Northern Ireland*, Belfast, The Blackstaff Press, [1996], 1998, pp. 252, pb.

Advocates a 'civic unionism' which acknowledges both the Britishness and Irishness of Northern Ireland. To quote from the Preface it 'accommodates questions of cultural identity, liberal emphases on the entitlements of individuals and a substantive understanding of politics in which the practice of dialogue is central'.

800. Rose, Richard, *Governing Without Consensus, An Irish Perspective*, London, Faber & Faber, 1971, pp.567; paperback edition, Beacon Press, 1971.

Standard and frequently cited work by an American political scientist based in Britain. Charts the origins and development of the divided community in Northern Ireland since the foundation of the state, and considers the problems of governance it gives rise to. Includes a discussion of the civil rights movement. Sees no immediately practicable solution to the problem and draws a comparison with the race problems in the United States. The analysis is supported by data from an extensive social survey of public opinion and informal discussions with people active in Northern Ireland politics.

801. Rowthorn, Bob & Naomi Wayne, *Northern Ireland: The Political Economy of Conflict*, Cambridge, Polity Press in association with Blackwell, 1988, pp.208, pb.

Analysis of the causes of conflict in Northern Ireland, dealing mainly with the period from partition to the Anglo-Irish Agreement of 1985, though with a brief survey of the longer historical background. Pays greater attention than the majority of accounts to economic and class factors.

802. Whyte, John, *Interpreting Northern Ireland*, Foreword by Garret Fitzgerald, Oxford, Clarendon Press, 1990, pp.328, pb.

Reviews the principal interpretations of the causes of conflict in Northern Ireland, including various Nationalist, Unionist and Marxist accounts, and proposed solutions. Concludes that both the traditional nationalist and traditional unionist interpretations had lost their popularity over the previous 20 years to be replaced by one prioritizing internal causes. Points also to the serious disagreements among Marxist commentators but acknowledges the major contribution a number of them, including McCann, Farrell, Bew, Gibbon and Patterson, have made to the literature, Suggests a new paradigm may be needed which, among other things, would take account of the contrast between different parts of Northern Ireland where areas only a few miles apart can differ enormously 'in religious mix, in economic circumstances, in the level of violence, in political attitudes.'

803. Whyte, John, 'How Much Discrimination Was There under the Unionist Regime, 1921-72?'in Gallagher, Tom and James O'Connell, eds., *Contemporary Irish Studies*, Manchester, Manchester University Press, 1983, pb., pp.1-35.

Detached assessment of the evidence. Concludes that while discrimination against Catholics in this period certainly existed, it was more marked in some policy areas than others – more marked in electoral practices (especially at local government level), public employment and policing, generally less so in private employment, public housing and regional policy. But he notes that geographically, also, there were marked differences, with discrimination being more widespread in the west, which had a higher Catholic population.

2.b The Search for a Settlement: the political process

804. Fay, Marie Therese, Mike Morrissey and Marie Smyth, *Northern Ireland's Troubles: The Human Costs*, London, Stirling, Virginia, Pluto Press, 1999, pp.229. pb.

Part I of this book sets out the context of the conflict in Northern Ireland, including a chronology of key events from the opening of the first Parliament there in 1921 to the Provisionl IRA ceasefire in September 1998, considers political, social and economic facets of the conflict, and reviews the principal interpretations of its causes. Part II examines the effects of the violence on individuals and groups and argues the need to address them if there is to be peace in the longer term.

805. Fearon, Kate, 'Northern Ireland Women's Coalition: institutionalizing a political voice and ensuring representation', in *Accord*, issue 13, 2002, pp.78-81. (*Accord* is published by the London-based Conciliation Resources. Issue 13 was entitled 'Owning the process: Public Participation in Peacemaking', edited by Catherine Barnes.)

The Northern Ireland Women's Coalition (NIWC) was initiated by women of various political affiliations, religious beliefs and occupations. It was institutionalized as a political party in 1996 so that its members would be eligible to take part in the all-party talks that culminated in the Good Friday Agreement. It also campaigned for the acceptance of the GFA in the referendums which followed its signing.

806. Hennessey, Thomas, *The Northern Ireland Peace Process: Ending the Troubles?*, Dublin, Gill & Macmillan, 2000, pp. 256.

Detailed account by an academic historian who acted as special advisor to the Unionist Party of the negotiations that led to the signing of the Good Friday Agreement of 1998. The author comments in the Introduction that 'what complicated the Northern Ireland conflict was the range of options which the central protagonists – Unionists and Nationalists – viewed as their preferred solution.' Historically, he states 'the Ulster Question has been a dispute concerning sovereignty and identity. Or to put it another way, it has been a dispute between states and nations. But neither Unionists nor Nationalists could agree which states were legitimate or the legitimacy of the opposing group's national identity'.

807. Irwin, Colin, *The People's Peace Process in Northern Ireland*, Basingstoke, Palgrave Macmillan 2002, pp 326.

Discusses the lessons learned from the negotiations leading to the Good Friday Agreement. Describes how opinion polls were used by politicians to explore what compromises their supporters might accept.

808. McCartney, Clem, ed., *Striking a Balance: The Northern Ireland Peace Process*, in *Accord*, Issue 8, 1999, London, Conciliation Resources.

Accounts of peace process from perspectives of various parties involved, including several members of the then recently formed Northern Ireland Executive. Clem McCartney writes on 'The Role of Civil Society' and Monica McWilliams and Kate Fearon of the Northern Ireland Women's Coalition on 'Problems of Implementation'.

809. McEvoy, Joanne, *Power-Sharing Executives:Governing in Bosnia, Macedonia, and Northern Ireland*, PA, University of Pennsylvania Press, 2014, pp. 288.

Comparative study of power sharing-initiatives, analyzing the different approaches in each case and the role of external actors. Author argues that the experience in Northern Ireland, despite many setbacks and false starts, has been relatively positive, though threatened by the rioting and quarrels that followed the decision in December 2010 to fly the Union flag at Stormont only on special occasions rather than every day as had previously been the case.

810. McEvoy, Joanne, *The Politics of Northern Ireland*, Politics Study Guides, Edinburgh, Edinburgh University Press, 2008, pp. 194, pb.

Discusses competing theoretical perspectives on the causes of the conflict and the political parties and paramilitaries involved. Records the various reforms and constitutional initiatives from the 1970s to the 1990s to find a settlement which culminated in the Good Friday Agreement, the setting up of a power-sharing Executive and Assembly, and finally, following the suspension of the Assembly between 2002 and 2007, the agreement between the DUP and Sinn Fein to co-operate in a power-sharing government.

811. Murray, Dominic, ed., *Protestant Perceptions of the Peace Process in Northern Ireland*, Limerick: Centre for Peace and Development Studies, University of Limerick, 2000, pp.173.

Contributions from Northern Ireland Protestants with backgrounds in politics, the media, education, religion and community work. Murray, himself from a nationalist background, stresses the importance of contesting the widely held view in the Republic of Ireland and beyond that the Unionist population of Northern Ireland is a homogeneous group, which is both intransigent and obstructive. His intention as editor, he states, is to illuminate the diversity which exists in the unionist community.

812. Tonge, Jonathan, *The New Northern Irish Politics.*, Basingstoke, Palgrave Macmillan, 2005, pp. 282.

Analyses the strengths and weaknesses of the constitutional arrangements embodied in the Good Friday Agreement. Argues that despite the difficult concessions unionists had to make, the GFA was a triumph for them politically since it embodied the principle of consent for any constitutional change in the province and the amendment of Articles 2 and 3 of the Republic's constitution. Rejects the proposition that the separate referendums on the GFA in Northern Ireland and the Irish Republic amounted to a genuine exercise in Irish self-determination, but expresses cautious optimism that the void left by 'the demise of traditional republicanism' can be filled within the broader EU context by a growing bi-nationalism and diminution of the north-south border.

2.c. Action at the Grassroots

Political reform and the moves towards a settlement were initially driven by grassroots mobilizations and campaigns. Chief among these campaigning organizations, as noted earlier, were the Derry Housing Action Committee and the Derry Citizens Action Campaign, the Northern Ireland Civil Rights Association and the more left wing People's Democracy (PD). There were also some later rights' campaigns, which are dealt with under 2.c.ii, and initiatives, and campaigns aimed specifically at ending inter-communal, paramilitary and state violence which are dealt with under c.iii

2.c.i Civil Rights Movement 1968-1973

813. Arthur, Paul, *The People's Democracy 1968-1973*, Belfast, Blackstaff Press, 1974, pp. 159.

Author was active in PD, but this nonetheless is a dispassionate and sometimes critical account of the movement, which had its origins among student activists at Queens University Belfast in 1968. Recounts internal debates and divisions and shows how PD moved from being a purely civil rights campaign to taking a radical socialist position, and campaigning for a workers' republic in a re-united Ireland.

814. Devlin, Bernadette, *The Price of My Soul*, London, Pan, 1969, pp. 206, pb.

Autobiography of one of the most dynamic student leaders of the civil rights movement. Recounts the emergence of People's Democracy (PD) at Queen's University Belfast, and includes vivid first-hand accounts of the August 1968 March in Derry, and the Belfast to Derry march by PD in January 1969 which was ambushed by a loyalist mob at Burntollet. Also recounts Devlin's election to the Westminster Parliament in April1969, her frustration at the limits to her power as an MP, and her participation in the Battle of the Bogside in August of that year.

815. McCann, Eamonn, *War and an Irish Town*, London, Pluto, 1980, pp. 176. (first edition published by Penguin 1974).

Describes the genesis of the civil rights and housing action campaign in Derry in which he played a leading role, and the civil rights march through the city in October 1968, which was attacked by the RUC and is now widely regarded as marking the start of the Troubles. Analyzes subsequent political developments from a radical socialist perspective and argues that the solution to the conflict lies in the creation of an all-Ireland workers' republic. Critical of what he regards as the apolitical stance of NICRA , and of the later Women Together and Peace People campaigns. McCann took part in the Battle of the Bogside in 1969 and the civil rights march in Derry on Bloody Sunday. Argues that there is war in Ireland ' because capitalism, to establish and preserve itself, created conditions which made war inevitable.'

816. McCluskey, Conn, *Up Off Their Knees: A Commentary on the Civil Rights Movement in Northern Ireland*, Republic of Ireland, ConnMcCkuskey & Associates, 1989, pp. 245, pb.

Account of origins and development of the movement by an activist who played a key role in its foundation.

817. O'Dochartaigh, Niall, *From Civil Rights to Armalites: Derry and the Birth of the Irish Troubles*, Cork, Cork University Press, 1997, & Palgrave Macmillan, 2005, pp.332, pb.

Describes the trajectory of resistance from largely nonviolent demonstrations, modeled on the US Civil Rights movement, to riots and finally to virtual civil war in Derry/Londonderry. O'Dochartaigh subscribes to the view that in conditions of civil disorder and conflict 'the local environment becomes ever more important as a focus of political activity.' A central thesis of the book is that 'occasions of violent confrontation play a crucial role in promoting the escalation and continuation of conflict'.

818. Prince, Simon and Geoffrey Warner, *Belfast and Derry in Revolt*, Dublin, Irish Academic Press, 2012, pp. 271.

Detailed account of the beginnings of the Troubles in these two cities. Argues that 5 October 1968, the date of the first civil rights march in Derry, which was attacked by the RUC and a loyalist mob, has a strong claim to be 'the second most significant date in Irish history' – after Easter week 1916.

819. Purdie, Bob, *Politics in the Streets: The Origins of the Civil Rights Movement in Northern Ireland*, Belfast, Blackstaff, 1990, pp. 286.

Argues that the movement made a strategic error in taking to the streets because of the connection between street demonstrations and sectarian conflict in Northern Ireland. Although activists drew inspiration from the US Civil Rights Movement they did not, in his view, take sufficient account of the different circumstances in the two countries.

2.c.ii. Later Campaigns for Rights

820. Campbell, Juleann, *Setting the Truth Free: The Inside Story of the Bloody Sunday Justice Campaign*, Dublin, Liberties Press, 2014, pp.256, pb.

Detailed account of the campaign set up by the families of the 13 people killed, and 14 injured, on 'Bloody Sunday' in Derry in 1972. The campaign set up in 1992 succeeded, in the face of intransigence by the British authorities and indifference or open hostility of many others, in forcing the government to institute a new inquiry under Lord Justice Saville. This concluded in 2010 that the demonstrators had been unarmed, that no stones or petrol bombs had been thrown and that the civilians were not posing any threat. British Prime Minister David Cameron made a public apology in Parliament, describing the killings as 'unjustified and unjustifiable.' The book is written by the niece of one of those who was killed, and includes the testimonies of eyewitnesses, and a foreword by the leading civil rights lawyer, Garreth Pierce.

821. Farrell, Michael, *Twenty Years On*, Dingle, Brandon, 1988, pp.192, pb.

Contributions by nine activists who had been involved in the Civil Rights movement in 1968. Contributors include Gerry Adams on his experiences as a republican in the civil rights campaign and the Provisionals'case for splitting with what became Official Sinn Fein and IRA; Bernadette (Devlin) McAliskey on her time in the British Parliament which she entitles 'a peasant in the halls of the great', and Michael Farrell on the 'Long March' from Belfast to Derry in January 1969 and subsequent developments. Carol Coulter describes the reverberations of the campaign in the South and Margaret Ward its influence in the development of feminism in Ireland.

822. Garvaghy Residents, *Garvaghy: A Community Under Siege*, Belfast, Beyond the Pale, 1999, pp. 171, pb.

Garvaghy Road, a Catholic area in mainly Protestant Portadown, has been the scene of confrontations down the years during the annual Orange Order parade on the weekend before 12 July, following a service in Drumcree Church. The Orange Order claims the right to march along the road; the residents say that they face abuse and violence when this happens and that there are alternative routes the parade could take. Resistance to the event has included sit-downs, a women's Peace and Justice Camp and the setting up of Radio Equality. Part 1 of the book is based mainly on the diaries of residents in July 1998 when the parade was banned and police and soldiers erected barricades and dug trenches to prevent the march from entering the road. Part 2 is an edited version of the Residents' submission in 1996 to the Parades Commission.

823. Ross, Stuart, F, *Smashing H-Block: The Popular Campaign Against Criminalization and the Irish Hunger Strikes 1976-1982.* Liverpool, University of Liverpool Press, 2011, pp.226.

In contrast to most accounts of the anti H-block campaign, this book focuses on the popular campaign outside the prison for the restoration of 'Special Category Status', originally accorded to both republican and loyalist prisoners in 1972 but phased out by the Labour Home Secretary, Merlyn Rees, in 1976. Ross maintains that the campaign that grew around the hunger strikes of 1981 and 1982 was 'perhaps the biggest and broadest solidarity movement since Vietnam', much of it driven from the bottom up by the republican grassroots, not its leadership. He also suggests that it propelled the Provisional IRA towards calling a ceasefire and shifting to a political strategy.

2.c.iii The Peace People and other initiatives to end the violence

The growing tension between the Protestant and Catholic communities in the 1970s and the rising violence by both republican and loyalist paramilitary groups led to a number of attempts to halt the violence and promote reconciliation, for example Witness for Peace created by a Protestant clergyman in 1972, and Women Together founded in 1970 to stop stone throwing and gang fights. But the most publicized and controversial campaign against violence was that of the Peace People, founded in 1976 after three young children were killed by a runaway IRA car whose driver had been shot by the army. Two women initiated the movement, Protestant Betty Williams, who saw the tragedy, and Catholic Mairead Corrigan, the children's aunt. The Peace People brought 10,000 and then 20,000 out onto the streets in Belfast in August, and 25,000 in Derry in September to demand an end to paramilitary violence. These demonstrations were followed by rallies and public events in more than a dozen towns and cities in Northern Ireland, the Irish Republic and Britain. By November 1976 the Peace People had over 80 local groups, offices in both Belfast and Derry and its own paper, *Peace by Peace.* The movement was criticized, especially by Provisional Sinn Fein, for its initial failure to condemn violence by the British Army and the Protestant-dominated RUC, and attacked by the militant Protestant leader of the Democratic Unionist Party, Ian Paisley, as a Catholic front. Over time, under the influence of the third key figure in the movement, former journalist Ciaran McKeown, the Peace People turned to long-term community organizing. See its website: http://www.peacepeople.com

Two periodicals which ran articles on the Peace People from a nonviolent perspective are *Peace News* (London) and the monthly *Dawn* (published by a collective from Belfast, Derry and Dublin). In the latter, see especially issues no. 25 (November 1976), the editorial on the Peace People leadership in no. 26 (Christmas 1976), and the analysis of Peace People strategy in nos. 27 and 28 (January and February 1977). *Dawn* also published a combined issue, 'Nonviolence in Irish History', no. 38-39, (April-May 1978), which traced nonviolence in Ireland back to the arrival of the Quakers in the 17th century, through the campaign of Daniel O'Connell for Catholic Emancipation, the Land League agitation in the 19th century and nonviolent elements in the national and labour movements (late 19th and early 20th centuries) to the Peace People.

824. Cory, Geoffrey, 'Political dialogue workshops: Deepening the peace process in Northern Ireland', *Conflict Resolution Quarterly*, Vol 30, Issue 1, 2012, pp. 53-80.

The author discusses the more than fifty residential three-day political dialogue workshops he facilitated between 1994 and 2007 at the Glencree Centre for Reconciliation near Dublin that brought together politicians from all parties in Britain and Ireland during the period of peace negotiations in Northern Ireland.

825. Deutsch, Richard, *Mairead Corrigan, Betty Williams*, Woodbury NY, Barrons, 1977, pp. 204. Foreword by Joan Baez.

Account of the genesis, development and programme of the Peace People by French journalist resident in Belfast at the time the movement began.

826. McKeown, Ciaran, *The Passion of Peace*, Belfast, Blackstaff Press, 1984, pp. 320.

McKeown was one of the group of student activists campaigning on civil rights issues at Queens University Belfast in the mid-1960s from which People's Democracy emerged in 1968. However, he opposed the Belfast to Derry march in January 1969 as likely to inflame sectarian divisions, and the Marxist direction to which the organization turned. Best known for his leading role in the Peace People whose origins and development he recounts in detail. Sets out his idea for a parliamentary system based not on political parties but on autonomous community groups.

827. O Connor, Fionnuala, 'Community politics in Northern Ireland', in Michael Randle, ed., *Challenge to Nonviolence*, Bradford, University of Bradford, 2002, pp. 207-22.pb.

Text of a talk given in June 1997 to the Nonviolent Research Project at Bradford University.. Discusses the development of community level political engagement and the vision of Ciaron McKeown of the Peace People that it could someday provide an alternative to the existing political system. She argues that Community politics up to that time (1997) was more developed in the Catholic/Nationalist community than in that of the Protestant/Unionist one but there too it had emerged in the previous five years or so. Former members of paramilitary groups were frequently involved because they had come to see the futility of the violence or because they wanted their own children to have a different life to the one they had experienced.

828. Overy, Bob, *How Effective Are Peace Movements?* Bradford School of Peace Studies and London, Housmans, 1982, pp. 78, pb.

Includes a sympathetic analysis of the Peace People pp. 30-38.

829. Wells, Ronald A, *People Behind the Peace: Community and Reconciliation in Northern Ireland,* Grand Rapids, Michigan, Eerdmans Pub, 1999. pp. 126.

Focuses on the contribution to the peace process in the lead-up to the 1998 Good Friday Agreement of three ecumenical Christian peace centres in Northern Ireland – the Corrymeela Community, the Christian Renewal Centre, and the Columbanus Community. The author, in contrast to the majority of commentators, identifies religious differences as the main cause of the conflict, though he argues that religion can be 'both cause of and cure for social conflict'.

J. Preparation and Training for Nonviolent Action

Movements that expect their nonviolent actions to be met with violence, and are concerned to avoid violent reactions by their own activists, often try to prepare themselves for such confrontations. However, nonviolence training has come to involve much more than that – a range of activities embracing personal empowerment, group formation, campaign planning, strategy development, and preparation and evaluation of protests.

Preparation for nonviolent action can be understood as part of a wider nonviolent lifestyle. Gandhi, who stressed the need for self-discipline, believed it would best be acquired through taking part in constructive activities. Today's activists are more likely to stress the importance of empowerment for engaging in nonviolent action. But they also see this as an attitude underpinning everyday behaviour.

Many materials used in nonviolent training overlap with other types of workshops – conflict transformation, pedagogy of the oppressed (Paolo Freire), theatre of the oppressed (Agosto Boal), nonviolent communication (Marshall Rosenberg), or the Alternatives to Violence programmes on institutional and domestic violence. Nonviolent action training has evolved, depending on what seems useful and practical in diverse contexts. Therefore workshop leaders have been eclectic in choosing and developing methods, using whatever works in their experience and culture.

This section does not cover all aspects of preparation, such as the technical practicalities of some forms of protest (tripods, lock-ons); nor does it cover legal issues. But two relevant sources for these are:

830. *Network for Climate Action: Guides to Taking Action* at: http://www.networkforclimateaction.org.uk which provides practical manuals on different types of protest, e.g. climbing fences, blockading.

831. Van der Zee, Bibi, *Rebel, Rebel: How to Start a Revolution*, London, Guardian Books, 2008, which is designed for British readership and gives legal as well as other practical advice.

I. Planning and Development of Campaigns

832. Martin, Brian, *Backfire Manual: Tactics Against Injustice*, available at:www.bmartin.cc/pubs/12bfm/12bfm.pdf

A guide to turning an opponent's violence to the campaign's advantage. For the wider theoretical analysis see: Martin, *Justice Ignited: The Dynamics of Backfire* (Introduction, 1.c.).

833. Moyer, Bill (with JoAnn McAllister, Mary Lou Finley, and Steven Soifer), *Doing Democracy: The MAP Model for Organizing Social Movements*, Gabriola Island, New Society Publishers, 2001, pp. 228.

From his central insight that some movements could not recognise when they were succeeding , Bill Moyer constructed his model MAP – Movement Action Plan -as a tool for strategic analysis for nonviolent movements. The book includes case studies of five US movements: civil rights, anti-nuclear energy, gay and lesbian, breast cancer and anti-globalization.

834. Rose, Chris, *How to Win Campaigns: 100 Steps to Success*, London, Earthscan, 2005, pp. 231.

Tips from an environmental campaigner and communications consultant who has worked for Greenpeace, among other organizations.

835. Shaw, Randy, *The Activist's Handbook: Winning Social Change in the 21st Century*, Berkeley CA, University of California Press, [2007] 2013 (2nd edition), pp. 304.

Urban activist focuses on how to achieve social change even in difficult environments.

836. *Turning the Tide*, Quaker Peace and Social Witness, London.

Information sheets on preparing for nonviolent action and nonviolent training resources and links to organizations offering training. Online at: http://www.turning-the-tide.org/resources

837. War Resisters' International, *Handbook for Nonviolent Campaigns*, 2nd edition, 2014, pp.232. Order from: http://www.wri-irg.org

Sections on 'Introduction to Nonviolence', 'Developing Strategic Campaigns', 'Organising Effective Actions', 'Case Studies' with examples from round the world, 'Training and Exercises' and advice on compiling one's own handbook and lists of helpful manuals, references and websites.

See also: Taylor, *Blockade: A Guide to Nonviolent Intervention* (545 D.5.) Part 2 is a manual for direct action.

228 A GUIDE TO CIVIL RESISTANCE – VOLUME 2

The Ruckus Society offers manuals and checklists on 'Action Planning', 'Media' and other topics, plus numerous links to other web pages. See: http://www.ruckus.org

2. Training for Nonviolent Action

838. Beck, Sanderson, *Nonviolent Action Handbook*, Goleta CA, World Peace Communications, 2002, pp. 95. Introductory texts, downloadable or as print copies from: World Peace Communications, 495 Whitman St, Goleta, CA 93117, USA. Online: http://www.san.beck.org/NAH-Contents. html

839. Desai, Narayan, *Handbook for Satyagrahis: A Manual for Volunteers of Total Revolution*, New Delhi, Gandhi Peace Foundation, 1980, pp. 57.

The founder of the Institute for Total Revolution outlines a Gandhian approach to nonviolence training.

840. Fisher, Simon, Dekha Ibrahin Abdi, Jawed Ludin, Richard Williams, Steven Smith and Sue Williams, *Working With Conflict: Skills and Strategies for Action*, London, Zed, 2000, pp. 185.

Includes exercises and advice on active nonviolence.

841. Hunter, Daniel and George Lakey, *Opening Space for Democracy: Training Manual for Third-Party Nonviolent Intervention*, Philadelphia PA, Training for Change, 2004. Much of this book can be downloaded from: http://www.training forchange.org

Devised as a training resource for the Nonviolent Peace Force, this manual contains hundreds of training activities, with special emphasis on team-building and defending human rights. It includes over 60 handouts, an integrated 23 day curriculum, and many tips for trainers.

842. Miller, Christopher A., *Strategic Nonviolent Conflict: A Training Manual*, Addis Ababa, University of Peace Africa Programme, 2006, pp. 142. Downloadable at: www.africa.upeace/org/resources.cfm

A manual derived mainly from writings and approach of Gene Sharp, Robert Helvey and Peter Ackerman and directed at an African audience.

843. Nonviolent Training Project, *Nonviolent Trainers Resources Manual*, Melbourne, 1995, pp. 211. Downloadable from: http://www.nonviolence.org.au

Wide ranging manual with sections on: 'Defining nonviolence', 'Power and conflict', 'Learning from other movements', 'Strategic frameworks',

'Nonviolence and communication', 'Working in groups', 'Preparing for nonviolent action'.

844. The Seeds for Change Network at: http://www.seedsforchange.org.uk Offers variety of workshops from practical organizing skills to action preparation. Although their own writing does not use the term nonviolence, their web page includes material on nonviolence reproduced from Turning the Tide.

See also: War Resisters' International, Handbook for Nonviolent Campaigns (837 J.1.) pp. 189-222.

Selected Titles on Nonviolent Action
and Movements:
in French, German and Spanish

Introduction

The purpose of this section is to indicate the existence of important works on the theory and practice of nonviolence and civil resistance in other languages and provide a preliminary introduction to key authors and titles in three major European languages.

It is designed partly to inform all those who might be interested, but in particular for those whose first language is not English and might find French, German or Spanish books and articles easier to read.

The French section includes works by Lanza del Vasto, an exponent of Gandhian nonviolence, and by two leading scholars in the field: Jean-Marie Muller and Jacques Semelin. The German titles include publications by Hildegard Goss-Mayr, who through the International Fellowship of Reconciliation played a key role (with her husband Jean Goss) in promoting nonviolent resistance to repressive regimes; and longstanding scholars of civil resistance, for example Theodor Ebert, as well as more recent theorists such as Martin Arnold, are also represented. The Spanish list includes titles from a significant literature on civil disobedience, and its expression in the major movement of resistance to conscription ('insumision') from 1988-2000. There is some cross-referencing between sections: for example Muller is listed in Spanish translation, and del Vasto and Semelin in German.

All literatures draw on the historical evolution of ideas of nonviolent resistance, for example the writings of Etienne de la Boetie on the potential of non-cooperation, Henry David Thoreau on civil disobedience, Tolstoy on refusal to cooperate with war and violence, and above all Gandhi's development of a theory and strategy of 'satyagraha'.

The Dutch anti-militarist Bart de Ligt wrote on the potential of mass noncooperation and defiance in the context of the 1930s in his influential

Conquest of Violence. More recently Gene Sharp's highly influential works elaborating on the potential of nonviolent action to overthrow repressive regimes have been widely translated from English – in particular his pamphlet *From Dictatorship to Democracy*, translated into 33 languages, including Spanish.

The titles in all three languages focus primarily on the theory of nonviolence and in particular the theory, strategy and methods of civil resistance (including civil disobedience), drawing on examples from a range of movements. In addition they list selected titles on Gandhi and the concept of nonviolent civilian defence (topics covered in the introductory section of Volume 1 of this Guide). A much more extended list of titles, also covering a wider range of movements using methods of nonviolent action, will in due course be available on our website: http://civilresistance.info

French Titles

Compiled by Veronique Dudouet

Theory, Methods and Examples

Bové, José et Gilles Luneau, *Pour la désobéissance civique*, Paris: La Découverte, 2004. pp.260.

This essay by leading politician and activist Bové and journalist Luneau traces the world history of civil disobedience and explains its current relevance.

Cervera-Marzal, Manuel, *Désobéir en démocratie: la pensée désobéissante de Thoreau à Martin Luther King*, Paris: Aux forges de Vulcain, 2013, pp.170.

Largely based on the author's PhD thesis, this book analyses three historical approaches to civil disobedience, from conservative and liberal philosophies to the applied theory of disobedience derived from Gandhi and Martin Luther King.

del Vasto, Lanza, *Technique de la Nonviolence*. Paris: Gallimard, 1988, pp.280.

Originally written in 1974, this essay explores the philosophy and strategy of nonviolence inspired by the author's meeting with Gandhi in 1937, and applies it to environmental and solidarity struggles as well as in the daily life of the Arch communities, which he founded across France.

La Boetie, Etienne, *Discours de la servitude volontaire*, Paris: Flammarion, 1983 (there are several editions), pp.217.

Renowned philosophical treatise on civil disobedience against tyranny, written by a young disciple of Montaigne in 1548.

Maurel, Olivier. *La non-violence active, 100 questions pour résister et agir*, Paris: Ed. La Plage, 2001, pp.121.

Manual presenting nonviolent strategies and tactics being used in contemporary environmental or social rights campaigns in France.

Mellon, Christian et Jacques Semelin. *La non-violence*, Paris: Presse Universitaire de France, 1994, pp128.

The authors offer a definition of nonviolence and its main components, before reviewing the history of nonviolent struggles as well as the past and future research agenda on civil resistance.

Muller, Jean-Marie, *Stratégie de l'action non-violente*, Paris: Le Seuil, Col. Points Politique, 1981, pp.256 [translations in Italian, Spanish, Polish, Croatian and Arabic].

This book has become a key reference on the subject-matter of nonviolent action, and notably was circulated clandestinely in Poland after 1981.

Muller, Jean-Marie, *Le Dictionnaire de la non-violence*, Paris: Le Relie de poche, 2005, pp. 410.

This encyclopaedia by leading French theorist compiles and analyses key words in the philosophy of nonviolence, as well as strategic components for effective nonviolent action.

Muller, Jean-Marie. *Le principe de non-violence*, Parcours philosophique, Paris: Desclée de Brouwer, 1995, pp.328. [translations in Portuguese, Italian and English].

The goal of this book is to develop a philosophical concept of nonviolence, aiming to challenge the ideology that violence is necessary, legitimate and honourable.

Quelquejeu, Bernard, *Sur les chemins de la non-violence – Etudes de philosophie morale et politique*, Paros: Vrin, 2010, pp. 224.

This collection of articles by the author gathers philosophical reflections on the ethics and politics of nonviolence, with reference to numerous classical and contemporary philosophers.

Renou. Xavier, *Petit manuel de désobéissance civile – à l'usage de ceux qui veulent vraiment changer le monde*, Paris: Syllepse, 2009, pp.142.

Training manual on civil disobedience addressed to political or social activists, it covers the theory and practice of nonviolent action, including strategy and advice on media and the law. The author is himself a trainer and former leader of Greenpeace on nuclear disarmament.

Sémelin, Jacques, *La non-violence expliquée à mes filles*. Paris: Le Seuil, 2000, pp.57. [translations in English, Spanish, Italian, Portuguese, Catalan, Japanese, Hebrew and Indonesian.]

Short manual on civil education on nonviolence in simple terms, in the form of a dialogue with the author's pre-teenage daughters.

Sharp, Gene, *De la dictature à la democratie : un cadre conceptuel pour la libération.* , Paris : L'Harmattan, 2009, pp. 137.

Translation of Sharp's manual on conducting nonviolent resistance written for and consulted by actvists in many parts of the world.

Nonviolent Defence
(including Resisting Coups and Lessons from the Second World War)

Sémelin, Jacques. *Sans armes face à Hitler: La résistance civile en Europe,* 1939-1943. Paris: Payot, 1998, pp.268. [Translations in German, English.]

Historical essay presenting and analysing various examples of civil resistance to Nazi occupation across Europe.

Sémelin, Jacques (2013).*Persécutions et entraides dans la France occupée. Comment 75% des juifs ont échappé à la mort,* Paris: Le Seuil/Les Arènes. 2013, pp.912.

Huge historiography which uncovers the role of civil servants in resisting the deportation of Jews during WWII occupation in France; based on several years of archival and interview-based research.

Marichez, Jeanet et Xavier Olagne, *La guerre par actions civiles: Identité d'une strategie de défense,* Paris: Fondation pour les Etudes de Defénse, 1998.

This book aims to sensitise policy-makers, and especially those active in the security sector, to the strategic utility of mass-based civil resistance, and its potential use for national defence purposes.

Mellon, Christian, Jean-Marie Muller et Jacques Sémelin, *La dissuasion civile.* Paris : Fondation des Etudes de Défense Nationale (FEDN), 1985, pp.204.

Study commissioned by the then French Defence Minister on the principles and techniques of nonviolent defence.

International Nonviolent Intervention and Accompaniment

Alternatives Non-Violentes (ANV), *L'intervention civile, une chance pour la paix,* ANV no. 124, 2002, pp. 80.

This special issue of the magazine *Alternatives Non-Violentes,* collects papers presented at a landmark conference organized at the French National Assembly in October 2001 on civil peace intervention.

Muller, Jean Marie, *Principes et méthodes de l'intervention civile.* Paris: Desclée de Brouwer, 1997, pp.176. [translations in Italian and Portuguese].

A key resource on the French approach to international civilian peace intervention as an alternative to military or humanitarian intervention in conflict zones.

People Power

Sémelin, Jacques, *La liberté au bout des ondes. Du coup de Prague à la chute du mur de Berlin*, Paris: Belfond, 1997. pp. 347.

This book provides accounts of the various peaceful revolutions in Eastern Europe against totalitarianism after 1948, culminating in 1989, with a specific emphasis on the role of media.

German Titles
(from Austria, Germany and Switzerland)

Compiled by Christine Schweitzer

Theory and Practice of Nonviolent Action

Arnold, Martin, *Guetekraft. Ein Wirkungsmodelaktiver Gewaltfreiheit nach Hildegard Goss-Mayr, Mohandas K. Gandhi und Bart de Ligt*, Baden-Baden: Nomos, 2011, 284pp.

Arnold, a Protestant cleric, explores the ideas of three protagonists of nonviolent resistance (Goss-Mayr, Gandhi and de Ligt) on how nonviolent action 'works'. The author, who does not use the German translation of 'nonviolence' but his own term 'the power of good', argues that, regardless of the origin and religion of the practitioners, the effects of nonviolence are basically the same. This volume – the fourth in a series – is a summary of his conclusions from three more detailed case studies, each published as a separate book, and derives from a dissertation undertaken late in the author's life.

Del Vasto, Lanza, *Die Macht der Friedfertigen. Radikale Alternativen zu Elend, Knechtschaft, Krieg und Revolte*, Freiberg/Heidelberg: F.H. Kerke, 1982, 320 pp.

Translation from French of 'The Power of the Peaceful', by well known nonviolent activist and theorist who drew inspiration from Gandhi.

Ebert, Theodor, *Gewaltfreier Aufstand. Alternative zum Buergerkrieg*, Waldkirchen: Waldkircher Verlagsgesellschaft, 1981 (4th edition), 253 pp.

Analysis of nonviolent resistance by leading German scholar of nonviolent uprisings, based on his dissertation. In this book Ebert outlines an often quoted series of steps in the escalation of nonviolent action.

Gerster, Petra mit Michael Gleich, *Die Friedensmacher*, Muenchen/Wien: Carl Hanser, 2005 260 pp. Mit CD: Peace Counts: Die Erfolge der Friedensmacher: ed. Institut fur Friedenspaedagogik.

The 'peace makers' is an exhibition of people from all over the world engaged in resistance and conflict transformation. The book, which the TV journalist Petra Gerster wrote with the producer of the exhibition, Michael Gleich, gives an impression of the range of nonviolent activism world-wide.

Goss-Mayr, Hildegard, *Der Mensch vor dem Unrecht. Spiritualitaet und Praxis gewaltloser Befreiung*, Wien/Muenchen/Zuerich:Europaverlag, 1981 (4th edition).

Theological approach to nonviolence and what the author terms 'nonviolent liberation'.

Goss-Mayr, Hildegard, *Wie Feinde Freunde werden. Mein Leben mit Jean Goss fuer Gewaltlosigkeit, Gerechtigkeit und Versoehnung*, Freiburg: Herder, 1996, 186 pp.

Goss-Mayr and Goss played a significant role in promoting nonviolent action and training internationally. This book is Goss-Mayr's biography and memories of their work in Latin America, Madagascar and the Philippines.

Jochheim, Gernot, *Die Gewaltfreie Aktion. Ideen und Methoden, Vorbilder und Wirkungen*, Hamburg: Rausch und Roehrig, 1984, 334 pp.

A general description of nonviolent action, its ideas, methods and effects.

Krippendorf, Ekkehart, *Staat und Krieg: Die historische Logik politischer Unvernunft*, Frankfurt a. Main: Edition Suhrkamp, 1985, 435 pp.

A 'classic' for grassroots activists. A study of the interdependence of the state, as a form of political organization, and war.

Nagler, Michael und Egon Spiegel, *Politik ohne Gewalt. Prinzipien, Praxis und Perspektiven der Gewaltfreiheit*, Berlin: Lit, 2008, 196 pp.

The American activist and academic Nagler and the German theologian Spiegel describe the principles, practices and perspectives of nonviolence.

Schweitzer, Christine, 'Soziale Verteidigung und Gewaltfreier Aufstand Reloaded. Neue Einblicke in zivilen Widerstand.' Ed.: Bund fuer Soziale Verteidigung, Hintergrund-und Diskussionspapier Nr. 41, Minden, 2015, 26 pp.: www.soziale-verteidigung.de

This paper summarizes the most recent English-language literature on civil resistance for a non-English speaking readership.

Schweitzer, Christine mit Joergen Johansen, 'Krieg verhindern oder stoppen. Der Beitrag von Friedensbewegungen. IFGK Arbeitspapier Nr. 26 July 2014, 81pp.: www.ifgk.de

Historical survey of the contribution of seven peace movements to halting or preventing the involvement of their own governments' in wars – from Sweden/Norway 1905 to Iraq 2003.

Steinweg, Reiner und Ulrike Laubenthal, eds., *Gewaltfreie Aktion. Erfahrungen und Analysen*, Frankfurt a. Main: Brandes & Apsel, 2011, 288 pp.

This book contains a number of articles on examples of nonviolent action, as well as more theoretical reflections on nonviolent action, both nationally and internationally.

Gandhi

Arnold, Martin,*Guetekraft – Gandhi's Satyagraha*, Overath: Bucken& Sulzer, 2011, 408 pp.

One in a series of four books analysing how nonviolent resistance works, focusing on Gandhi. [See comments under Arnold in section above.]

My Life is my message: Das Leben und Wirken von M.K. Gandhi, ed. Gandhi Informationszentrum, Kassel: Weber, Zucht & Co., 1988.

This book gives an insight into Gandhi's life (including a chronology), as well as a chronology of events in India and South Africa, plus speeches and articles by Gandhi on truth, nonviolence, civil disobedience, etc.

Sternstein, Wolfgang, *Gandhi und Jesus. Das Ende des Fundamentalismus*, Guetersloh: Guetersloher Verlagsgesellschaft, 2009, 368 pp.

The Ploughshares activist Wolfgang Sternstein compares Gandhi's ideas of religion and ethics with the teaching of Jesus. He contrasts both to fundamentalism and dogmatism of any kind.

Civilian-based Defence

Boserup, Anders and Andrew Mack, *Krieg ohne Waffen*, Reinbek b. Hamburg: Rohwohlt, 1980 [1974 1st edition], 156 pp.

One of the best conceptualizations of civilian-based defence, enriched with examples of civil resistance.

Ebert, Theodor, *Soziale Verteidigung*. Vol. 1: *Historische Erfahrungen und Grundzuege der Strategie*, 1981, 193pp; Vol. 2. *Formen und Bedingungen des Zivilen Widerstands*, Waldkirch: Waldkircher Verlag, 1981, 194 pp.

Ebert has researched important examples of earlier nonviolent resistance, e.g. the 1953 East German uprising, and has been a leading theorist of nonviolent action and civil defence since the 1960s. Both books are compilations of articles Ebert wrote on the subject in the 1970s.

Graswurzelrevolution, Sonderheft Soziale Verteidigung, Nr 98/99, November 1985.

'Grassroots Revolution' is a nonviolent-libertarian-anarchist magazine. This special issue focuses on an anarchistic approach to 'social defence' as opposed to proposals for governments to adopt civilian-based defence.

Jochheim, Gernot, *Frauenprotest in der Rosenstrasse. Berlin 1943. Bericht, Dokumente. Hintergrunde,* Berlin: Hentrich&Hentrich, 2002, 223 pp.

Study of important and rare example of open protest against Gestapo, by German wives demanding release of their German Jewish husbands who had been arrested.

Mez, Lutz, *Ziviler Widerstand in Norwegen,* Frankfurt: Haag & Herchen, 1976, 376 pp.

The resistance by Norwegian teachers and other civil society groups to Quisling's attempt to impose fascist ideology during th e German occupation is one of the most important and successful examples of resistance during World War Two.

Mueller, Barbara, *Passiver Widerstand in Ruhrkampf. Eine Fallstudie zur gewaltlosen zwischenstaatlichen Konfliktaustragung und ihren Erfolgsbedingungen,* Muenster: Lit, 1995, 529 pp.

The officially organized German resistance to the French occupation of the Ruhr in 1923 is an especially relevant case study for proponents of civilian-based defence.

Semelin, Jacques, *Ohne Waffen gegen Hitler: Eine Studie zum zivilen Widerstand in Europa,* Frankfur a Main: dipa Verlag, 1995, 302 pp.

Translation from French of authoritative scholarly study of forms of civil resistance in German-occupied Europe in World War Two.

Nonviolent Intervention

Buettner, Christian W., *Friedenbrigaden: Zivile Konfliktbearbeitung mit gewaltfreien Methoden,* Muenster: Lit Verlag, 1995, 147 pp.

On different peace brigade projects, including the Gandhian-inspired Shanti Sena.

Evers, Tilman, ed., *Ziviler Friedendienst. Fachleute fur den Frieden. Idee – Erfahrungen-Ziele,* Opladen: Leske & Budrich, 2000, 380 pp.

Compilation of articles on the rationale, history and practice of the Civilian Peace Service (CPS) in Germany. The CPS, which started in 2000, is a governmentally financed programme with implementers both from state and non-state organizations.

Heinemann-Grueder, Andreas und Isabella Bauer, eds., *Zivile Konfliktbearbeitung. Vom Anspruch zur Wirklichkeit,* Opladen/Berlin/ Toronto: Barbara Budrich, 2013, 246 pp.

This book, which deals with international approaches to conflict transformation, has been compiled by two researchers/practitioners with a background in the Civil Peace Service.

Mueller, Barbara, *Balkan Peace Team 1994-2001. Mit Freiwilligenteams in gewaltfreiem Einsatz in Krisenregionen, Bildungsvereinigung Arbeit und Leben,* Niedersachsen: Braunschweig, 2004, 240 pp.

A description and evaluation of the work of the international Balkan Peace Team that worked in Croatia and Serbia/Kosovo in the 1990s.

Spanish Titles

Compiled by Jesús Castañar and Javier Gárate

Nonviolence and Nonviolent Action in Historical Perspective

Casado da Rocha, Antonio, *La Desobediencia Civil a partir de Thoreau*, San Sebastian, Gakoa Lubruak, 2002, 133 pp.

This essay updates Thoreau's thought in the light of later additions by academics and activists. Starting from Thoreau's own context, and using extracts from his classic text and other unpublished fragments available in Spanish, the author recreates Thoreau's thinking for today.

Castañar, Jesús, *Teoría e Historia de la Revolución Noviolenta*, Barcelona, Virus, 2012, 327 pp. Available at: http://viruseditorial.net/pdf/teoria-e-historia-de-la-accion-no-violenta-baja.pdf

This is a historical review of nonviolent ideas and movements from the first recorded strike in ancient Egypt to the 21st century. It connects the concepts of revolution and transformatión in each era with the historical movements which often inspired them. There are chapters on Tolstoy, Gandhi and other theorists of nonviolent action, e.g. Bart de Ligt and Gene Sharp, as well as chapters on conscientious objection, nonviolent resistance to Hitler and opposition to other dictatorships round the world, but no detailed examples after the 1960s. Instead it focuses on different approaches to nonviolent action, from the 'pragmatic' approaches of Sharp and Ackerman to the principled commitment to nonviolence of Burrowes, Martin and Lakey.

Ortega, Pere y Alejandro Pozo, *Noviolencia y Transformación social*, Barcelona, Icaria, 2005, 131 pp.

This book is an introduction to some of the classic theories and movements of nonviolent action, based on the studies of Sharp and Ackerman, which have not yet been translated into Spanish. But it provides a personal interpretation derived from the principled approach to nonviolent action. A very good starting point for beginners in this subject.

Randle, Michael, *Resistencia Civil*, Barcelona, Paidos, 1998, 262 pp.

Translation from English of 1994 study of the evolution of the concepts and practice of nonviolent action since the 18th century to 1991, the trends promoting its use, and its dynamics. The second part examines nonviolent civilian defence.

Schell, Jonathan, *El mundo inconquistable. Poder, no violencia y voluntad popular*, Madrid, Galaxia Gutenberg, 2005, 528 pp.

Translation from English of 2005 study exploring historical trends leading to greater role for nonviolence, Gandhi's innovative thought and the role of unarmed protest in some earlier revolutions. Then focuses in particular on the ideas of the resisters in Eastern Europe in the 1970s and 1980s and on the cooperative concept of power.

VV,AA. *Noviolencia. La transformacion creative del conflict social* Medellin, Gobernacion de Antiquoia, 01-05-2004,168 pp. Available online at: http://www.saliendodelcallejon.pnud.org.co/documentos.shtmll?x=4678

This as an introductory book on nonviolence by various authors (Equipo Plan Congruente de Paz y Nonviolencia), centred on the classics: Thoreau, Gandhi and Luther King. It provides exercise sheets for students and develops the concept of 'kingian' nonviolence (following Martin Luther King's approach).

Civil Resistance in Practice

Hernández Delgado, Esperanza, *Resistencia civil artesana de paz: Experiencias indígenas, afrodescendientes y campesinas*, Bogotá, Editorial de la Universidad Javeriana, 2004, 468 pp.

This is a key book about the Colombian peace communities and the civil resistance of indigenous peoples, Afro Americans and peasants in the context of a bloody civil war. It focuses in particular on the civil resistance of the Nasa people (Paez) in the Cauca department. This is not only the strongest movement (with their Indigenous Guard able to confront guerrillas, the army and paramilitaries), but also the one which has lasted longest and influenced the others. In addition there are studies of the Asociacíon Campesina Integral del Atrato (ACIA), Asociación de Trabajadores Campesinos de Carare (ATCC), Comunidad de Paz de San José de Apartadó and the Asamblea Municipal Constituyente de Tarso.

Ormazabal, Sabino, *500 ejemplos de noviolencia. Otra forma de contar la historia*, Bilbao, Fundación Manu Robles-Arangiz, 2009. Available at: http://www.mrafundazioa.eus/es/centro-de-documentacion/libros/500-ejemplos-de-no-violencia-otra-forma-de-contar-la-historia

This book is a compendium of many examples of nonviolent action, mainly in the Basque country, but also from the rest of the world. The examples are presented individually, without a connecting link, so this is not a history, but a compendium of cases.

Sandoval Forero, Eduardo Andrés, *La Guardia Indígena Nasa y el Arte de la Resistencia Pacífica*, Ediciones Colección Étnica: Diálogos Interculturales, Fundación Hemera, Columbia, 2008, 143 pp. Available free at: http://www. imagocatalunya.org/descargas/GUARDIA_INGID ENA_NASA.pdf

This book combines an anthropological with a political approach, describing the origin, development and activities of the Indigenous Guard of the Nasa People of Cauca (Colombia) with testimonies from some of their leaders.

Sharp, Gene, *De la dictadura a la democracia. Un sistema conceptual para la liberación*. Boston, Albert Einstein Institution, 2003, 91 pp.

The first English edition of this widely influential booklet, which gives advice on planning and implementing nonviolent campaigns to those resisting repression, was published in 1993.

Shock, Kurt, *Insurrecciones no armadas*, Bogotá, 2008, 305 pp. (e índice analítico)

Translation by Freddy Cante (who contributes a Foreword) of 2005 study which explores issues of strategy and dynamics in nonviolent campaigns seeking political transformation, and discusses reasons for success illustrated by campaigns in South Africa, the Philippines, Nepal and Thailand, and for failure in China 1989 and Burma 1988.

Nonviolent (Civilian) Defence

Arias, Gonzalo (editor), *El proyecto politico d e la Noviolencia*, Madrid, Nueva Utopía, 1995. (First edition was printed illegally in 1973 during the Franco dictatorship.) 204 pp.

This is a compilation of texts on nonviolent alternatives to accepting unjust rule, starting from the classics, e.g. Thoreau, Tolstoy, Gandhi, Gregg and Ramamurti, and providing translations of important contemporary European authors, such as Muller, Ebert, Colbere or Frognier. The second appendix of the second edition offers a summary of the nonviolent movement in Spain up to 1995.

Colectivo Utopía Contagiosa, *Política Noviolenta y Lucha Social. Alternativa Noviolenta a la defensa militar*, Madrid, Ecologistas en Acción, 2012, 302 pp.

This book summarizes the long term work of the two person collective Utopía Contagiosa on defense alternatives from an antimilitarist point of view. The model of military defense is challenged from a nonviolence- cooperation paradigm which conflicts with the hegemonic paradigm of domination and violence. The authors then propose transarmament, suggesting criteria, methodological orientations and a two-phase implementation, together with several proposals for sectorial transarmament for debate.

López Martínez, Mario, *Ni paz ni guerra, sino todo lo contrario. Ensayos sobre defensa y resistencia civil*, Granada, Ano-Lugar, 2012, 134 pp.

Professor Lopez presents the concepts of civil defense, people power, civil resistance, nonviolent defense and peace building. Although the book is a compilation of articles, it has a structural connection, and the many references provide the reader with more than an introduction – a full map of sources to research the ideas presented.

Proyecto AUPA, *Defensa Popular Noviolenta*, Zaragoza, Ediciones Mambrú, 1989, 40 pp.

This pamphlet was for a long time the only publication on the history of nonviolent movements, reviewing classical cases such as the resistance to the Kapp Putsch, the Salt March led by Gandhi and the Prague Spring among others.

Civil Disobedience in Theory and Practice

Dalmau Lliso, Juan Carlos, *La Objecion Fiscal a los gastos militares*, Madrid, Technos, 1996.

Study of the Spanish tax resistance campaign against military expenditure, launched in the early1980s and still continuing.

Falcon Tella, Maria Jose, *La Desobediencia Civil*, Monografias Juridicas, Madrid/Barcelona, Macello Pons, 2000, 570 pp.

A study of civil disobedience from a legal standpoint.

Iglésias Turrión, Páblo, *Desobedientes. De Chiapas a Madrid*, Madrid, Editorial Popular, 2011, 260 pp.

This book was written in 2011 by the present leader of the radical party 'Podemos', just before he bécame a TV star. His aim is to explain the genealogy of the 15M movement, linking it with'Juvenal sin Futuro' (Youth without a Future) and 'Democracia Real Ya' (True Democracy), and connecting these with the lessons learned in the anti-globalization movement at the beginning of the 21st century, and with the Italian 'Disobedienti'.

Lastra, Antonio (editor), *Desobediencia civil. Historia y antologia de un concepto*, Madrid, Technos, 2012, 308 pp.

Primarily a compilation of texts on civil disobedience from a philosophical perspective, using texts from George Anastaplo, G.E. Lessing, Ralph Waldo Emerson and Henry David Thoreau, plus chapter 6 from John Rawls's *Theory of Justice*. Tolstoy is represented by chapters 14 and 15 from his novel *War and Peace*, and there is an appendix with two short classic texts from Gandhi and Martin Luther King.

Pérez, José Antonio, *Manual Práctico para la Desobediencia Civil*, Pamplona, Amiela, 1994, 254 pp.

This is a handbook explaining the scope of civil disobedience written in a readable, non-technical style. The first two chapters cover the origins and traditions of disobedience, followed by practical examples. Emphasis is given to tax resistance and conscientious objection to military service, with detailed explanantions how to engage in both, plus examples of letters to send to the administration. There are also chapters on theoretical issues arising.

Insumisión

Aguirre, Xavier y Rafael Ajangiz; Ibarra, Pedro y Rafael Sainz de Rozas, *La insumisión, un singular ciclo histórico de desobediencia civil*, Madrid, Tecnos, 1998, 171 pp.

Primarily an account of the movement of conscientious objection and 'insumision' in Spain, but including analysis and proposals. It was written by university teachers who joined the movement and assisted from inside. Published in the final stage of the movement, when the end of conscription was announced. but there were still objectors jailed in military prisons.

Beristan, Carlos M., *La insumisión encarcelada*, Barcelona, Virus, 1992, 158 pp.

A compilation of the voices and experiences of seven objectors in prison, as well as of their relatives and supporting groups, in the context of the first years of the campaign of disobedience to military service in Spain. This book arose out of the need to train activists to face jail.

Domínguez, Rosario, *La Insumisión. Una forma de vida*, Madrid, La Malatesta Editorial, 2012, 147 pp.

Tells the story of the *insumisos* from the point of view of one of the mothers. It begins with a summary of the historical process and then introduces a personal narrative of the experience of trials and jail, and the struggle of the conscientious objectors' mothers association. Includes press articles and pictures which illustrate each element of the story.

Ibarra, Pedro (editor), *Objeción e insumisión, claves ideológicas y socials*, Madrid, Fundamentos, 1992, 319 pp.

This collective work analyzes the origins and early stages of conscientious objection and *insumision* in Spain, its ideological debates and evolution. It includes an analysis of the national and international political context, a chapter on alternative civilian service in the Federal Republic of Germany, and a guide to becoming an objector.

Movimiento de Objeción de Conciencia, *En Legitima Desobediencia*, Madrid, Proyecto Editorial Traficantes de Sueños, 2002, 348 pp. Available on the internet at:

http://www.antimilitaristas.org/IMG/pdf/LIBRO.pdf

This is the major compilation of declarations, press statements and articles by the protagonists of the *insumisión* campaign at the time of their disobedience. Therefore it includes accounts of various stages of movement, such as the formation of the first objectors' groups, and defiance of the Conscientious Objection Act, and the struggle inside the prison in Pamplona. There are also manifestoes, letters of support and internal documents which record these struggles and others that arose out of them: for example the gender issue raised by antimilitarist-feminist women, and the campaign against military expenditure involving tax refusal.

Oliver, Pedro, *La utopía insumisa de Pepe Beunza. Una objeción subversiva durante el franquismo*, Barcelona, Virus, 2002, 174 pp.

A book about the beginning of the conscientious objection movement in Spain, which tells the story of Pepe Beunza, the first C.O. in Spain who embarked on disobedience under the Franco dictatorship. It is not only about Pepe's personal experience, but also an account of the supporting campaigns and of the next conscientious objectors and the creation of MOC, the C.O. movement that still exists.

Author Index